Fiction Goes to Court

Favorite Stories of Lawyers and the Law Selected by Famous Lawyers

edited by

ALBERT P. BLAUSTEIN

GREENWOOD PRESS, PUBLISHERS
WESTPORT, CONNECTICUT

Library of Congress Cataloging in Publication Data

Blaustein, Albert P 1921- ed.
Fiction goes to court.

Reprint of the 1954 ed. published by Holt, New York.
1. Lawyers--Fiction. 2. Short stories, American.
3. Short stories, English. I. Title.
[PZ1.B574Fi9] [PS648.L3] 813'.01 77-2827
ISBN 0-8371-9522-5

Originally published in 1954 by Henry Holt and Company, New York

Reprinted with the permission of Albert P. Blaustein

Reprinted in 1977 by Greenwood Press, Inc.

Library of Congress catalog card number 77-2827

ISBN 0-8371-9522-5

Printed in the United States of America

The editor wishes to thank the authors, publishers, and literary representatives for permission to reprint the following stories:

"The *Corpus Delicti*," by Melville Davisson Post. Reprinted from *The Strange Schemes of Randolph Mason,* by Melville Davisson Post; copyright, 1896, by G. P. Putnam's Sons.

"The Dog Andrew," by Arthur Train. Reprinted from *Tutt and Mr. Tutt,* by Arthur Train; copyright, 1920, by the Curtis Publishing Company; 1920, by Charles Scribner's Sons; 1948, by Helen C. Train. Used by permission of the publishers.

"Board of Inland Revenue *v*. Haddock: The Negotiable Cow," by A. P. Herbert. Reprinted from *Uncommon Law,* by A. P. Herbert; copyright, 1933, by Doubleday and Company, Inc. Used by permission of Sir Alan Herbert, *Punch*, and the publishers.

"The Juryman," by John Galsworthy. Reprinted from *Five Tales,* by John Galsworthy; copyright, 1918, by Charles Scribner's Sons; 1948, by Ada Galsworthy. Used by permission of the publishers.

"The Blushing Beginner and the Bearded Juryman," by O (Theo Mathew). Reprinted from *Forensic Fables,* by O; published by Butterworth and Company. Used by permission of the author and publishers.

"The Law and the Profits," by Octavus Roy Cohen. Reprinted from *Sunclouds,* by Octavus Roy Cohen; published by Dodd, Mead and Company; copyright, 1923, 1924, by Octavus Roy Cohen. Used by permission of the author.

"Boys Will Be Boys," by Irvin S. Cobb. Reprinted from *The Saturday Evening Post,* the Curtis Publishing Company; copyright, 1918, by Irvin S. Cobb. Used by permission of the copyright owners.

"Coroner de Luxe," by Ruel McDaniel. Reprinted from *Vinegarroon,* by Ruel McDaniel; published by Southern Publishers; copyright, 1936, by Ruel McDaniel. Used by permission of the author.

"The Barrister," by A. A. Milne. Reprinted from the book, *The Pocket Milne,* published by E. P. Dutton and Company, Inc.; copyright, 1941, by A. A. Milne. Used by permission of the publishers.

"Tomorrow," by William Faulkner. Reprinted from *Knight's Gambit,* by William Faulkner; copyright, 1940, by the Curtis Publishing Company. Used by permission of Random House, Inc.

"Triumph of Justice," by Irwin Shaw. Reprinted from *Mixed Company,* by Irwin Shaw; copyright, 1940, by Irwin Shaw. Used by permission of Random House, Inc.

"A Wasted Day," by Richard Harding Davis. Reprinted from *Once Upon a Time,* by Richard Harding Davis; copyright, 1910, by Charles Scribner's Sons; 1938, by Hope Harding Davis Kehrig. Used by permission of the publishers.

"Doowinkle, Attorney," by Harry Klingsberg. Reprinted from *The Saturday Evening Post,* September 18, 1943; copyright, 1943, by the Curtis Publishing Company. Used by permission of the author.

"Coroner's Inquest," by Marc Connelly. Reprinted from *Collier's;* copyright, 1930, by Marc Connelly. Used by permission of the author.

Preface

Nowhere in the world of fiction can one find more fascinating stories with greater general interest than those dealing with law and lawyers. And no wonder. For law and the administration of justice are not confined to the legal profession. They are everybody's business—and everybody is interested in the tales which have translated the drama and the humor of legal battles from the courtroom to the printed page. Legal themes have long served as the basis for the greatest and most popular literature of the English-speaking world—the kind of literature that has been enjoyed by lawyer and nonlawyer alike.

But lawyers have a special stake in lawyer fiction. The lawyer is, by nature, an omnivorous reader. He has to be. For every lawyer must devote much of his working day to plowing through the *wherefores* and *whereases* of his clients' contracts and briefs—and then spend additional hours perusing the reports, the advance sheets, the reviews, etc., to keep up to date with the ever-changing patterns of the law.

And when reading for business is finally done, the lawyer still keeps on reading about the law; he takes a busman's holiday by relaxing with lawyer fiction.

It is no surprise to find that the best judges of legal fiction are the attorneys themselves. And the fact that they are good judges is borne out by the list of favorite stories selected by some of America's outstanding lawyers.

In this anthology are eighteen stories chosen from the favorite reading of the legal profession. Here are stories portraying the majesty of the law, the drama of its human conflict, and the humor which is an inevitable by-product of the administration of justice in a democracy. Here are stories about great lawyers—and about neophytes at the bar. Here are such old friends as Mr. Tutt, old Judge Priest, the indomitable Perry Mason, and the great mythical firm of Forbes, Hathaway, Bryan and Devore. Here also are the astute Rupert Carleton, lawyer Evans Chew, and even a few laymen who would play the lawyer's role. But more important, these are great stories selected by lawyers who have read the best—stories which have been enjoyed by outstanding members of the bench and bar.

And here, also, are some of those *"outstanding"* lawyers. The word *"outstanding"* well warrants both the quotes and the italics, for there are no statistics that would enable any editor to designate the eighteen contributors to this anthology as THE outstanding lawyers of the Anglo-American world. That they are outstanding, however, cannot be denied. They are some of the top figures of the legal profession—leaders of the bench and of the bar, and lawyers who have achieved world-wide recognition for their service to government and in their roles as law teacher, soldier, banker, and author.

Heading the list—as he heads so many lists of great attorneys—is John W. Davis, the man who has earned the title of "Mr. Lawyer" from the members of his profession. Candidate for President of the United States 'way back in 1924, he has been accorded every honor that the American bar has been able to bestow upon an acknowledged leader. Advocacy is his forte, and not only does he head one of the nation's largest firms but he has the distinction of having appeared before the U. S. Supreme Court more often than any other lawyer in history.

Three other outstanding practicing lawyers—and outstanding advocates—have also named stories for the collection: William J. Donovan, Lloyd Paul Stryker, and Jerry Giesler.

Better known to most Americans as Colonel "Wild Bill" Donovan of the Fighting 69th in World War I and as Major General William J. Donovan of the OSS in World War II, Lawyer Donovan is among the most distinguished members of the American bar. Senior partner of a top-drawer New York law firm, his background includes the post of Assistant Attorney General of the United States, the candidacy for governor of New York State and, more recently, the position as U. S. ambassador to Thailand.

Lloyd Paul Stryker is a name which has become synonymous with some of the greatest courtroom battles of our day—and a name which has won a permanent niche in the world of legal literature. His best-selling biography of Thomas Erskine, entitled *For the Defense*, was followed this year by the widely acclaimed *The Art of Advocacy.*

Often described as "the most sensational advocate in the land," California's Jerry Giesler has achieved much fame and acclaim as counsel for Rudolph Valentino, John Barrymore, Charles Chaplin, Errol Flynn, and other noted Hollywoodians who have combined litigation with cinematography. He has been in the public eye since 1912 when his first boss, Earl Rogers, became ill, and Giesler successfully defended Clarence Darrow on a jury-fixing charge.

Top lawyers in government have joined the top practitioners in this anthology—leading lawyers on the bench, leading lawyers in the Congress, and leading lawyers on the American political scene.

Highest legal posts in the Anglo-American Common Law world are Chief Justice of the United States and Lord High Chancellor of Great Britain—posts that have been honored by the late Honorable Fred M. Vinson of Kentucky and England's the Right Honorable Lord Gavin Turnbull Simonds. And aiding and abetting these leaders of the bench in naming favorite tales for this collection is a third distinguished jurist, Honorable Tom C. Clark of Texas, Associate Justice of the United States Supreme Court.

Two thirds of the members of Congress are likewise members of the bar, and two of their most popular representatives are Estes Kefauver and Sam Rayburn. Senator Kefauver, whose prowess as counsel and advocate has long been common knowledge to the people of Tennessee, became one of the nation's best-known lawyers during the course of his successful and widely televised crime-busting investigations in 1951.

No lawyer has given greater service to the legislature than Texas' Sam Rayburn. A member of the House of Representatives for more than forty years, he has served several terms as Speaker of the House and is presently Democratic leader of the lower chamber.

Number-two man in American political life today is both the top lawyer in government and the top lawyer in the GOP, California's Richard M. Nixon, Vice-President of the United States. His story in this anthology is followed by the favorite tale of the top lawyer in the Democratic Party, former Illinois Governor Adlai E. Stevenson, Democratic candidate for President in 1952.

Representing lawyers in business are John J. McCloy, chairman of the board of the Chase National Bank, and Eric Johnston, president of the Motion Picture Association of America.

Lawyer McCloy, who has been associated with three of New York's largest law firms during his busy career at the bar, gave valuable service to government as Assistant Secretary of War during most of World War II and as the first U. S. High Commissioner for Germany. He was president of the World Bank prior to his assignment in Germany and took over the reins at the Chase National Bank in 1953.

Lawyer Johnston has long been one of the nation's top men of business. He organized, developed, and headed many retail, distributing, and manufacturing corporations and has been a director of banks, airlines, electric companies, and others too numerous to mention. From 1942 to 1946 he was president of the Chamber of Commerce of the United States and became the motion picture czar in 1945. He served government on the Defense Mobilization Board and in the Economic Stabilization Agency, and has been a special ambassador for President Eisenhower in the Near East.

Erle Stanley Gardner, Elmer Rice, and Oscar Hammerstein,

2d, are three men of law who have deserted the workaday lawyers' world to become famous men of letters.

One of America's top mystery writers, Lawyer Gardner occupies a distinctive position in this anthology: He is not only a selector of a favorite tale but has had one of his own short stories selected by another outstanding member of the bar. Author of nearly one hundred detective novels under his own name and under such pseudonyms as A. A. Fair, Charles J. Kenny, and Carleton Kendrake, Gardner has still found time to be active in the work of the various bar associations. He has also spearheaded "The Court of Last Resort," which has performed yeoman service in aiding those who have been unjustly convicted of alleged criminal offenses.

Pulitzer Prize playwright Elmer Rice also left the practice of the law to devote his full time to literary efforts, but Lawyer Rice never stopped writing about his profession. His plays include *Counsellor-at-Law*, *On Trial*, and *For the Defense*.

Pulitzer Prize librettist Oscar Hammerstein, 2d, went from law to literature at a very early stage in his career. Although he studied law at Columbia, he was soon drawn to the theater, and his successes, ranging from *Rose Marie* in the early twenties to the recent *South Pacific,* forestalled practice at the bar.

Samuel Williston and Roscoe Pound fall into a special category. Divorced from the spotlight of the courtroom and the publicity-conscious worlds of popular writing, big business, and politics, they are nevertheless better known among lawyers than any of the other contributors to this anthology. And it would be difficult, if not impossible, to find two lawyers more admired and respected than these two venerable teachers of the law.

Patriarch of the legal profession, nonagenarian Williston is the oldest member of the American Bar Association, both in point of age and in length of membership, and was the winner of the A.B.A.'s first Gold Medal Award for "conspicuous service to American jurisprudence." Long a distinguished professor at Harvard Law School, he is one of the world's truly great legal scholars; and it is unlikely that even one lawyer in the United States today has failed to receive some part of his legal education from a Williston treatise.

Octogenarian Pound, a law teacher for more than fifty years, is one of the most famous of Harvard's many famous law school deans. Author of literally hundreds of books and articles, he is one of the prime spokesmen of the legal profession and a frequent representative of the American bar in international legal circles.

These are the "selectors"—the outstanding lawyers who have named favorite stories for *Fiction Goes to Court*. The judgment of these selectors is attached hereto and submitted herewith for the concurrence of the great American reading jury.

Contents

The Corpus Delicti

by:

MELVILLE DAVISSON POST

selected by:

JOHN W. DAVIS

Melville Davisson Post was an old friend of my West Virginia days—a friend who sometimes borrowed my law books to do research for his magnificent lawyer stories. Perhaps his best known and my favorite is "The Corpus Delicti."

S.S. JOHN W. DAVIS

That man Mason," said Samuel Walcott, "is the mysterious member of this club. He is more than that; he is the mysterious man of New York."

"I was much surprised to see him," answered his companion, Marshall St. Clair, of the great law firm of Seward, St. Clair & De Muth. "I had lost track of him since he went to Paris as counsel for the American stockholders of the Canal Company. When did he come back to the States?"

"He turned up suddenly in his ancient haunts about four months ago," said Walcott, "as grand, gloomy, and peculiar as Napoleon ever was in his palmiest days. The younger members of the club call him 'Zanona Redivivus.' He wanders through the house usually late at night, apparently without noticing anything or anybody. His mind seems to be deeply and busily at work, leaving his bodily self to wander as it may happen to. Naturally, strange stories are told of him; indeed, his individuality and his habit of doing some unexpected thing, and doing it in such a marvelously original manner that men who are experts at it look on in wonder, cannot fail to make him an object of interest.

"He has never been known to play at any game whatever, and

yet one night he sat down to the chess table with old Admiral Du Brey. You know the admiral is the great champion since he beat the French and English officers in the tournament last winter. Well, you also know that the conventional openings at chess are scientifically and accurately determined. To the utter disgust of Du Brey, Mason opened the game with an unheard-of attack from the extremes of the board. The old admiral stopped and, in a kindly, patronizing way, pointed out the weak and absurd folly of his move and asked him to begin again with some one of the safe openings. Mason smiled and answered that if one had a head that he could trust he should use it; if not, then it was the part of wisdom to follow blindly the dead forms of some man who had a head. Du Brey was naturally angry and set himself to demolish Mason as quickly as possible. The game was rapid for a few moments. Mason lost piece after piece. His opening was broken and destroyed and its utter folly apparent to the lookers-on. The admiral smiled and the game seemed all one-sided, when, suddenly, to his utter horror, Du Brey found that his king was in a trap. The foolish opening had been only a piece of shrewd strategy. The old admiral fought and cursed and sacrificed his pieces, but it was of no use. He was gone. Mason checkmated him in two moves and arose wearily.

" 'Where in Heaven's name, man,' said the old admiral, thunderstruck, 'did you learn that masterpiece?'

" 'Just here,' replied Mason. 'To play chess, one should know his opponent. How could the dead masters lay down rules by which you could be beaten, sir? They had never seen you'; and thereupon he turned and left the room. Of course, St. Clair, such a strange man would soon become an object of all kinds of mysterious rumors. Some are true and some are not. At any rate, I know that Mason is an unusual man with a gigantic intellect. Of late he seems to have taken a strange fancy to me. In fact, I seem to be the only member of the club that he will talk with, and I confess that he startles and fascinates me. He is an original genius, St. Clair, of an unusual order."

"I recall vividly," said the younger man, "that before Mason went to Paris he was considered one of the greatest lawyers of this city and he was feared and hated by the bar at large. He came here, I believe, from Virginia and began with the high-grade criminal practice. He soon became famous for his powerful and ingenious defenses. He found holes in the law through which his clients escaped, holes that by the profession at large were not suspected to exist, and that frequently astonished the judges. His ability caught the attention of the great corporations. They tested him and found in him learning and unlimited resources. He pointed out methods by which they could evade obnoxious statutes, by which they could comply with the apparent letter of the law and yet violate its spirit, and advised them well in that most important of all things, just how far they could bend the law without breaking it. At the time he left for Paris he had a vast clientage and was in the midst of a brilliant career. The day he took passage from New York, the bar lost sight of him. No matter how great a man may be, the wave soon closes over him in a city like this. In a few years Mason was forgotten. Now only the older practitioners would recall him, and they would do so with hatred and bitterness. He was a tireless, savage, uncompromising fighter, always a recluse."

"Well," said Walcott, "he reminds me of a great world-weary cynic, transplanted from some ancient mysterious empire. When I come into the man's presence I feel instinctively the grip of his intellect. I tell you, St. Clair, Randolph Mason is the mysterious man of New York."

At this moment a messenger boy came into the room and handed Mr. Walcott a telegram. "St. Clair," said that gentleman, rising, "the directors of the Elevated are in session, and we must hurry." The two men put on their coats and left the house.

Samuel Walcott was not a club man after the manner of the Smart Set, and yet he was in fact a club man. He was a bachelor in the latter thirties, and resided in a great silent house on the avenue. On the street he was a man of substance, shrewd and progressive, backed by great wealth. He had various corporate interests in the larger syndicates, but the basis and foundation of his fortune was real estate. His houses on the avenue were the best possible property, and his elevator row in the importers' quarter was indeed a literal gold mine. It was known that, many years before, his grandfather had died and left him the property, which, at that time, was of no great value. Young Walcott had gone out into the gold fields and had been lost sight of and forgotten. Ten years afterward he had turned up suddenly in New York and taken possession of his property, then vastly increased in value. His speculations were almost phenomenally successful, and, backed by the now-enormous value of his real property, he was soon on a level with the merchant princes. His judgment was considered sound, and he had the full confidence of his business associates for safety and caution. Fortune heaped up riches around him with a lavish hand. He was unmarried and the halo of his wealth caught the keen eye of the matron with marriageable daughters. He was invited out, caught by the whirl of society, and tossed into its maelstrom. In a measure he reciprocated. He kept horses and a yacht. His dinners at Delmonico's and the club were above reproach. But with all he was a silent man with a shadow deep in his eyes, and seemed to court the society of his fellows, not because he loved them, but because he either hated or feared solitude. For years the strategy of the matchmaker had gone gracefully afield, but Fate is relentless. If she shields the victim from the traps of men, it is not because she wishes him to escape, but because she is pleased to reserve him for her own trap. So it happened that, when Virginia St. Clair assisted Mrs. Miriam Steuvisant at her midwinter reception, this same Samuel Walcott fell deeply and hopelessly and utterly in love, and it was so apparent to the beaten generals present that Mrs. Miriam Steuvisant applauded herself, so to speak, with encore after encore. It was good to see this courteous, silent man literally at the feet of the young debutante. He was there of right. Even the mothers of marriageable daughters admitted that. The young girl was brown-haired, brown-eyed, and tall enough, said the experts, and of the blue blood royal, with all the grace, courtesy, and inbred genius of such princely heritage.

Perhaps it was objected by the censors of the Smart Set that Miss St. Clair's frankness and honesty were a trifle old-fashioned, and that she was a shadowy bit of a puritan; and perhaps it was of these same qualities that Samuel Walcott received his hurt. At any rate the hurt was there and deep, and the new actor stepped up into the old, time-worn, semitragic drama, and began his role with a tireless, utter sincerity that was deadly dangerous if he lost.

II

Perhaps a week after the conversation between St. Clair and Walcott, Randolph Mason stood in the private waiting room of the club with his hands behind his back.

He was a man apparently in the middle forties; tall and reasonably broad across the shoulders; muscular without being either stout or lean. His hair was thin and of a brown color, with erratic streaks of gray. His forehead was broad and high and of a faint reddish color. His eyes were restless, inky black, and not overlarge. The nose was big and muscular and bowed. The eyebrows were black and heavy, almost bushy. There were heavy furrows running from the nose downward and outward to the corners of the mouth. The mouth was straight and the jaw was heavy and square.

Looking at the face of Randolph Mason from above, the expression in repose was crafty and cynical; viewed from below upward, it was savage and vindictive, almost brutal; while from the front, if looked squarely in the face, the stranger was fascinated by the animation of the man and at once concluded that his expression was fearless and sneering. He was evidently of Southern extraction and a man of unusual power.

A fire smoldered on the hearth. It was a crisp evening in the early fall, and with that far-off touch of melancholy which ever heralds the coming winter, even in the midst of a city. The man's face looked tired and ugly. His long white hands were clasped tight together. His entire figure and face wore every mark of weakness and physical exhaustion; but his eyes contradicted. They were red and restless.

In the private dining room the dinner party was in the best of spirits. Samuel Walcott was happy. Across the table from him was Miss Virginia St. Clair, radiant, a tinge of color in her cheeks. On either side, Mrs. Miriam Steuvisant and Marshall St. Clair were brilliant and lighthearted. Walcott looked at the young girl and the measure of his worship was full. He wondered for the thousandth time how she could possibly love him and by what earthly miracle she had come to accept him, and how it would be always to have her across the table from him, his own table in his own house.

They were about to rise from the table when one of the waiters entered the room and handed Walcott an envelope. He thrust it quickly into his pocket. In the confusion of rising the others did not notice him, but his face was ash-white and his hands trembled violently as he placed the wraps around the bewitching shoulders of Miss St. Clair.

"Marshall," he said, and despite the powerful effort his voice was hollow, "you will see the ladies safely cared for, I am called to attend a grave matter."

"All right, Walcott," answered the young man, with cheery good nature, "you are too serious, old man; trot along."

"The poor dear," murmured Mrs. Steuvisant, after Walcott had helped them to the carriage and turned to go up the steps of the club, "the poor dear is hard hit, and men are such funny creatures when they are hard hit."

Samuel Walcott, as his fate would, went direct to the private writing room and opened the door. The lights were not turned on and in the dark he did not see Mason motionless by the mantel shelf. He went quickly across the room to the writing table, turned on one of the lights, and, taking the envelope from his pocket, tore it open. Then he bent down by the light to read the contents. As his eyes ran over the paper, his jaw fell. The skin drew away from his cheekbones and his face seemed literally to sink in. His knees gave way under him and he would have gone down in a heap had it not been for Mason's long arms that closed around him and held him up. The human economy is ever mysterious. The moment the new danger threatened, the latent power of the man as an animal, hidden away in the centers of intelligence, asserted itself. His hand clutched the paper and, with a half slide, he turned in Mason's arms. For a moment he stared up at the ugly man whose thin arms felt like wire ropes.

"You are under the deadfall, aye," said Mason. "The cunning of my enemy is sublime."

"Your enemy?" gasped Walcott. "When did you come into it? How in God's name did you know it? How your enemy?"

Mason looked down at the wide, bulging eyes of the man.

"Who should know better than I?" he said. "Haven't I broken through all the traps and plots that she could set?"

"She? She trap you?" The man's voice was full of horror.

"The old schemer," muttered Mason. "The cowardly old schemer, to strike in the back; but we can beat her. She did not count on my helping you—I, who know her so well."

Mason's face was red, and his eyes burned. In the midst of it all he dropped his hands and went over to the fire. Samuel Walcott arose, panting, and stood looking at Mason, with his hands behind him on the table. The naturally strong nature and the rigid school in which the man had been trained presently began to tell. His composure in part returned and he thought rapidly. What did this strange man know? Was he simply making shrewd guesses, or had he some mysterious knowledge of this matter? Walcott could not know that Mason meant only Fate, that he believed her to be his great enemy. Walcott had never before doubted his own ability to meet any emergency. This mighty jerk had carried him off his feet. He was unstrung and panic-stricken. At any rate this man had promised help. He would take it. He put the paper and envelope carefully into his pocket, smoothed out his rumpled coat, and going over to Mason touched him on the shoulder.

"Come," he said, "if you are to help me we must go."

The man turned and followed him without a word. In the hall Mason put on his hat and overcoat, and the two went out into the street. Walcott hailed a cab, and the two were driven to his house on the avenue. Walcott took out his latchkey, opened the door, and led the way into the library. He turned on the light and motioned Mason to seat himself at the table. Then he went into another room and presently returned with a bundle of papers and a decanter of brandy. He poured out a glass of the liquor and offered it to Mason. The man shook his head. Walcott poured the contents of the glass down his own throat. Then he set the decanter down and drew up a chair on the side of the table opposite Mason.

"Sir," said Walcott, in a voice deliberate, ındeed, but as hollow as a sepulcher, "I am done for. God has finally gathered up the ends of the net, and it is knotted tight."

"Am I not here to help you?" said Mason, turning savagely. "I can beat Fate. Give me the details of her trap."

He bent forward and rested his arms on the table. His streaked gray hair was rumpled and on end, and his face was ugly. For a moment Walcott did not answer. He moved a little into the shadow; then he spread the bundle of old yellow papers out before him.

"To begin with," he said, "I am a living lie, a gilded, crime-made sham, every bit of me. There is not an honest piece anywhere. It is all lie. I am a liar and a thief before men. The property which I possess is not mine, but stolen from a dead man. The very name which I bear is not my own, but is the bastard child of a crime. I am more than all that—I am a murderer; a murderer before the law; a murderer before God; and worse than a murderer before the pure woman whom I love more than anything that God could make."

He paused for a moment and wiped the perspiration from his face.

"Sir," said Mason, "this is all drivel, infantile drivel. What you are is of no importance. How to get out is the problem, how to get out."

Samuel Walcott leaned forward, poured out a glass of brandy, and swallowed it.

"Well," he said, speaking slowly, "my right name is Richard Warren. In the spring of 1879 I came to New York and fell in with the real Samuel Walcott, a young man with a little money and some property which his grandfather had left him. We became friends and concluded to go to the Far West together. Accordingly we scraped together what money we could lay our hands on, and landed in the gold-mining regions of California. We were young and inexperienced, and our money went rapidly. One April morning we drifted into a little shack camp, away up in the Sierra Nevadas, called Hell's Elbow. Here we struggled and starved for perhaps a year. Finally, in utter desperation, Walcott married the daughter of a Mexican gambler, who ran an eating house and a poker joint. With them we lived from hand to mouth in a wild, God-forsaken way for several years. After a time the woman began to take a strange fancy to me. Walcott finally noticed it and grew jealous.

One night, in a drunken brawl, we quarreled, and I killed him. It was late at night, and, besides the woman, there were four of us in the poker room—the Mexican gambler, a half-breed devil called Cherubim Pete, Walcott, and myself. When Walcott fell, the half-breed whipped out his weapon and fired at me across the table; but the woman, Nina San Croix, struck his arm, and, instead of killing me, as he intended, the bullet mortally wounded her father, the Mexican gambler. I shot the half-breed through the forehead and turned round, expecting the woman to attack me. On the contrary, she pointed to the window and bade me wait for her on the cross trail below.

"It was fully three hours later before the woman joined me at the place indicated. She had a bag of gold dust, a few jewels that belonged to her father, and a package of papers. I asked her why she had stayed behind so long, and she replied that the men were not killed outright and that she had brought a priest to them and waited until they had died. This was the truth, but not all the truth. Moved by superstition or foresight, the woman had induced the priest to take down the sworn statements of the two dying men, seal it, and give it to her. This paper she brought with her. All this I learned afterward. At the time I knew nothing of this damning evidence.

"We struck out together for the Pacific coast. The country was lawless. The privations we endured were almost past belief. At times the woman exhibited cunning and ability that were almost genius; and through it all, often in the very fingers of death, her devotion to me never wavered. It was doglike and seemed to be her only object on earth. When we reached San Francisco, the woman put these papers into my hands." Walcott took up the yellow package and pushed it across the table to Mason.

"She proposed that I assume Walcott's name, and that we come boldly to New York and claim the property. I examined the papers, found a copy of a will by which Walcott inherited the property, a bundle of correspondence, and sufficient documentary evidence to establish his identity beyond the shadow of a doubt. Desperate gambler as I now was, I quailed before the daring plan of Nina San Croix. I urged that I, Richard Warren, would be known, that the attempted fraud would be detected and would result in investigation and perhaps unearth the whole horrible matter.

"The woman pointed out how much I resembled Walcott, what vast changes ten years of such life as we had led would naturally be expected to make in men, how utterly impossible it would be to trace back the fraud to Walcott's murder at Hell's Elbow, in the wild passes of the Sierra Nevadas. She bade me remember that we were both outcasts, both crime-branded, both enemies of man's law and God's; that we had nothing to lose; we were both sunk to the bottom. Then she laughed and said that she had not found me a coward until now, but that if I had turned chicken-hearted, that was the end of it, of course. The result was, we sold the gold dust and jewels in San Francisco, took on such evidences of civilization as possible, and purchased passage to New York on the best steamer we could find.

"I was growing to depend on the bold gambler spirit of this woman, Nina San Croix; I felt the need of her strong, profligate nature. She was of a queer breed and a queerer school. Her mother was the daughter of a Spanish engineer and had been stolen by the Mexican, her father. She herself had been raised and educated as best as might be in one of the monasteries along the Rio Grande, and had there grown to womanhood before her father, fleeing into the mountains of California, carried her with him.

"When we landed in New York I offered to announce her as my wife, but she refused, saying that her presence would excite comment and perhaps attract the attention of Walcott's relatives. We therefore arranged that I should go alone into the city, claim the property, and announce myself as Samuel Walcott, and that she should remain under cover until such time as we would feel the ground safe under us.

"Every detail of the plan was fatally successful. I established my identity without difficulty and secured the property. It had increased vastly in value, and I, as Samuel Walcott, soon found myself a rich man. I went to Nina San Croix in hiding and gave her a large sum of money, with which she purchased a residence in a retired part of the city, far up in a northern suburb. Here she lived secluded and unknown while I remained in the city, living here as a wealthy bachelor.

"I did not attempt to abandon the woman, but went to her from time to time in disguise and under cover of the greatest secrecy. For a time everything ran smooth: the woman was still devoted to me above everything else and thought always of my welfare first and seemed content to wait so long as I thought best. My business expanded. I was sought after and consulted and drawn into the higher life of New York, and more and more felt that the woman was an albatross on my neck. I put her off with one excuse after another. Finally she began to suspect me and demanded that I should recognize her as my wife. I attempted to point out the difficulties. She met them all by saying that we should both go to Spain, there I could marry her, and we could return to America and drop into my place in society without causing more than a passing comment.

"I concluded to meet the matter squarely once for all. I said that I would convert half of the property into money and give it to her, but that I would not marry her. She did not fly into a storming rage as I had expected, but went quietly out of the room and presently returned with two papers, which she read. One was the certificate of her marriage to Walcott duly authenticated; the other was the dying statement of her father, the Mexican gambler, and of Samuel Walcott, charging me with murder. It was in proper form and certified by the Jesuit priest.

" 'Now,' she said, sweetly, when she had finished, 'which do you prefer, to recognize your wife or to turn all the property over to Samuel Walcott's widow and hang for his murder?'

"I was dumfounded and horrified. I saw the trap that I was in and I consented to do anything she should say if she would only destroy the papers. This she refused to do. I pleaded with her and implored her to destroy them. Finally she gave them to me with a great show of returning confidence, and I tore them into bits and threw them into the fire.

"That was three months ago. We arranged to go to Spain and do as she said. She was to sail this morning and I was to follow. Of course I never intended to go. I congratulated myself on the fact that all trace of evidence against me was destroyed and that her grip was now broken. My plan was to induce her to sail, believing that I would follow. When she was gone I would marry Miss St. Clair, and if Nina San Croix should return

I would defy her and lock her up as a lunatic. But I was reckoning like an infernal ass, to imagine for a moment that I could thus hoodwink such a woman as Nina San Croix.

"Tonight I received this." Walcott took the envelope from his pocket and gave it to Mason. "You saw the effect of it; read it and you will understand why. I felt the death hand when I saw her writing on the envelope."

Mason took the paper from the envelope. It was written in Spanish and ran:

> Greeting to Richard Warren.
>
> The great Señor does his little Nina injustice to think she would go away to Spain and leave him in the beautiful America. She is not so thoughtless. Before she goes, she shall be, Oh so very rich! and the dear Señor shall be, Oh so very safe! The archbishop and the kind church hate murderers.
>
> *Nina San Croix.*
>
> Of course, fool, the papers you destroyed were copies.
>
> *N. San C.*

To this was pinned a line in a delicate, aristocratic hand, saying that the archbishop would willingly listen to Madam San Croix's statement if she would come to him on Friday morning at eleven.

"You see," said Walcott desperately, "there is no possible way out. I know the woman—when she decides to do a thing that is the end of it. She has decided to do this."

Mason turned around from the table, stretched out his long legs, and thrust his hands deep into his pockets. Walcott sat with his head down, watching Mason hopelessly, almost indifferently, his face blank and sunken. The ticking of the bronze clock on the mantel shelf was loud, painfully loud. Suddenly Mason drew his knees in and bent over, put both his bony hands on the table, and looked at Walcott.

"Sir," he said, "this matter is in such shape that there is only one thing to do. This growth must be cut out at the roots, and cut out quickly. This is the first fact to be determined, and a fool would know it. The second fact is that you must do it yourself. Hired killers are like the grave and the daughters of the horse leech—they cry always, 'Give, Give.' They are only palliatives, not cures. By using them you swap perils. You simply take a stay of execution at best. The common criminal would know this. These are the facts of your problem. The master plotters of crime would see here but two difficulties to meet:

"A practical method for accomplishing the body of the crime.

"A cover for the criminal agent.

"They would see no farther, and attempt to guard no farther. After they had provided a plan for the killing and a means by which the killer could cover his trail and escape from the theater of the homicide, they would believe all the requirements of the problems met and would stop. The greatest, the very giants among them, have stopped here and have been in great error.

"In every crime, especially in the great ones, there exists a third element, pre-eminently vital. This third element the master plotters have either overlooked or else have not had the genius to construct. They plan with rare cunning to baffle the victim. They plan with vast wisdom, almost genius, to baffle the trailer. But they fail utterly to provide any plan for baffling the punisher. Ergo, their plots are fatally defective and often result in ruin. Hence the vital necessity for providing the third element—the escape *ipso jure*."

Mason arose, walked around the table, and put his hand firmly on Samuel Walcott's shoulder. "This must be done tomorrow night," he continued; "you must arrange your business matters tomorrow and announce that you are going on a yacht cruise, by order of your physician, and may not return for some weeks. You must prepare your yacht for a voyage, instruct your men to touch at a certain point on Staten Island, and wait until six o'clock day after tomorrow morning. If you do not come aboard by that time, they are to go to one of the South American ports and remain until further orders. By this means your absence for an indefinite period will be explained. You will go to Nina San Croix in the disguise which you have always used, and from her to the yacht, and by this means step out of your real status and back into it without leaving traces. I will come here tomorrow evening and furnish you with everything that you shall need and give you full and exact instructions in every particular. These details you must execute with the greatest care, as they will be vitally essential to the success of my plan."

Through it all Walcott had been silent and motionless. Now he arose, and in his face there must have been some premonition of protest, for Mason stepped back and put out his hand. "Sir," he said, with brutal emphasis, "not a word. Remember that you are only the hand, and the hand does not think." Then he turned around abruptly and went out of the house.

III

The place which Samuel Walcott had selected for the residence of Nina San Croix was far up in a northern suburb of New York. The place was very old. The lawn was large and ill-kept; the house, a square old-fashioned brick, was set far back from the street and partly hidden by trees. Around it all was a rusty fence. The place had the air of genteel ruin, such as one finds in the Virginias.

On a Thursday of November, about three o'clock in the afternoon, a little man, driving a dray, stopped in the alley at the rear of the house. As he opened the back gate an old Negro woman came down the steps from the kitchen and demanded to know what he wanted. The drayman asked if the lady of the house was in. The old Negro answered that she was asleep at this hour and could not be seen.

"That is good," said the little man; "now there won't be any row. I brought up some cases of wine which she ordered from our house last week and which the boss told me to deliver at once, but I forgot it until today. Just let me put it in the cellar now, Auntie, and don't say a word to the lady about it and she won't ever know that it was not brought up on time."

The drayman stopped, fished a silver dollar out of his pocket, and gave it to the old Negro. "There now, Auntie," he said, my job depends upon the lady not knowing about this wine; keep it mum."

"Dat's all right, honey," said the old servant, beaming like a May morning. "De cellar door is open, carry it all in and put it in de back part and nobody ain't never going to know how long it has been in dar."

The old Negro went back into the kitchen and the little man began to unload the dray. He carried in five wine cases and stowed them away in the back part of the cellar as the old woman had directed. Then, after having satisfied himself that no one was watching, he took from the dray two heavy paper sacks, presumably filled with flour, and a little bundle wrapped in an old newspaper; these he carefully hid behind the wine cases in the cellar. After a while he closed the door, climbed on his dray, and drove off down the alley.

About eight o'clock in the evening of the same day a Mexican sailor dodged in the front gate and slipped down to the side of the house. He stopped by the window and tapped on it with his finger. In a moment a woman opened the door. She was tall, lithe, and splendidly proportioned, with a dark Spanish face and straight hair. The man stepped inside. The woman bolted the door and turned round.

"Ah," she said, smiling, "it is you, Señor? How good of you!"

The man started. "Whom else did you expect?" he said quickly.

"Oh!" laughed the woman, "perhaps the archbishop."

"Nina!" said the man, in a broken voice that expressed love, humility, and reproach. His face was white under the black sunburn.

For a moment the woman wavered. A shadow flitted over her eyes, then she stepped back. "No," she said, "not yet."

The man walked across to the fire, sank down in a chair, and covered his face with his hands. The woman stepped up noiselessly behind him and leaned over the chair. The man was either in great agony or else he was a superb actor, for the muscles of his neck twitched violently and his shoulders trembled.

"Oh," he muttered, as though echoing his thoughts, "I can't do it, I can't!"

The woman caught the words and leaped up as though some one had struck her in the face. She threw back her head. Her nostrils dilated and her eyes flashed.

"You can't do it!" she cried. "Then you do love her! You shall do it! Do you hear me? You shall do it! You killed him!

You got rid of him! but you shall not get rid of me. I have the evidence, all of it. The archbishop will have it tomorrow. They shall hang you! Do you hear me? They shall hang you for this murder!"

The woman's voice rose; it was loud and shrill. The man turned slowly round without looking up, and stretched out his arms toward the woman. She stopped and looked down at him. The fire glittered for a moment and then died out of her eyes, her bosom heaved and her lips began to tremble. With a cry she flung herself into his arms, caught him around the neck, and pressed his face up close against her cheek.

"Oh! Dick, Dick," she sobbed, "I do love you so! I can't live without you! Not another hour, Dick! I do want you so much, so much, Dick!"

The man shifted his right arm quickly, slipped a great Mexican knife out of his sleeve, and passed his fingers slowly up the woman's side until he felt the heart beat under his hand, then he raised the knife, gripped the handle tight, and drove the keen blade into the woman's bosom. The hot blood gushed out over his arm and down on his leg. The body, warm and limp, slipped down in his arms. The man got up, pulled out the knife, and thrust it into a sheath at his belt, unbuttoned the dress, and slipped it off the body. As he did this a bundle of papers dropped upon the floor; these he glanced at hastily and put into his pocket. Then he took the dead woman up in his arms, went out into the hall, and started to go up the stairway. The body was relaxed and heavy, and for that reason difficult to carry. He doubled it up into an awful heap, with the knees against the chin, and walked slowly and heavily up the stairs and out into the bathroom. There he laid the corpse down on the tiled floor. Then he opened the window, closed the shutters, and lighted the gas. The bathroom was small and contained an ordinary steel tub, porcelain lined, standing near the window and raised about six inches above the floor. The sailor went over to the tub, pried up the metal rim of the outlet with his knife, removed it, and fitted into its place a porcelain disk which he took from his pocket; to this disk was attached a long platinum wire, the end of which he fastened on the outside of the tub. After he had done this he went back to the body, stripped off its clothing, put it down in the tub, and began to dismember it with the great Mexican knife. The blade was strong and sharp as a razor. The man worked rapidly and with the greatest care.

When he had finally cut the body into as small pieces as possible, he replaced the knife in its sheath, washed his hands, and went out of the bathroom and downstairs to the lower hall. The sailor seemed perfectly familiar with the house. By a side door he passed into the cellar. There he lighted the gas, opened one of the wine cases, and, taking up all the bottles that he could conveniently carry, returned to the bathroom. There he poured the contents into the tub on the dismembered body and then returned to the cellar with the empty bottles, which he replaced in the wine cases. This he continued to do until all the cases but one were emptied and the bathtub was more than half full of liquid. This liquid was sulfuric acid.

When the sailor returned to the cellar with the last empty wine bottles, he opened the fifth case, which really contained wine, took some of it out, and poured a little into each of the empty bottles in order to remove any possible odor of the sulfuric acid. Then he turned out the gas and brought up to the bathroom with him the two paper flour sacks and the little heavy bundle. These sacks were filled with nitrate of soda. He set them down by the door, opened the little bundle, and took out two long rubber tubes, each attached to a heavy gas burner, not unlike the ordinary burners of a small gas stove. He fastened the tubes to two of the gas jets, put the burners under the tub, turned the gas on full, and lighted it. Then he threw into the tub the woman's clothing and the papers which he had found on her body, after which he took up the two heavy sacks of nitrate of soda and dropped them carefully into the sulfuric acid. When he had done this he went quickly out of the bathroom and closed the door.

The deadly acids at once attacked the body and began to destroy it; as the heat increased, the acids boiled and the destructive process was rapid and awful. From time to time the sailor opened the door of the bathroom cautiously and, holding a wet towel over his mouth and nose, looked in at his horrible work. At the end of a few hours there was only a swimming mass in the tub. When the man looked at four o'clock, it was all a thick, murky liquid. He turned off the gas quickly and stepped back out of the room. For perhaps half an hour he waited in the hall; finally, when the acids had cooled so that they no longer gave off fumes, he opened the door and went in, took hold of the platinum wire and, pulling the porcelain disk from the stopcock, allowed the awful contents of the tub to run out. Then he turned on the hot water, rinsed the tub clean, and replaced the metal outlet. Removing the rubber tubes, he cut them into pieces, broke the porcelain disk, and, rolling up the platinum wire, washed it all down the sewer pipe.

The fumes had escaped through the open window; this he now closed and set himself to putting the bathroom in order, and effectually removing every trace of his night's work. The sailor moved around with the very greatest degree of care. Finally, when he had arranged everything to his complete satisfaction, he picked up the two burners, turned out the gas, and left the bathroom, closing the door after him. From the bathroom he went directly to the attic, concealed the two rusty burners under a heap of rubbish, and then walked carefully and noiselessly down the stairs and through the lower hall. As he opened the door and stepped into the room where he had killed the woman, two police officers sprang out and seized him. The man screamed like a wild beast taken in a trap, and sank down.

"Oh! oh!" he cried, "it was no use! It was no use to do it!" Then he recovered himself in a manner and was silent. The officers handcuffed him, summoned the patrol, and took him at once to the station house. There he said he was a Mexican sailor and that his name was Victor Ancona; but he would say nothing further. The following morning he sent for Randolph Mason and the two were long together.

IV

The obscure defendant charged with murder had little reason to complain of the law's delays. The morning following the arrest of Victor Ancona, the newspapers published long sensational articles, denounced him as a fiend, and convicted him. The grand jury, as it happened, was in session. The preliminaries were soon arranged and the case was railroaded into trial. The indictment contained a great many counts and charged the prisoner with the murder of Nina San Croix by striking, stabbing, choking, poisoning, and so forth.

The trial had continued for three days and had appeared so overwhelmingly one-sided that the spectators who were crowded into the courtroom had grown to be violent and bitter partisans, to such an extent that the police watched them closely. The attorneys for the People were dramatic and denunciatory and forced their case with arrogant confidence. Mason, as counsel for the prisoner, was indifferent and listless. Throughout the entire trial he had sat almost motionless at the table, his gaunt form bent over, his long legs drawn up under his chair, and his weary, heavy-muscled face, with its restless eyes, fixed and staring out over the heads of the jury, was like a tragic mask. The bar, and even the judge, believed that the prisoner's counsel had abandoned his case.

The evidence was all in and the People rested. It had been shown that Nina San Croix had resided for many years in the house in which the prisoner was arrested; that she had lived by herself, with no other companion than an old Negro servant; that her past was unknown, and that she received no visitors, save the Mexican sailor, who came to her house at long intervals. Nothing whatever was shown tending to explain who the prisoner was or whence he had come. It was shown that on Tuesday preceding the killing the archbishop had received a communication from Nina San Croix, in which she said she desired to make a statement of the greatest import, and asking for an audience. To this the archbishop replied that he would willingly grant her a hearing if she would come to him at eleven o'clock on Friday morning. Two policemen testified that about eight o'clock on the night of Thursday they had noticed the prisoner slip into the gate of Nina San Croix's residence and go down to the side of the house, where he was admitted; that his appearance and seeming haste had attracted their attention; that they had concluded that it was some clandestine amour and out of curiosity had both slipped down to the house and endeavored to find a position from which they could see into the room, but were unable to do so and were about to go back to the street when they heard a woman's voice cry out in great anger, "I know that you love her and that you want to get rid of me, but you shall not do it! You murdered him, but you shall not murder me! I have all the evidence to convict you of murdering him! The archbishop will have it tomorrow! They shall hang you! Do you hear me? They shall hang you for this murder!" that thereupon one of the policemen proposed that they should break into the house and see what was wrong, but the other had urged that it was only the usual lovers' quarrel and if they should interfere they would find nothing upon which a charge could be based and would only be laughed at by the chief; that they had waited and listened for a time, but hearing nothing further had gone back to the street and contented themselves with keeping strict watch on the house.

The People proved further, that on Thursday evening Nina San Croix had given the old Negro domestic a sum of money and dismissed her, with the instruction that she was not to return until sent for. The old woman testified that she had gone directly to the house of her son and later had discovered that she had forgotten some articles of clothing which she needed; that thereupon she had returned to the house and had gone up the back way to her room—this was about eight o'clock; that while there she had heard Nina San Croix's voice in great passion and remembered that she had used the words stated by the policemen; that these sudden, violent cries had frightened her greatly and she had bolted the door and been afraid to leave the room; shortly thereafter, she had heard heavy footsteps ascending the stairs, slowly and with great difficulty, as though someone were carrying a heavy burden; that therefore her fear had increased and that she had put out the light and hidden under the bed. She remembered hearing the footsteps moving about upstairs for many hours, how long she could not tell. Finally, about half-past four in the morning she crept out, opened the door, slipped downstairs, and ran out into the street. There she had found the policemen and requested them to search the house.

The two officers had gone to the house with the woman. She had opened the door and they had just had time to step back into the shadow when the prisoner entered. When arrested, Victor Ancona had screamed with terror and cried out, "It was no use! It was no use to do it!"

The chief of police had come to the house and instituted a careful search. In the room below, from which the cries had come, he found a dress which was identified as belonging to Nina San Croix and which she was wearing when last seen by the domestic about six o'clock that evening. This dress was covered with blood and had a slit about two inches long in the left side of the bosom, into which the Mexican knife, found on the prisoner, fitted perfectly. These articles were introduced in evidence, and it was shown that the slit would be exactly over the heart of the wearer, and that such a wound would certainly result in death. There was much blood on one of the chairs and on the floor. There was also blood on the prisoner's coat and the leg of his trousers, and the heavy Mexican knife was also bloody. The blood was shown by the experts to be human blood.

The body of the woman was not found, and the most rigid and tireless search failed to develop the slightest trace of the corpse, or the manner of its disposal. The body of the woman had disappeared as completely as though it had vanished into the air.

When counsel announced that he had closed for the People, the judge turned and looked gravely down at Mason. "Sir," he said, "the evidence for the defense may now be introduced."

Randolph Mason arose slowly and faced the judge.

"If your Honor please," he said, speaking slowly and distinctly, "the defendant has no evidence to offer." He paused while a murmur of astonishment ran over the court room. "But, if your Honor please," he continued, "I move that the jury be directed to find the prisoner not guilty."

The crowd stirred. The counsel for the People smiled. The judge looked sharply at the speaker over his glasses. "On what ground?" he said curtly.

"On the ground," replied Mason, "that the *corpus delicti* has not been proven."

"Ah!" said the judge, for once losing his judicial gravity.

Mason sat down abruptly. The senior counsel for the prosecution was on his feet in a moment.

"What!" he said. "The gentleman bases his motion on a

failure to establish the *corpus delicti*? Does he jest or has he forgotten the evidence? The term *'corpus delicti'* is technical and means the body of the crime, or the substantial fact that a crime has been committed. Does anyone doubt it in this case? It is true that no one actually saw the prisoner kill the decedent and that he has so successfully hidden the body that it has not been found, but the powerful chain of circumstances, clear and close-linked, proving motive, the criminal agency, and the criminal act, is overwhelming.

"The victim in this case is on the eve of making a statement that would prove fatal to the prisoner. The night before the statement is to be made he goes to her residence. They quarrel. Her voice is heard, raised high in the greatest passion, denouncing him, and charging that he is a murderer, that she has the evidence and will reveal it, that he shall be hanged and that he shall not be rid of her. Here is the motive for the crime, clear as light. Are not the bloody knife, the bloody dress, the bloody clothes of the prisoner, unimpeachable witnesses to the criminal act? The criminal agency of the prisoner has not the shadow of a possibility to obscure it. His motive is gigantic. The blood on him, and his despair when arrested, cry, 'Murder! murder!' with a thousand tongues.

"Men may lie, but circumstances cannot. The thousand hopes and fears and passions of men may delude or bias the witness. Yet it is beyond the human mind to conceive that a clear, complete chain of concatenated circumstances can be in error. Hence it is that the greatest jurists have declared that such evidence, being rarely liable to delusion or fraud, is safest and most powerful. The machinery of human justice cannot guard against the remote and improbable doubt. The inference is persistent in the affairs of men. It is the only means by which the human mind reaches the truth. If you forbid the jury to exercise it, you bid them work after first striking off their hands. Rule out the irresistible inference, and the end of justice is come in this land; and you may as well leave the spider to weave his web through the abandoned courtroom."

The attorney stopped, looked down at Mason with a pompous sneer, and retired to his place at the table. The judge sat thoughtful and motionless. The jurymen leaned forward in their seats.

"If your Honor please," said Mason, rising, "this is a matter of law, plain, clear, and so well settled in the State of New York that even counsel for the People should know it. The question before your Honor is simple. If the *corpus delicti,* the body of the crime, has been proven, as required by the laws of the commonwealth, then this case should go to the jury. If not, then it is the duty of this court to direct the jury to find the prisoner not guilty. There is here no room for judicial discretion. Your Honor has but to recall and apply the rigid rule announced by our courts prescribing distinctly how the *corpus delicti* in murder must be proven.

"The prisoner here stands charged with the highest crime. The law demands, first, that the crime, as a fact, be established. The fact that the victim is indeed dead must first be made certain before anyone can be convicted for her killing, because, so long as there remains the remotest doubt as to the death, there can be no certainty as to the criminal agent, although the circumstantial evidence indicating the guilt of the accused may be positive, complete, and utterly irresistible. In murder the *corpus delicti,* or body of the crime, is composed of two elements:

"Death, as a result.

"The criminal agency of another as the means.

"It is the fixed and immutable law of this state, laid down in the leading case of Ruloff *v.* The People, and binding upon this court, that both components of the *corpus delicti* shall not be established by circumstantial evidence. There must be direct proof of one or the other of these two component elements of the *corpus delicti.* If one is proven by direct evidence, the other may be presumed; but both shall not be presumed from circumstances, no matter how powerful, how cogent, or how completely overwhelming the circumstances may be. In other words, no man can be convicted of murder in the State of New York unless the body of the victim be found and identified, or there be direct proof that the prisoner did some act adequate to produce death, and did it in such a manner as to account for the disappearance of the body."

The face of the judge cleared and grew hard. The members

of the bar were attentive and alert; they were beginning to see the legal escape open up. The audience were puzzled; they did not yet understand. Mason turned to the counsel for the People. His ugly face was bitter with contempt.

"For three days," he said, "I have been tortured by this useless and expensive farce. If counsel for the People had been other than play-actors, they would have known in the beginning that Victor Ancona could not be convicted for murder, unless he were confronted in this courtroom with a living witness, who had looked into the dead face of Nina San Croix; or, if not that, a living witness who had seen him drive the dagger into her bosom.

"I care not if the circumstantial evidence in this case were so strong and irresistible as to be overpowering; if the judge on the bench, if the jury, if every man within sound of my voice, were convinced of the guilt of the prisoner to the degree of certainty that is absolute; if the circumstantial evidence left in the mind no shadow of the remotest improbable doubt; yet, in the absence of the eyewitness, this prisoner cannot be punished, and this court must compel the jury to acquit him."

The audience now understood, and they were dumfounded. Surely this was not the law. They had been taught that the law was common sense, and this, this was anything else.

Mason saw it all and grinned. "In its tenderness," he sneered, "the law shields the innocent. The good law of New York reaches out its hand and lifts the prisoner out of the clutches of the fierce jury that would hang him."

Mason sat down. The room was silent. The jurymen looked at each other in amazement. The counsel for the People arose. His face was white with anger, and incredulous.

"Your Honor," he said, "this doctrine is monstrous. Can it it be said that, in order to evade punishment, the murderer has only to hide or destroy the body of the victim or sink it into the sea? Then, if he is not seen to kill, the law is powerless and the murderer can snap his finger in the face of retributive justice. If this is the law, then the law for the highest crime is a dead letter. The great commonwealth winks at murder and invites every man to kill his enemy, provided he kill him in secret and hide him. I repeat, your Honor"—the man's voice was now loud and angry and rang through the courtroom—"that this doctrine is monstrous!"

"So said Best, and Story, and many another," muttered Mason, "and the law remained."

"The court," said the judge, abruptly, "desires no further argument."

The counsel for the People resumed his seat. His face lighted up with triumph. The court was going to sustain him.

The judge turned and looked down at the jury. He was grave, and spoke with deliberate emphasis.

"Gentlemen of the jury," he said, "the rule of Lord Hale obtains in this state and is binding upon me. It is the law as stated by counsel for the prisoner: that to warrant conviction of murder there must be direct proof either of the death, as of the finding and identification of the corpse, or of criminal violence adequate to produce death, and exerted in such a manner as to account for the disappearance of the body; and it is only when there is direct proof of the one that the other can be established by circumstantial evidence. This is law and cannot now be departed from. I do not presume to explain its wisdom. Chief Justice Johnson has observed, in the leading case, that it may have its probable foundation in the idea that where direct proof is absent as to both the fact of the death and of criminal violence capable of producing death, no evidence can rise to the degree of moral certainty that the individual is dead by criminal intervention, or even lead by direct inference to this result; and that, where the fact of death is not certainly ascertained, all inculpatory circumstantial evidence wants the key necessary for its satisfactory interpretation and cannot be depended on to furnish more than probable results. It may be, also, that such a rule has some reference to the dangerous possibility that a general preconception of guilt, or a general excitement of popular feeling, may creep in to supply the place of evidence, if, upon other than direct proof of death or a cause of death, a jury are permitted to pronounce a prisoner guilty.

"In this case the body has not been found and there is no direct proof of criminal agency on the part of the prisoner, although the chain of circumstantial evidence is complete and irresistible in the highest degree. Nevertheless, it is all circumstantial evidence, and under the laws of New York the prisoner cannot be punished. I have no right of discretion. The law does not permit a conviction in this case, although every one of us may be morally certain of the prisoner's guilt. I am, therefore, gentlemen of the jury, compelled to direct you to find the prisoner not guilty."

"Judge," interrupted the foreman, jumping up in the box, "we cannot find that verdict under our oath; we know that this man is guilty."

"Sir," said the judge, "this is a matter of law in which the wishes of the jury cannot be considered. The clerk will write a verdict of not guilty, which you, as foreman, will sign."

The spectators broke out into a threatening murmur that began to grow and gather volume. The judge rapped on his desk and ordered the bailiffs promptly to suppress any demonstration on the part of the audience. Then he directed the foreman to sign the verdict prepared by the clerk. When this was done he turned to Victor Ancona; his face was hard and there was a cold glitter in his eyes.

"Prisoner at the bar," he said, "you have been put to trial before this tribunal on a charge of cold-blooded and atrocious murder. The evidence produced against you was of such powerful and overwhelming character that it seems to have left no doubt in the minds of the jury, nor indeed in the mind of any person present in this courtroom.

"Had the question of your guilt been submitted to these twelve arbiters, a conviction would certainly have resulted and the death penalty would have been imposed. But the law, rigid, passionless, even-eyed, has thrust in between you and the wrath of your fellows and saved you from it. I do not cry out against the impotency of the law; it is perhaps as wise as imperfect humanity could make it. I deplore, rather, the genius of evil men who, by cunning design, are enabled to slip through the fingers of this law. I have no word of censure or admonition for you, Victor Ancona. The law of New York compels me to acquit you. I am only its mouthpiece, with my individual wishes throttled. I speak only those things which the law directs I shall speak.

"You are now at liberty to leave this courtroom, not guiltless of the crime of murder, perhaps, but at least rid of its punishment. The eyes of men may see Cain's mark on your brow, but the eyes of the law are blind to it." When the audience fully realized what the judge had said they were amazed and silent. They knew as well as men could know that Victor Ancona was guilty of murder, and yet he was now going out of the courtroom free. Could it happen that the law protected only against the blundering rogue? They had heard always of the boasted completeness of the law which magistrates from time immemorial had labored to perfect, and now when the skillful villain sought to evade it, they saw how weak a thing it was.

V

The wedding march of *Lohengrin* floated out from the Episcopal Church of St. Mark, clear and sweet, and perhaps heavy with its paradox of warning. The theater of this coming contract before high heaven was a wilderness of roses worth the taxes of a county. The high caste of Manhattan, by the grace of the checkbook, were present, clothed in Parisian purple and fine linen, cunningly and marvelously wrought.

Over in her private pew, ablaze with jewels and decked with fabrics from the deft hand of many a weaver, sat Mrs. Miriam Steuvisant as imperious and self-complacent as a queen. To her it was all a kind of triumphal procession, proclaiming her ability as a general. With her were a choice few of the *genus homo,* which obtains at the five-o'clock teas, instituted, say the sages, for the purpose of sprinkling the holy water of Lethe.

"Czarina," whispered Reggie Du Puyster, leaning forward, "I salute you. The ceremony *sub jugum* is superb."

"Walcott is an excellent fellow," answered Mrs. Steuvisant, "not a vice, you know, Reggie."

"Aye, Empress," put in the others, "a purist taken in the net. The clean-skirted one has come to the altar. *Vive la vertu!*"

Samuel Walcott, still sunburned from his cruise, stood before the chancel with the only daughter of the blue-blooded St. Clairs. His face was clear and honest and his voice firm. This was life and not romance. The lid of the sepulcher had closed and he had slipped from under it. And now, and ever after, the hand red with murder was clean as any.

The minister raised his voice, proclaiming the holy union before God, and this twain, half pure, half foul, now by divine ordinance one flesh, bowed down before it. No blood cried from the ground. The sunlight of high noon streamed down through the windowpanes like a benediction.

Back in the pew of Mrs. Miriam Steuvisant, Reggie Du Puyster turned down his thumb. *"Habet!"* he said.

The Dog Andrew

by:

ARTHUR TRAIN

selected by:

RICHARD M. NIXON

Like so many members of the bar, I have always enjoyed taking a "busman's holiday" by relaxing with fiction about law and the legal profession. Like so many members of the bar, my favorite author is Arthur Train, whose "Mr. Tutt" stories have inspired and given pleasure to two generations of American lawyers. One of his best and my choice is "The Dog Andrew."

S.S. RICHARD M. NIXON

"Every dog is entitled to one bite."—UNREPORTED OPINION OF THE APPELLATE DIVISION OF THE NEW YORK SUPREME COURT.

"Now see here!" shouted Mr. Appleboy, coming out of the boathouse, where he was cleaning his morning's catch of perch, as his neighbor Mr. Tunnygate crashed through the hedge and cut across Appleboy's parched lawn to the beach. "See here, Tunnygate, I won't have you trespassing on my place! I've told you so at least a dozen times! Look at the hole you've made in that hedge, now! Why can't you stay in the path?"

His ordinarily good-natured countenance was suffused with anger and perspiration. His irritation with Mr. Tunnygate had reached the point of explosion. Tunnygate was a thankless friend and he was a great cross to Mr. Appleboy. Aforetime the two had been intimate in the fraternal, taciturn intimacy characteristic of fat men, an attraction perhaps akin to that exerted for one another by celestial bodies of great mass, for it is a fact that stout people do gravitate toward one another—and hang or float in placid juxtaposition, perhaps merely as a physical result of their avoirdupois. So Appleboy and Tunnygate had swum into each other's spheres of influence, either blown by the dallying winds of chance or drawn by some mysterious animal magnetism, and, being both addicted to the delights of the soporific sport sanctified by Izaak Walton, had raised unto themselves portable temples upon the shores of Long Island Sound in that part of the geographical limits of the Greater City known as Throggs Neck.

Every morn during the heat of the summer months Appleboy would rouse Tunnygate or conversely Tunnygate would rouse Appleboy, and each in his own wobbly skiff would row out to the spot which seemed most propitious to the piscatorial art. There, under two green umbrellas, like two fat rajahs in their shaking howdahs upon the backs of two white elephants, the friends would sit in solemn equanimity awaiting the evasive cunner, the vagrant perch or cod, or the occasional flirtatious eel. They rarely spoke and when they did the edifice of their conversation—their Tower of Babel, so to speak—was monosyllabic. Thus:

"Huh! Ain't had a bite!"

"Huh!"

"Huh!"

Silence for forty minutes. Then: "Huh! Had a bite?"

"Nope!"

"Huh!"

That was generally the sum total of their interchange. Yet it satisfied them, for their souls were in harmony. To them it was pregnant of unutterable meanings, of philosophic mysteries more subtle than those of the esoterics, of flowers and poetry, of bird song and twilight, of all the nuances of softly whispered avowals, of the elusive harmonies of love's half-fainting ecstasy.

"Huh!"

"Huh!"

And then into this Eden—only not by virtue of the excision of any vertebra such as was originally necessary in the case of Adam—burst woman. There was silence no longer. The air was rent with clamor; for both Appleboy and Tunnygate, within a month of one another, took unto themselves wives. Wives after their own image!

For a while things went well enough; it takes ladies a few weeks to find out each other's weak points. But then the new Mrs. Tunnygate unexpectedly yet undeniably began to exhibit the serpent's tooth, the adder's tongue, or the cloven hoof—as the reader's literary traditions may lead him to prefer. For no obvious reason at all she conceived a violent hatred of Mrs. Appleboy, a hatred that waxed all the more virulent on account of its object's innocently obstinate refusal to comprehend or recognize it. Indeed Mrs. Tunnygate found it so difficult to rouse Mrs. Appleboy into a state of belligerency sufficiently interesting that she soon transferred her energies to the more worthy task of making Appleboy's life a burden to him.

To this end she devoted herself with a truly Machiavellian ingenuity, devising all sorts of insults, irritations, and annoyances, and adding to the venom of her tongue the inventive cunning of a Malayan witch doctor. The Appleboys' flowerpots mysteriously fell off the piazza, their tholepins disappeared, their milk bottles vanished, Mr. Appleboy's fish lines acquired a habit of derangement equaled only by barbed-wire entanglements, and his clams went bad! But these things might have been borne had it not been for the crowning achievement of her malevolence, the invasion of the Appleboys' cherished lawn, upon which they lavished all that anxious tenderness which otherwise they might have devoted to a child.

It was only about twenty feet by twenty, and it was bordered by a hedge of moth-eaten privet, but anyone who has ever attempted to induce a blade of grass to grow upon a sand dune will fully appreciate the deviltry of Mrs. Tunnygate's malignant mind. Already there was a horrid rent where Tunnygate had floundered through at her suggestion in order to save going round the pathetic grass plot which the Appleboys had struggled to create where Nature had obviously intended a floral vacuum. Undoubtedly it had been the sight of Mrs. Appleboy with her small watering pot patiently encouraging the recalcitrant blades that had suggested the malicious thought to Mrs. Tunnygate that maybe the Appleboys didn't own that far up the beach. They didn't—that was the mockery of it. Like many others they had built their porch on their boundary line, and, as Mrs. Tunnygate pointed out, they were claiming to own something that wasn't theirs. So Tunnygate, in daily obedience to his spouse, forced his way through the hedge to the beach, and daily the wrath of the Appleboys grew until they were driven almost to desperation.

Now when the two former friends sat fishing in their skiffs they either contemptuously ignored one another or, if they "Huh-Huhed!" at all the "Huhs!" resembled the angry growls of infuriated beasts. The worst of it was that the Appleboys couldn't properly do anything about it. Tunnygate had, as Mrs. Tunnygate sneeringly pointed out, a perfect legal right to push his way through the hedge and tramp across the lawn, and she didn't propose to allow the Appleboys to gain any rights by proscription, either. Not much!

Therefore, when Mr. Appleboy addressed to Mr. Tunnygate the remarks with which this story opens, the latter insolently replied in words, form, or substance that Mr. Appleboy could go to hell. Moreover, as he went by Mr. Appleboy he took pains to kick over a clod of transplanted sea grass, nurtured by Mrs. Appleboy as the darling of her bosom, and designed to give an air of verisimilitude to an otherwise bare and unconvincing surface of sand. Mr. Appleboy almost cried with vexation.

"Oh!" he ejaculated, struggling for words to express the full content of his feeling. "Gosh, but you're—mean!"

He hit it! Curiously enough, that was exactly the word! Tunnygate was mean—and his meanness was second only to that of the fat hippopotama, his wife.

Then, without knowing why, for he had no formulated ideas as to the future and probably only intended to try to scare Tunnygate with vague threats, Appleboy added: "I warn you not to go through that hedge again! Understand—I warn you! And if you do I won't be responsible for the consequences!"

He really didn't mean a thing by the words, and Tunnygate knew it.

"Huh!" retorted the latter contemptuously. "You!"

Mr. Appleboy went inside the shack and banged the door. Mrs. Appleboy was peeling potatoes in the kitchen-living room.

"I can't stand it!" he cried weakly. "He's driving me wild!"

"Poor lamb!" soothed Mrs. Appleboy, peeling an interminable rind. "Ain't that just a sweetie? Look! It's most as long as your arm!"

She held it up, dangling between her thumb and forefinger.

Then, with a groan she dropped it at his feet. "I know it's a real burden to you, deary!" she sighed.

Suddenly they both bent forward with startled eyes, hypnotized by the peel upon the floor.

Unmistakably it spelt "dog"! They looked at one another significantly.

"It is a symbol!" breathed Mrs. Appleboy in an awed whisper.

"Whatever it is, it's some grand idea!" exclaimed her husband. "Do you know anybody who's got one? I mean a—a—"

"I know just what you mean," she agreed. "I wonder we never thought of it before! But there wouldn't be any use in getting any dog!"

"Oh, no!" he concurred. "We want a real—dog!"

"One you know about!" she commented.

"The fact is," said he, rubbing his forehead, "if they know about 'em they do something to 'em. It ain't so easy to get the right kind."

"Oh, we'll get one!" she encouraged him. "Now Aunt Eliza up to Livonia used to have one. It made a lot of trouble and they ordered her—the selectmen did—to do away with it. But she only pretended she had—she didn't really—and I think she's got him yet."

"Gee!" said Mr. Appleboy tensely. "What sort was it?"

"A bull!" she replied. "With a big white face."

"That's the kind!" he agreed excitedly. "What was its name?"

"Andrew," she answered.

"That's a queer name for a dog!" he commented. "Still, I don't care what his name is, so long as he's the right kind of dog! Why don't you write to Aunt Eliza tonight?"

"Of course Andrew may be dead," she hazarded. "Dogs do die."

"Oh, I guess Andrew isn't dead!" he said hopefully. "That tough kind of dog lasts a long time. What will you say to Aunt Eliza?"

Mrs. Appleboy went to the dresser and took a pad and pencil from one of the shelves.

"Oh, something like this," she answered, poising the pencil over the pad in her lap:

Dear Aunt Eliza: I hope you are quite well. It is sort of lonely living down here on the beach and there are a good many rough characters, so we are looking for a dog for companionship and protection. Almost any kind of healthy dog would do and you may be sure he would have a good home. Hoping to see you soon. Your affectionate niece, *Bashemath.*

"I hope she'll send us Andrew," said Appleboy.

"I guess she will!" nodded Bashemath.

"What on earth is that sign?" wrathfully demanded Mrs. Tunnygate one morning about a week later as she looked across the Appleboys' lawn from her kitchen window. "Can you read it, Herman?"

Herman stopped trying to adjust his collar and went out on the piazza.

"Something about 'dog,'" he declared finally.

"Dog!" she exclaimed. "They haven't got a dog!"

"Well," he remarked, "that's what the sign says: 'Beware of the dog'! And there's something above it. Oh! 'No crossing this property. Trespassing forbidden.'"

"What impudence!" avowed Mrs. Tunnygate. "Did you ever know such people! First they try and take land that don't belong to them, and then they go and lie about having a dog. Where are they, anyway?"

"I haven't seen 'em this morning," he answered. "Maybe they've gone away and put up the sign so we won't go over. Think that'll stop us!"

"In that case they've got another think comin'!" she retorted angrily. "I've a good mind to have you go over and tear up the whole place!"

"'N pull up the hedge?" he concurred eagerly. "Good chance!"

Indeed, to Mr. Tunnygate it seemed the supreme opportunity both to distinguish himself in the eyes of his blushing bride and to gratify that perverse instinct inherited from our cave-dwelling ancestors to destroy utterly—in order, perhaps, that they may never seek to avenge themselves upon us—those whom we have wronged. Accordingly Mr. Tunnygate girded himself with his suspenders and, with a gleam of fiendish exultation in his eye, stealthily descended from his porch and crossed to the hole in the hedge. No one was in sight except two barefooted searchers after clams a few hundred yards farther up the beach and a man working in a field half a mile away. The bay shimmered in the broiling August sun and from a distant grove came the rattle and wheeze of locusts. Throggs Neck blazed in silence, and utterly silent was the house of Appleboy.

With an air of bravado, but with a slightly accelerated heartbeat, Tunnygate thrust himself through the hole in the hedge and looked scornfully about the Appleboy lawn. A fierce rage worked through his veins. A lawn! What effrontery! What business had these condescending second-raters to presume to improve a perfectly good beach which was satisfactory to other folks? He'd show 'em! He took a step in the direction of the transplanted sea grass. Unexpectedly the door of the Appleboy kitchen opened.

"I warned you!" enunciated Mr. Appleboy with unnatural calmness, which with another background might have struck almost anybody as suspicious.

"Huh!" returned the startled Tunnygate, forced under the circumstances to assume a nonchalance that he did not altogether feel. "You!"

"Well," repeated Mr. Appleboy. "Don't ever say I didn't!"

"Pshaw!" ejaculated Mr. Tunnygate disdainfully.

With premeditation and deliberation, and with undeniable malice aforethought, he kicked the nearest bunch of sea grass several feet in the air. His violence carried his leg high in the air and he partially lost his equilibrium. Simultaneously a white streak shot from beneath the porch and something like a red-hot poker thrust itself savagely into an extremely tender part of his anatomy.

"Ouch! O—o—oh!" he yelled in agony. "Oh!"

"Come here, Andrew!" said Mr. Appleboy mildly. "Good doggy! Come here!"

But Andrew paid no attention. He had firmly affixed himself to the base of Mr. Tunnygate's personality without any intention of being immediately detached. And he had selected that place, taken aim, and discharged himself with an air of confidence and skill begotten of lifelong experience.

"Oh! O—o—oh!" screamed Tunnygate, turning wildly and clawing through the hedge, dragging Andrew after him. "Oh! O—oh!"

Mrs. Tunnygate rushed to the door in time to see her spouse lumbering up the beach with a white object gyrating in the air behind him.

"What's the matter?" she called out languidly. Then perceiving the matter she hastily followed. The Appleboys were standing on their lawn, viewing the whole proceeding with ostentatious indifference.

Up the beach fled Tunnygate, his cries becoming fainter and fainter. The two clam diggers watched him curiously but made no attempt to go to his assistance. The man in the field leaned luxuriously upon his hoe and surrendered himself to unalloyed delight. Tunnygate was now but a white flicker against the distant sand. His wails had a dying fall: "O—o—oh!"

"Well, we warned him!" remarked Mr. Appleboy to Bashemath with a smile in which, however, lurked a slight trace of apprehension.

"We certainly did!" she replied. Then after a moment she added a trifle anxiously: "I wonder what will happen to Andrew!"

Tunnygate did not return. Neither did Andrew. Secluded in their kitchen-living room the Appleboys heard a motor arrive and through a crack in the door saw it carry Mrs. Tunnygate away bedecked as for some momentous ceremonial. At four o'clock, while Appleboy was digging bait, he observed another motor making its wriggly way along the dunes. It was fitted longitudinally with seats, had a wire grating and was marked N.Y.P.D. Two policemen in uniform sat in front. Instinctively Appleboy realized that the gods had called him. His heart sank among the clams. Slowly he made his way back to the lawn where the wagon had stopped outside the hedge.

"Hey there!" called out the driver. "Is your name Appleboy?" Appleboy nodded.

"Put your coat on, then, and come along," directed the other. "I've got a warrant for you."

"Warrant?" stammered Appleboy dizzily.

"What's that?" cried Bashemath, appearing at the door. "Warrant for what?"

The officer slowly descended and handed Appleboy a paper. "For assault," he replied. "I guess you know what for, all right!"

"We haven't assaulted anybody," protested Mrs. Appleboy heatedly. "Andrew—"

"You can explain all that to the judge," retorted the cop. "Meanwhile put on your duds and climb in. If you don't expect to spend the night at the station you'd better bring along the deed of your house so you can give bail."

"But who's the warrant for?" persisted Mrs. Appleboy.

"For Enoch Appleboy," retorted the cop wearily. "Can't you read?"

"But Enoch didn't do a thing!" she declared. "It was Andrew!"

"Who's Andrew?" inquired the officer of the law mistrustfully.

"Andrew's a dog," she explained.

"Mr. Tutt," announced Tutt, leaning against his senior partner's doorjamb with a formal-looking paper in his hand, "I have landed a case that will delight your legal soul."

"Indeed?" queried the elder lawyer. "I have never differentiated between my legal soul and any other I may possess. However, I assume from your remark that we have been retained in a matter presenting some peculiarly absurd, archaic, or otherwise interesting doctrine of law?"

"Not directly," responded Tutt. "Though you will doubtless find it entertaining enough, but indirectly—atmospherically, so to speak—it touches upon doctrines of jurisprudence, of religion and of philosophy, replete with historic fascination."

"Good!" exclaimed Mr. Tutt, laying down his stogy. "What kind of a case is it?"

"It's a dog case!" said the junior partner, waving the paper. "The dog bit somebody."

"Ah!" exclaimed Mr. Tutt, perceptibly brightening. "Doubtless we shall find a precedent in Oliver Goldsmith's famous elegy:

"And in that town a dog was found,
As many dogs there be,
Both mongrel, puppy, whelp, and hound,
And curs of low degree."

"Only," explained Tutt, "in this case, though the man recovered of the bite, the dog refused to die!"

"And so they want to prosecute the dog? It can't be done. An animal hasn't been brought to the bar of justice for several centuries."

"No, no!" interrupted Tutt. "They don't——"

"There was a case," went on Mr. Tutt reminiscently. "Let me see—at Sauvigny, I think it was—about 1457, when they tried a sow and three pigs for killing a child. The court assigned a lawyer to defend her, but like many assigned counsel he couldn't think of anything to say in her behalf. As regards the little pigs he did enter the plea that no animus was shown, that they had merely followed the example of their mother, and that at worst they were under age and irresponsible. However, the court found them all guilty, and the sow was publicly hanged in the market place."

"What did they do with the three little pigs?" inquired Tutt with some interest.

"They were pardoned on account of their extreme youth," said Mr. Tutt, "and turned loose again—with a warning."

"I'm glad of that!" sighed Tutt. "Is that a real case?"

"Absolutely," replied his partner. "I've read it in the Sauvigny records."

"I'll be hanged!" exclaimed Tutt. "I never knew that animals were ever held personally responsible."

"Why, of course they were!" said Mr. Tutt. "Why shouldn't they be? If animals have souls why shouldn't they be responsible for their acts?"

"But they haven't any souls!" protested Tutt.

"Haven't they now?" remarked the elder lawyer. "I've seen many an old horse that had a great deal more conscience than his master. And on general principles wouldn't it be far more just and humane to have the law deal with a vicious animal that had injured somebody than to leave its punishment to an irresponsible and arbitrary owner who might be guilty of extreme brutality?"

"If the punishment would do any good—yes!" agreed Tutt.

"Well, who knows?" meditated Mr. Tutt. "I wonder if it ever does any good? But anybody would have to agree that responsibility for one's acts should depend upon the degree of one's intelligence—and from that point of view many of our friends are really much less responsible than sheep.

"Which, as you so sagely point out, would, however, be a poor reason for letting their families punish them in case they did wrong. Just think how such a privilege might be abused! If Uncle John didn't behave himself as his nephews thought proper they could simply set upon him and briskly beat him up."

"Yes, of course, the law even today recognizes the right to exercise physical discipline within the family. Even homicide is excusable, under Section 1054 of our code, when committed in lawfully correcting a child or servant."

"That's a fine relic of barbarism!" remarked Tutt. "But the child soon passes through that dangerous zone and becomes entitled to be tried for his offenses by a jury of his peers; the animal never does."

"Well, an animal couldn't be tried by a jury of his peers, anyhow," said Mr. Tutt.

"I've seen juries that were more like nanny goats than men!" commented Tutt. "I'd like to see some of our clients tried by juries of geese or woodchucks."

"The field of criminal responsibility is the no man's land of the law," mused Mr. Tutt. "Roughly, mental capacity to understand the nature of one's acts is the test, but it is applied arbitrarily in the case of human beings and a mere point of time is taken beyond which, irrespective of his actual intelligence, a man is held accountable for whatever he does. Of course that is theoretically unsound. The more intelligent a person is the more responsible he should be held to be and the higher the quality of conduct demanded of him by his fellows. Yet after twenty-one all are held equally responsible—unless they're actually insane. It isn't equity! In theory no man or animal should be subject to the power of discretionary punishment on the part of another—even his own father or master. I've often wondered what earthly right we have to make the animals work for us—to bind them to slavery when we denounce slavery as a crime. It would horrify us to see a human being put up and sold at auction. Yet we tear the families of animals apart, subject them to lives of toil, and kill them whenever we see fit. We say we do this because their intelligence is limited and they cannot exercise any discrimination in their conduct, that they are always in the zone of irresponsibility and so have no rights. But I've seen animals that were shrewder than men, and men who were vastly less intelligent than animals."

"Right-o!" assented Tutt. "Take Scraggs, for instance. He's no more responsible than a chipmunk."

"Nevertheless, the law has always been consistent," said Mr. Tutt, "and has never discriminated between animals any more than it has between men on the ground of varying degrees of intelligence. They used to try 'em all, big and little, wild and domesticated, mammals and invertebrates."

"Oh, come!" exclaimed Tutt. "I may not know much law, but—"

"Between 1120 and 1740 they prosecuted in France alone no less than ninety-two animals. The last one was a cow."

"A cow hasn't much intelligence," observed Tutt.

"And they tried fleas," added Mr. Tutt.

"They have a lot!" commented his junior partner. "I knew a flea once, who——"

"They had a regular form of procedure," continued Mr. Tutt, brushing the flea aside, "which was adhered to with the utmost technical accuracy. You could try an individual animal, either in person or by proxy, or you could try a whole family, swarm, or herd. If a town was infested by rats, for example, they first assigned counsel—an advocate, he was called—and then the defendants were summoned three times publicly to appear. If they didn't show up on the third and last call they were tried *in absentia,* and if convicted were ordered out of the country before a certain date under penalty of being exorcised."

"What happened if they were exorcised?" asked Tutt curiously.

"It depended a good deal on the local power of Satan," answered the old lawyer dryly. "Sometimes they became even more prolific and destructive than they were before, and sometimes they promptly died. All the leeches were prosecuted at Lausanne in 1451. A few selected representatives were brought into court, tried, convicted, and ordered to depart within a fixed period. Maybe they didn't fully grasp their obligations or perhaps were just acting contemptuously, but they didn't depart and so were promptly exorcised. Immediately they began to die off and before long there were none left in the country."

"I know some rats and mice I'd like to have exorcised," mused Tutt.

"At Autun in the fifteenth century the rats won their case," said Mr. Tutt.

"Who got 'em off?" asked Tutt.

"M. Chassensée, the advocate appointed to defend them. They had been a great nuisance and were ordered to appear in court. But none of them turned up. M. Chassensée therefore argued that a default should not be taken because *all* the rats had been summoned, and some were either so young or so old and decrepit that they needed more time. The court thereupon granted him an extension. However, they didn't arrive on the day set, and this time their lawyer claimed that they were under duress and restrained by bodily fear—of the townspeople's cats. That all these cats, therefore, should first be bound over to keep the peace! The court admitted the reasonableness of this, but the townsfolk refused to be responsible for their cats and the judge dismissed the case!"

"What did Chassensée get out of it?" inquired Tutt.

"There is no record of who paid him or what was his fee."

"He was a pretty slick lawyer," observed Tutt. "Did they ever try birds?"

"Oh, yes!" answered Mr. Tutt. "They tried a cock at Basel in 1474—for the crime of laying an egg."

"Why was that a crime?" asked Tutt. "I should call it a *tour de force.*"

"Be that as it may," said his partner, "from a cock's egg is hatched the cockatrice, or basilisk, the glance of whose eye turns the beholder to stone. Therefore they tried the cock, found him guilty, and burned him and his egg together at the stake. That is why cocks don't lay eggs now."

"I'm glad to know that," said Tutt. "When did they give up trying animals?"

"Nearly two hundred years ago," answered Mr. Tutt. "But for some time after that they continued to try inanimate objects for causing injury to people. I've heard they tried one of the first locomotives that ran over a man and declared it forfeit to the crown as a deodand."

"I wonder if you couldn't get 'em to try Andrew," hazarded Tutt, "and maybe declare him forfeited to somebody as a deodand."

"Deodand means 'given to God,' " explained Mr. Tutt.

"Well, I'd give Andrew to God—if God would take him," declared Tutt devoutly.

"But who is Andrew?" asked Mr. Tutt.

"Andrew is a dog," said Tutt, "who bit one Tunnygate, and now the grand jury have indicted not the dog, as it is clear from your historical disquisition they should have done, but the dog's owner, Mr. Enoch Appleboy."

"What for?"

"Assault in the second degree with a dangerous weapon."

"What was the weapon?" inquired Mr. Tutt simply.

"The dog."

"What are you talking about?" cried Mr. Tutt. "What nonsense!"

"Yes, it is nonsense!" agreed Tutt. "But they've done it all the same. Read it for yourself!" And he handed Mr. Tutt the indictment.

The Grand Jury of the County of New York by this indictment accuse Enoch Appleboy of the crime of assault in the second degree, committed as follows:

Said Enoch Appleboy, late of the Borough of Bronx, City and County aforesaid, on the 21st day of July, in the year of our Lord one thousand nine hundred and fifteen, at the Borough and County aforesaid, with force and arms in and upon one Herman Tunnygate, in the peace of the State and People then and there being, feloniously did willfully and wrongfully make an assault in and upon the legs and body of him the said Herman Tunnygate, by means of a certain dangerous weapon, to wit: one dog, of the form, style, and breed known as "bull," being of the name of "Andrew," then and there being within control of the said Enoch Appleboy, which said dog, being of the name of "Andrew," the said Enoch Appleboy did then and there feloniously, willfully, and wrongfully incite, provoke, and encourage, then and there being, to bite him, the said Herman Tunnygate, by means whereof said dog "Andrew" did then and there grievously bite the said Herman Tunnygate in and upon the legs and body of him, the said Herman Tunnygate, and the said Enoch Appleboy thus then and there feloniously did willfully and wrongfully cut, tear, lacerate, and bruise, and did then and there by the means of the dog "Andrew" aforesaid feloniously, willfully, and wrongfully inflict grievous bodily harm upon the said Herman Tunnygate, against the form of the statute in such case made and provided, and against the peace of the People of the State of New York and their dignity.

"That," asserted Mr. Tutt, wiping his spectacles, "is a document worthy of preservation in the Congressional Library. Who drew it?"

"Don't know," answered Tutt! "but whoever he was he was a humorist!"

"It's no good. There isn't any allegation of *scienter* in it," affirmed Mr. Tutt.

"What of it? It says he assaulted Tunnygate with a dangerous weapon. You don't have to set forth that he knew it was a dangerous weapon if you assert that he did it willfully. You don't have to allege in an indictment charging an assault with a pistol that the defendant knew it was loaded."

"But a dog is different!" reasoned Mr. Tutt. "A dog is not *per se* a dangerous weapon. Saying so doesn't make it so, and that part of the indictment is bad on its face—unless, to be sure, it means that he hit him with a dead dog, which, it is clear from the context, he didn't. The other part—that he set the dog on him—lacks the allegation that the dog was vicious and that Appleboy knew it: in other words an allegation of *scienter*. It ought to read that said Enoch Appleboy—'well knowing that said dog Andrew was a dangerous and ferocious animal and would, if incited, provoked and encouraged, bite the legs and body of him the said Herman—did then and there feloniously, willfuly, and wrongfully incite, provoke, and encourage the said Andrew, and so forth.' "

"I get you!" exclaimed Tutt enthusiastically. "Of course an allegation of *scienter* is necessary! In other words you could demur to the indictment for insufficiency?"

Mr. Tutt nodded.

"But in that case they'd merely go before the grand jury and find another—a good one. It's much better to try and knock the case out on the trial once and for all."

"Well, the Appleboys are waiting to see you," said Tutt. "They are in my office. Bonnie Doon got the case for us off his local district leader, who's a member of the same lodge of the Abyssinian Mysteries—Bonnie's been Supreme Exalted Ruler of the Purple Mountain for over a year—and he's pulled in quite a lot of good stuff, not all dog cases either! Appleboy's an Abyssinian too."

"I'll see them," consented Mr. Tutt, "but I'm going to have you try the case. I shall insist upon acting solely in an advisory capacity. Dog trials aren't in my line. There are some things which are *infra dig*—even for Ephraim Tutt."

Mr. Appleboy sat stolidly at the bar of justice, pale but resolute. Beside him sat Mrs. Appleboy, also pale but even more resolute. A jury had been selected without much manifest attention by Tutt, who had nevertheless managed to slip an Abyssinian brother on the back row, and an ex-dog fancier for Number Six. Also among those present were a delicatessen man from East Houston Street, a dealer in rubber novelties, a plumber, and the editor of *Baby's World*. The foreman was almost as fat as Mr. Appleboy, but Tutt regarded this as an even break on account of the size of Tunnygate. As Tutt confidentially whispered to Mrs. Appleboy, it was as rotten a jury as he could get.

Mrs. Appleboy didn't understand why Tutt should want a rotten jury, but she nevertheless imbibed some vicarious confidence from this statement and squeezed Appleboy's hand encouragingly. For Appleboy, in spite of his apparent calm, was a very much frightened man, and under the creases of his floppy waistcoat his heart was beating like a tom-tom. The penalty for assault in the second degree was ten years in state's prison, and life with Bashemath, even in the vicinity of the Tunnygates, seemed sweet. The thought of breaking stones under the summer sun—it was a peculiarly hot summer—was awful. Ten years! He could never live through it! And yet as his glance fell upon the Tunnygates, arrayed in their best finery and sitting with an air of importance upon the front bench of the courtroom, he told himself that he would do the whole thing over again—yes, he would! He had only stood up for his rights, and Tunnygate's blood was upon his own head—or wherever it was. So he squeezed Bashemath's hand tenderly in response.

Upon the bench Judge Witherspoon, assigned from somewhere upstate to help keep down the ever-lengthening criminal calendar of the Metropolitan District, finished the letter he was writing to his wife in Genesee County, sealed it, and settled back in his chair. An old war horse of the country bar, he had in his time been mixed up in almost every kind of litigation, but as he looked over the indictment he with difficulty repressed a smile. Thirty years ago he'd had a dog case himself; also of the form, style, and breed known as bull.

"You may proceed, Mr. District Attorney!" he announced, and little Pepperill, the youngest of the D.A.'s staff, just out of the law school, begoggled and with his hair plastered evenly down on either side of his small round head, rose with serious mien, and with a high piping voice opened the prosecution.

It was, he told them, a most unusual and hence most important case. The defendant Appleboy had maliciously procured a savage dog of the most vicious sort and loosed it upon the innocent complainant as he was on his way to work, with the result that the latter had nearly been torn to shreds. It was a horrible, dastardly, incredible, fiendish crime. He would expect them to do their full duty in the premises, and they should hear Mr. Tunnygate's story from his own lips.

Mr. Tunnygate limped with difficulty to the stand and, having been sworn, gingerly sat down—partially. Then turning his broadside to the gaping jury he recounted his woes with indignant gasps.

"Have you the trousers which you wore upon that occasion?" inquired Pepperill.

Mr. Tunnygate bowed solemnly and lifted from the floor a

paper parcel which he untied and from which he drew what remained of that now historic garment.

"These are they," he announced dramatically.

"I offer them in evidence," exclaimed Pepperill, "and I ask the jury to examine them with great care."

They did so.

Tutt waited until the trousers had been passed from hand to hand and returned to their owner; then, rotund, chipper, and birdlike as ever, began his cross-examination much like a woodpecker attacking a stout stump. The witness had been an old friend of Mr. Appleboy's, had he not? Tunnygate admitted it, and Tutt pecked him again. Never had done him any wrong, had he? Nothing in particular. Well, any wrong? Tunnygate hesitated. Why, yes, Appleboy had tried to fence in the public beach that belonged to everybody. Well, did that do the witness any harm? The witness declared that it did; compelled him to go round when he had a right to go across. Oh! Tutt put his head on one side and glanced at the jury. How many feet? About twenty feet. Then Tutt pecked a little harder.

"Didn't you tear a hole in the hedge and stamp down the grass when by taking a few extra steps you could have reached the beach without difficulty?"

"I—I simply tried to remove an illegal obstruction!" declared Tunnygate indignantly.

"Didn't Mr. Appleboy ask you to keep off?"

"Sure—yes!"

"Didn't you obstinately refuse to do so?"

Mr. Pepperill objected to "obstinately" and it was stricken out.

"I wasn't going to stay off where I had a right to go," asserted the witness.

"And didn't you have warning that the dog was there?"

"Look here!" suddenly burst out Tunnygate. "You can't hector me into anything. Appleboy never had a dog before. He got a dog just to sick him on me! He put up a sign 'Beware of the dog,' but he knew that I'd think it was just a bluff. It was a plant, that's what it was! And just as soon as I got inside the hedge that dog went for me and nearly tore me to bits. It was a rotten thing to do and you know it!"

He subsided, panting.

Tutt bowed complacently.

"I move that the witness' remarks be stricken out on the grounds first, that they are unresponsive; second, that they are irrelevant, incompetent, and immaterial; third, that they contain expressions of opinion and hearsay; and fourth, that they are abusive and generally improper."

"Strike them out!" directed Judge Witherspoon. Then he turned to Tunnygate. "The essence of your testimony is that the defendant set a dog on you, is it not? You had quarreled with the defendant, with whom you had formerly been on friendly terms. You entered on premises claimed to be owned by him, though a sign warned you to beware of a dog. The dog attacked and bit you? That's the case, isn't it?"

"Yes, your Honor."

"Had you ever seen that dog before?"

"No, sir."

"Do you know where he got it?"

"My wife told me——"

"Never mind what your wife told you. Do you——"

"He don't know where the dog came from, judge!" suddenly called out Mrs. Tunnygate in strident tones from where she was sitting. "But I know!" she added venomously. "That woman of his got it from——"

Judge Witherspoon fixed her coldly with an impassive and judicial eye.

"Will you kindly be silent, madam? You will no doubt be given an opportunity to testify as fully as you wish. That is all, sir, unless Mr. Tutt has some more questions."

Tutt waved the witness from the stand contemptuously.

"Well, I'd like a chance to testify!" shrilled Mrs. Tunnygate, rising in full panoply.

"This way, madam," said the clerk, motioning her round the back of the jury box. And she swept ponderously into the offing like a full-rigged bark and came to anchor in the witness chair, her chin rising and falling upon her heaving bosom like the figurehead of a vessel upon a heavy harbor swell.

Now it has never been satisfactorily explained just why the character of an individual should be in any way deducible from such irrelevant attributes as facial anatomy, bodily structure, or the shape of the cranium. Perhaps it is not, and in reality we discern disposition from something far more subtle—the tone of voice, the expression of the eyes, the lines of the face, or even from an aura unperceived by the senses. However that may be, the wisdom of the Constitutional safeguard guaranteeing that every person charged with crime shall be confronted by the witnesses against him was instantly made apparent when Mrs. Tunnygate took the stand, for without hearing a word from her firmly compressed lips the jury simultaneously swept her with one comprehensive glance and turned away. Students of women, experienced adventurers in matrimony, these plumbers, bird merchants, "delicatessens," and the rest looked, perceived and comprehended that here was the very devil of a woman—a virago, a shrew, a termagant, a natural-born trouble-maker; and they shivered and thanked God that she was Tunnygate's and not theirs; their unformulated sentiment best expressed in Pope's immortal couplet:

Oh woman, woman! when to ill thy mind
Is bent, all hell contains no fouler fiend.

She had said no word. Between the judge and jury nothing had passed, and yet through the alpha rays of that mysterious medium of communication by which all men as men are united where woman is concerned, the thought was directly transmitted and unanimously acknowledged that here for sure was a hellcat!

It was as naught to them that she testified to the outrageous illegality of the Appleboys' territorial ambitions, the irascibility of the wife, the violent threats of the husband; or that Mrs. Appleboy had been observed to mail a suspicious letter shortly before the date of the canine assault. They disregarded her. Yet when Tutt upon cross-examination sought to attack her credibility by asking her various pertinent questions, they unhesitatingly accepted his implied accusations as true, though under the rules of evidence he was bound by her denials.

Peck 1: "Did you not knock Mrs. Appleboy's flower pots off the piazza?" he demanded significantly.

"Never! I never did!" she declared passionately.

But they knew in their hearts that she had.

Peck 2: "Didn't you steal her milk bottles?"

"What a lie! It's absolutely false!"

Yet they knew that she did.

Peck 3: "Didn't you tangle up their fish lines and take their tholepins?"

"Well, I never! You ought to be ashamed to ask a lady such questions!"

They found her guilty.

"I move to dismiss, your Honor," chirped Tutt blithely at the conclusion of her testimony.

Judge Witherspoon shook his head.

"I want to hear the other side," he remarked. "The mere fact that the defendant put up a sign warning the public against the dog may be taken as some evidence that he had knowledge of the animal's vicious propensities. I shall let the case go to the jury unless this evidence is contradicted or explained. Reserve your motion."

"Very well, your Honor," agreed Tutt, patting himself upon the abdomen. "I will follow your suggestion and call the defendant. Mr. Appleboy, take the stand."

Mr. Appleboy heavily rose, and the heart of every fat man upon the jury, and particularly that of the Abyssinian brother upon the back row, went out to him. For just as they had known without being told that the new Mrs. Tunnygate was a vixen, they realized that Appleboy was a kind, good-natured man—a little soft, perhaps, like his clams, but no more dangerous. Moreover, it was plain that he had suffered and was, indeed, still suffering, and they had pity for him. Appleboy's voice shook and so did the rest of his person as he recounted his ancient friendship for Tunnygate and their piscatorial association, their common matrimonial experiences, the sudden change in the temperature of the society of Throggs Neck, the malicious destruction of their property and the unexplained aggressions of Tunnygate upon the lawn. And the jury, believing, understood.

Then like the sword of Damocles the Bessemer voice of Pepperill severed the general atmosphere of amiability: "Where did you get that dog?"

Mr. Appleboy looked round helplessly, distress pictured in every feature.

"My wife's aunt lent it to us."

"How did she come to lend it to you?"

"Bashemath wrote and asked for it."

"Oh! Did you know anything about the dog before you sent for it?"

"Of your own knowledge?" interjected Tutt sharply.

"Oh, no!" returned Appleboy.

"Didn't you know it was a vicious beast?" sharply challenged Pepperill.

"Of your own knowledge?" again warned Tutt.

"I'd never seen the dog."

"Didn't your wife tell you about it?"

Tutt sprang to his feet, wildly waving his arms.

"I object; on the ground that what passed between husband and wife upon this subject must be regarded as confidential."

"I will so rule," said Judge Witherspoon, smiling. "Excluded."

Pepperill shrugged his shoulders.

"I would like to ask a question," interpolated the editor of *Baby's World*.

"Do!" exclaimed Tutt eagerly.

The editor, who was a fat editor, rose in an embarrassed manner.

"Mr. Appleboy!" he began.

"Yes, sir!" responded Appleboy.

"I want to get this straight. You and your wife had a row with the Tunnygates. He tried to tear up your front lawn. You warned him off. He kept on doing it. You got a dog and put up a sign and when he disregarded it you sicked the dog on him. Is that right?"

He was manifestly friendly, merely a bit cloudy in the cerebellum. The Abyssinian brother pulled him sharply by the coattails.

"Sit down," he whispered hoarsely. "You're gumming it all up."

"I didn't sick Andrew on him!" protested Appleboy.

"But I say, why shouldn't he have?" demanded the baby's editor. "That's what anybody would do!"

Pepperill sprang frantically to his feet.

"Oh, I object! This juryman is showing bias. This is entirely improper."

"I am, am I?" sputtered the fat editor angrily. "I'll show you——"

"You want to be fair, don't you?" whined Pepperill. "I've proved that the Appleboys had no right to hedge in the beach!"

"Oh, pooh!" sneered the Abyssinian, now also getting to his feet. "Supposing they hadn't? Who cares a damn? This man Tunnygate deserved all he's got!"

"Gentlemen! Gentlemen!" expostulated the judge firmly. "Take your seats or I shall declare a mistrial. Go on, Mr. Tutt. Call your next witness."

"Mrs. Appleboy," called out Tutt, "will you kindly take the chair?" And that good lady, looking as if all her adipose existence had been devoted to the production of the sort of pies that mother used to make, placidly made her way to the witness stand.

"Did you know that Andrew was a vicious dog?" inquired Tutt.

"No!" answered Mrs. Appleboy firmly. "I didn't."

O woman!

"That is all," declared Tutt with a triumphant smile.

"Then," snapped Pepperill, "why did you send for him?"

"I was lonely," answered Bashemath unblushingly.

"Do you mean to tell this jury that you didn't know that that dog was one of the worst biters in Livornia?"

"I do!" she replied. "I only knew Aunt Eliza had a dog. I didn't know anything about the dog personally."

"What did you say to your aunt in your letter?"

"I said I was lonely and wanted protection."

"Didn't you hope the dog would bite Mr. Tunnygate?"

"Why, no!" she declared. "I didn't want him to bite anybody."

At that the delicatessen man poked the plumber in the ribs and they both grinned happily at one another.

Pepperill gave her a last disgusted look and sank back in his seat.

"That is all!" he ejaculated feebly.

"One question, if you please, madam," said Judge Witherspoon. "May I be permitted to"—he coughed as a suppressed snicker ran round the court—"that is—may I not—er——Oh, look here! How did you happen to have the idea of getting a dog?"

Mrs. Appleboy turned the full moon of her homely countenance upon the court.

"The potato peel came down that way!" she explained blandly.

"What!" exploded the dealer in rubber novelties.

"The potato peel—it spelled 'dog,' " she repeated artlessly.

"Lord!" deeply suspirated Pepperill. "What a case! Carry me out!"

"Well, Mr. Tutt," said the judge, "now I will hear what you may wish to say upon the question of whether this issue should be submitted to the jury. However, I shall rule that the indictment is sufficient."

Tutt elegantly rose.

"Having due respect to your Honor's ruling as to the sufficiency of the indictment I shall address myself simply to the question *scienter*. I might, of course, dwell upon the impropriety of charging the defendant with criminal responsibility for the act of another free agent even if that agent be an aminal—but I will leave that, if necessary, for the Court of Appeals. If anybody were to be indicted in this case I hold it should have been the dog Andrew. Nay, I do not jest! But I can see by your Honor's expression that any argument upon that score would be without avail."

"Entirely," remarked Witherspoon. "Kindly go on!"

"Well," continued Tutt, "the law of this matter needs no elucidation. It has been settled since the time of Moses."

"Of whom?" inquired Witherspoon. "You don't need to go back farther than Chief Justice Marshall so far as I am concerned."

Tutt bowed.

"It is an established doctrine of the common law both of England and America that it is wholly proper for one to keep a domestic animal for his use, pleasure, or protection, until, as Dykeman, J., says in Muller *v.* McKesson, 10 Hun., 45, 'some vicious propensity is developed and brought out to the knowledge of the owner.' Up to that time the man who keeps a dog or other animal cannot be charged with liability for his acts. This has always been the law.

"In the twenty-first chapter of Exodus at the twenty-eighth verse it is written: 'If an ox gore a man or a woman, that they die; then the ox shall be surely stoned, and his flesh shall not be eaten; but the owner of the ox shall be quit. But if the ox were wont to push with his horn in time past, and it hath been testified to his owner, and he hath not kept him in, but that he hath killed a man or a woman; the ox shall be stoned, and his owner also shall be put to death.'

"In the old English case of Smith *v.* Pehal, 2 Strange, 1264, it was said by the court: 'If a dog has once bit a man, and the owner having notice thereof keeps the dog, and lets him go about or lie at his door, an action will lie against him at the suit of a person who is bit, though it happened by such person's treading on the dog's toes; for it was owing to his not hanging the dog on the first notice. And the safety of the king's subjects ought not afterwards to be endangered.' That is sound law; but it is equally good law that "if a person with full knowledge of the evil propensities of an animal wantonly excites him or voluntarily and unnecessarily puts himself in the way of such an animal he would be adjudged to have brought the injury upon himself, and ought not to be entitled to recover. In such a case it cannot be said in a legal sense that the keeping of the animal, which is the gravamen of the offense, produced the injury.'

"Now in the case at bar, first there is clearly no evidence that this defendant knew or ever suspected that the dog Andrew was otherwise than of a mild and gentle disposition. That is, there is no evidence whatever of *scienter*. In fact, except in this single instance there is no evidence that Andrew ever bit anybody. Thus, in the word of Holy Writ the defendant Appleboy should be quit, and in the language of our own courts he must be held harmless. Secondly, moreover, it appears that the complainant deliberately put himself in the way of the dog Andrew, after full warning. I move that the jury be directed to return a verdict of not guilty."

"Motion granted," nodded Judge Witherspoon, burying his nose in his handkerchief. "I hold that every dog is entitled to one bite."

"Gentlemen of the jury," chanted the clerk: "How say you? Do you find the defendant guilty or not guilty?"

"Not guilty," returned the foreman eagerly, amid audible evidences of satisfaction from the Abyssinian brother, the *Baby's World* editor, and the others. Mr. Appleboy clung to Tutt's hand, overcome by emotion.

"Adjourn court!" ordered the judge. Then he beckoned to Mr. Appleboy. "Come up here!" he directed.

Timidly Mr. Appleboy approached the dais.

"Don't do it again!" remarked his Honor shortly.

"Eh? Beg pardon, your Honor, I mean——"

"I said: 'Don't do it again!' " repeated the judge with a twinkle in his eye. Then lowering his voice he whispered: "You see I come from Livornia, and I've known Andrew for a long time."

As Tutt guided the Appleboys out into the corridor the party came face to face with Mr. and Mrs. Tunnygate.

"Huh!" sneered Tunnygate.

"Huh!" retorted Appleboy.

Board of Inland Revenue v. Haddock; Rex v. Haddock The Negotiable Cow

by:

A. P. HERBERT

selected by:

ADLAI E. STEVENSON

I am afraid my reading in the field of lawyer stories has been limited in the last thirteen years of almost incessant government work. But I do recall with infinite pleasure A. P. Herbert's The Uncommon Law. *One of that collection of engaging stories which I remember particularly is the most excellent tale, "The Negotiable Cow."*

S.S. ADLAI E. STEVENSON

"Was the cow crossed?"

"No, your worship, it was an open cow."

These and similar passages provoked laughter at Bow Street today when the Negotiable Cow case was concluded.

Sir Joshua Hoot, K.C. (appearing for the Public Prosecutor): Sir Basil, these summonses, by leave of the court, are being heard together, an unusual but convenient arrangement.

The defendant, Mr. Albert Haddock, has for many months, in spite of earnest endeavors on both sides, been unable to establish harmonious relations between himself and the Collector of Taxes. The collector maintains that Mr. Haddock should make over a large part of his earnings to the government. Mr. Haddock replies that the proportion demanded is excessive, in view of the inadequate services or consideration which he himself has received from that Government. After an exchange of endearing letters, telephone calls, and even checks, the sum demanded was reduced to fifty-seven pounds; and about this sum the exchange of opinions continued.

On the 31st of May the collector was diverted from his respectable labors by the apparition of a noisy crowd outside his windows. The crowd, Sir Basil, had been attracted by Mr.

Haddock, who was leading a large white cow of malevolent aspect. On the back and sides of the cow were clearly stenciled in red ink the following words:

> *To the London and Literary Bank, Ltd.*
> Pay the Collector of Taxes, who is no gentleman, or Order, the sum of fifty-seven pounds (and may he rot!)
>
> *Pounds 57/0/0* *Albert Haddock*

Mr. Haddock conducted the cow into the collector's office, tendered it to the collector in payment of income tax and demanded a receipt.

Sir Basil String: Did the cow bear the statutory stamp?

Sir Joshua: Yes, a twopenny stamp was affixed to the dexter horn. The collector declined to accept the cow, objecting that it would be difficult or even impossible to pay the cow into the bank. Mr. Haddock, throughout the interview, maintained the friendliest demeanor[1]; and he now remarked that the collector could endorse the cow to any third party to whom he owed money, adding that there must be many persons in that position. The collector then endeavored to endorse the check——

Sir Basil String: Where?

Sir Joshua: On the back of the check, Sir Basil, that is to say, on the abdomen of the cow. The cow, however, appeared to resent endorsement, and adopted a menacing posture. The collector, abandoning the attempt, declined finally to take the check. Mr. Haddock led the cow away and was arrested in Trafalgar Square for causing an obstruction. He has also been summoned by the Board of Inland Revenue for nonpayment of income tax.

Mr. Haddock, in the witness box, said that he had tendered a check in payment of income tax, and if the commissioners did not like his check they could do the other thing. A check was only an order to a bank to pay money to the person in possession of the check or a person named on the check. There was nothing in statute or customary law to say that that order must be written on a piece of paper of specified dimensions. A check, it was

---

[1] *Mars est celare martem.* (Selden, *Mare Clausum,* lib. 1, c. 21.)

well known, could be written on a piece of notepaper. He himself had drawn checks on the backs of menus, on napkins, on handkerchiefs, on the labels of wine bottles; all these checks had been duly honored by his bank and passed through the Bankers' Clearing House. He could see no distinction in law between a check written on a napkin and a check written on a cow. The essence of each document was a written order to pay money, made in the customary form and in accordance with statutory requirements as to stamps, etc. A check was admittedly not legal tender in the sense that it could not lawfully be refused; but it was accepted by custom as a legitimate form of payment. There were funds in his bank sufficient to meet the cow; the commissioners might not like the cow, but, the cow having been tendered, they were estopped from charging him with failure to pay. (Mr. Haddock here cited Spowers v. The Strand Magazine, Lucas v. Finck, and Wadsworth v. The Metropolitan Water Board.)

As to the action of the police, Mr. Haddock said it was a nice thing if in the heart of the commercial capital of the world a man could not convey a negotiable instrument down the street without being arrested. He had instituted proceedings against Constable Boot for false imprisonment.

Cross-examined as to motive, witness said that he had no check-forms available and, being anxious to meet his obligations promptly, had made use of the only material to hand. Later he admitted that there might have been present in his mind a desire to make the Collector of Taxes ridiculous. But why not? There was no law against deriding the income tax.[2]

Sir Basil String (after the hearing of further evidence): This case has at least brought to the notice of the court a citizen who is unusual both in his clarity of mind and integrity of behavior. No thinking man can regard those parts of the Finance Acts which govern the income tax with anything but contempt. There may be something to be said—not much—for taking from those who have inherited wealth a certain proportion of that wealth for the service of the state and the benefit of the poor and needy; and those who by their own ability, brains, industry, and

---

[2] *Cf. Magna Carta: Jus ridendi nulli negabimus.*

exertion have earned money may reasonably be invited to surrender a small portion of it toward the maintenance of those public services by which they benefit, to wit, the police, the navy, the army, the public sewers, and so forth. But to compel such individuals to bestow a large part of their earnings upon other individuals, whether by way of pensions, unemployment grants, or education allowances, is manifestly barbarous and indefensible. Yet this is the law. The original and only official basis of taxation was that individual citizens, in return for their money, received collectively some services from the state, the defense of their property and persons, the care of their health, or the education of their children. All that has now gone. Citizen A, who has earned money, is commanded simply to give it to citizens B, C, and D, who have not, and by force of habit this has come to be regarded as a normal and proper proceeding, whatever the comparative industry or merits of citizens A, B, C, and D. To be alive has become a virtue, and the mere capacity to inflate the lungs entitles citizen B to a substantial share in the laborious earnings of citizen A. The defendant, Mr. Haddock, repels and resents this doctrine, but, since it has received the sanction of Parliament, he dutifully complies with it. Hampered by practical difficulties, he took the first steps he could to discharge his legal obligations to the state. Paper was not available, so he employed instead a favorite cow. Now, there can be nothing obscene, offensive, or derogatory in the presentation of a cow by one man to another. Indeed, in certain parts of our Empire the cow is venerated as a sacred animal. Payment in kind is the oldest form of payment, and payment in kind more often than not meant payment in cattle. Indeed, during the Saxon period, Mr. Haddock tells us, cattle were described as *viva pecunia,* or "living money," from their being received as a payment on most occasions, at certain regulated prices.[3] So that, whether the check was valid or not, it was impossible to doubt the validity of the cow; and whatever the collector's distrust of the former it was at least his duty to accept the latter and credit Mr. Haddock's account with its value. But, as Mr. Haddock protested in his able argument, an order to pay

---

[3] Mandeville uses *Catele* for "price." (Wharton's *Law Lexicon.*)

is an order to pay, whether it is made on the back of an envelope or on the back of a cow. The evidence of the bank is that Mr. Haddock's account was in funds. From every point of view, therefore the Collector of Taxes did wrong, by custom if not by law, in refusing to take the proffered animal, and the summons issued at his instance will be discharged.

As for the second charge, I hold again that Constable Boot did wrong. It cannot be unlawful to conduct a cow through the London streets. The horse, at the present time a much less useful animal, constantly appears in those streets without protest, and the motor car, more unnatural and unattractive still, is more numerous than either animal. Much less can the cow be regarded as an improper or unlawful companion when it is invested (as I have shown) with all the dignity of a bill of exchange.

If people choose to congregate in one place upon the apparition of Mr. Haddock with a promissory cow, then Constable Boot should arrest the people, not Mr. Haddock. Possibly, if Mr. Haddock had paraded Cockspur Street with a paper check for one million pounds made payable to bearer, the crowd would have been as great, but that is not to say that Mr. Haddock would have broken the law. In my judgment Mr. Haddock has behaved throughout in the manner of a perfect knight, citizen, and taxpayer. The charge brought by the Crown is dismissed; and I hope with all my heart that in his action against Constable Boot Mr. Haddock will be successful. What is the next case, please?

The Juryman

by:

JOHN GALSWORTHY

selected by:

FRED M. VINSON

It is more than coincidence that some of the greatest legal writing has been done by lawyers who have left active practice to devote their lives to literature. And some of the best of this writing is the work of lawyer John Galsworthy —in novels, in plays, and in short stories. The short story which is my particular favorite is his excellent "Juryman."

S.S. FRED M. VINSON

I

"Don't you see, brother, I was reading yesterday the Gospel about Christ, the little Father; how He suffered, how He walked on the earth. I suppose you have heard about it?"

"Indeed, I have," replied Stepanuitch; "but we are people in darkness; we can't read."—TOLSTOI.

Mr. Henry Bosengate, of the London Stock Exchange, seated himself in his car that morning during the Great War with a sense of injury. Major in a Volunteer Corps; member of all the local committees; lending this very car to the neighboring hospital, at times even driving it himself for their benefit; subscribing to funds, so far as his diminished income permitted—he was conscious of being an asset to the country, and one whose time could not be wasted with impunity. To be summoned to sit on a jury at the local assizes, and not even the grand jury at that! It was in the nature of an outrage.

Strong and upright, with hazel eyes and dark eyebrows, pinkish-brown cheeks, a forehead white, well shaped, and getting high, with grayish hair glossy and well-brushed, and a trim mustache, he might have been taken for that colonel of Volunteers which indeed he was in a fair way of becoming.

His wife had followed him out under the porch, and stood bracing her supple body clothed in lilac linen. Red rambler roses formed a sort of crown to her dark head; her ivory-colored face had in it just a suggestion of the Japanese.

Mr. Bosengate spoke through the whirr of the engine.

"I don't expect to be late, dear. This business is ridiculous. There oughtn't to *be* any crime in these days."

His wife—her name was Kathleen—smiled. She looked very pretty and cool, Mr. Bosengate thought. To one bound on this dull and stuffy business everything he owned seemed pleasant—the geranium beds beside the gravel drive, his long, red brick house mellowing decorously in its creepers and ivy, the little clock tower over stables now converted to a garage, the dovecote, masking at the other end the conservatory which adjoined the billiard room. Close to the red brick lodge his two children, Kate and Harry, ran out from under the acacia trees and waved to him, scrambling bare-legged on to the low, red, ivy-covered wall which guarded his domain of eleven acres. Mr. Bosengate waved back, thinking, Jolly couple—by Jove, they are! Above their heads, through the trees, he could see right away to some downs, faint in the July heat haze. And he thought, Pretty a spot as one could have got, so close to town!

Despite the war he had enjoyed these last two years more than any of the ten since he built Charmleigh and settled down to semirural domesticity with his young wife. There had been a certain piquancy, a savor added to existence, by the country's peril, and all the public service and sacrifice it demanded. His chauffeur was gone, and one gardener did the work of three. He enjoyed—positively enjoyed—his committee work; even the serious decline of business and increase of taxation had not much worried one continually conscious of the national crisis and his own part therein. The country had wanted waking up, wanted a lesson in effort and economy; and the feeling that he had not spared himself in these strenuous times had given a zest to those quiet pleasures of bed and board which, at his age, even the most patriotic could retain with a good conscience. He had denied himself many things—new clothes, presents for Kathleen and the children, travel, and that pineapple house which he had been on the point of building when the war broke out; new wine, too, and cigars, and membership of the two clubs which he had never used in the old days. The hours had seemed fuller and longer, sleep better earned—wonderful, the things one could do without when put to it! He turned the car into the high road, driving dreamily, for he was in plenty of time. The war was going pretty well now; he was no fool optimist, but now that conscription was in force, one might reasonably hope for its end within a year. Then there would be a boom, and one might let oneself go a little. Visions of theaters and supper with his wife at the Savoy afterward, and cosy night drives back into the sweet-smelling country behind your own chauffeur once more teased a fancy which even now did not soar beyond the confines of domestic pleasures. He pictured his wife in new dresses by Jay—she was fifteen years younger than himself, and "paid for dressing" as they said. He had always delighted—as men older than their wives will—in the admiration she excited from others not privileged to enjoy her charms. Her rather queer and ironical beauty, her cool, irreproachable wifeliness, was a constant balm to him. They would give dinner parties again, have their friends down from town, and he would once more enjoy sitting at the foot of the dinner table while Kathleen sat at the head, with the light soft on her ivory shoulders, behind flowers she had arranged in that original way of hers, and fruit which he had grown in his hothouses; once more he would take legitimate interest in the wine he offered to his guests—once more stock that Chinese cabinet wherein he kept cigars. Yes—there was a certain satisfaction in these days of privation, if only from the anticipation they created.

The sprinkling of villas had become continuous on either side of the high road; and women going to shop, tradesmen's boys delivering victuals, young men in khaki, began to abound. Now and then a limping or bandaged form would pass—some bit of human wreckage! and Mr. Bosengate would think mechanically, Another of those poor devils! Wonder if we've had his case before us!

Running his car into the best hotel garage of the little town, he made his way leisurely over to the court. It stood back from the market place, and was already lapped by a sea of persons having, as in the outer ring at race meetings, an air of business at which one must not be caught out, together with a soaked or flushed appearance. Mr. Bosengate could not resist putting his handkerchief to his nose. He had carefully drenched it with lavender water, and to this fact owed, perhaps, his immunity from the post of foreman on the jury—for, say what you will about the English, they have a deep instinct for affairs.

He found himself second in the front row of the jury box, and through the odor of "Sanitas" gazed at the judge's face expressionless up there, for all the world like a bewigged bust. His fellows in the box had that appearance of falling between two classes characteristic of jurymen. Mr. Bosengate was not impressed. On one side of him the foreman sat, a prominent upholsterer, known in the town as "Gentleman Fox." His dark and beautifully brushed and oiled hair and mustache, his radiant linen, gold watch and chain, the white piping to his waistcoat, and a habit of never saying "Sir" had long marked him out from commoner men; he undertook to bury people too, to save them trouble; and was altogether superior. On the other side Mr. Bosengate had one of those men who, except when they sit on juries, are never seen without a little brown bag, and the appearance of having been interrupted in a drink. Pale and shiny, with large, loose eyes shifting from side to side, he had an underdone voice and uneasy, flabby hands. Mr. Bosengate disliked sitting next to him. Beyond this commercial traveler sat a dark pale young man with spectacles; beyond him again, a short old man with gray mustache, mutton chops, and innumerable wrinkles; and the front row was completed by a chemist. The three immediately behind, Mr. Bosengate did not thoroughly master; but the three at the end of the second row he learned in their order of an oldish man in a gray suit, given to winking; an inanimate person with the mouth of a mustachioed codfish, over whose long bald crown three wisps of damp hair were carefully arranged; and a dried, dapperish, clean-shorn man, whose mouth seemed terrified lest it should be surprised without a smile. Their first and second verdicts were recorded without the necessity for withdrawal, and Mr. Bosengate was already sleepy when the third case was called. The sight of khaki revived his drooping attention. But what a weedy-looking specimen! This prisoner had a truly nerveless, pitiable, dejected air. If he had ever had a military bearing it had shrunk into him during his confinement. His ill-shaped brown tunic, whose little brass buttons seemed trying to keep smiling, struck Mr. Bosengate as ridiculously short, used though he was to such things. Absurd, he thought—Lumbago! Just where they ought to be covered! Then the officer and gentleman stirred in him, and he added to himself, Still, there must be some distinction made! The little soldier's visage had once perhaps been tanned but was now the color of dark dough; his large brown eyes with white showing below the iris, as so often in the eyes of very nervous people, wandered from face to face, of judge, counsel, jury, and public. There were hollows in his cheeks, his dark hair looked damp; around his neck he wore a bandage. The commercial traveler on Mr. Bosengate's left turned, and whispered: *"Felo de se!* My hat! what a guy!" Mr. Bosengate pretended not to hear—he could not bear that fellow!—and slowly wrote on a bit of paper: "Owen Lewis." Welsh! Well, he looked it—not at all an English face. Attempted suicide—not at all an English crime! Suicide implied surrender, a putting-up of hands to Fate—to say nothing of the religious aspect of the matter. And suicide in khaki seemed to Mr. Bosengate particularly abhorrent; like turning tail in face of the enemy; almost meriting the fate of a deserter. He looked at the prisoner, trying not to give way to this prejudice. And the prisoner seemed to look at him, though this, perhaps, was fancy.

The counsel for the prosecution, a little, alert, gray, decided man, above military age, began detailing the circumstances of the crime. Mr. Bosengate, though not particularly sensitive to atmosphere, could perceive a sort of current running through the court. It was as if jury and public were thinking rhythmically in obedience to the same unexpressed prejudice of which he himself was conscious. Even the Caesarlike pale face up there, presiding, seemed in its ironic serenity responding to that current.

"Gentlemen of the jury, before I call my evidence, I direct your attention to the bandage the accused is still wearing. He gave himself this wound with his army razor, adding, if I may say so, insult to the injury he was inflicting on his country. He pleads not guilty; and before the magistrates he said that absence from his wife was preying on his mind"—the advocate's close lips widened. "Well, gentlemen, if such an excuse is to weigh with us in these days, I'm sure I don't know what's to happen to the Empire."

No, by George! thought Mr. Bosengate.

The evidence of the first witness, a roommate who had caught the prisoner's hand, and of the sergeant, who had at once been summoned, was conclusive, and he began to cherish a hope that they would get through without withdrawing, and he would be home before five. But then a hitch occurred. The regimental doctor failed to respond when his name was called; and the judge, having for the first time that day showed himself capable of human emotion, intimated that he would adjourn until the morrow.

Mr. Bosengate received the announcement with equanimity. He would be home even earlier! And gathering up the sheets of paper he had scribbled on, he put them in his pocket and got up. The would-be suicide was being taken out of the court —a shambling drab figure with shoulders hunched. What good were men like that in these days! What good! The prisoner looked up. Mr. Bosengate encountered in full the gaze of those large brown eyes, with the white showing underneath. What a suffering, wretched, pitiful face! A man had no business to give you a look like that! The prisoner passed on down the stairs, and vanished. Mr. Bosengate went out and across the market place to the garage of the hotel where he had left his car. The sun shone fiercely and he thought, I must do some watering in the garden. He brought the car out, and was about to start the engine, when someone passing said, "Good evenin'. Seedy-lookin' beggar that last prisoner, ain't he? We don't want men of that stamp." It was his neighbor on the jury, the commercial traveler, in a straw hat, with a little brown bag already in his hand and the froth of an interrupted drink on his mustache. Answering curtly, "Good evening!" and thinking: Nor of yours, my friend! Mr. Bosengate started the car with unnecessary clamor. But as if brought back to life by the commercial traveler's remark, the prisoner's figure seemed to speed along too, turning up at Mr. Bosengate his pitifully unhappy eyes. Want of his wife!—queer excuse that for trying to put it out of his power ever to see her again. Why! Half a loaf, even a slice, was better than no bread. Not many of that neurotic type in the Army—thank heaven! The lugubrious figure vanished, and Mr. Bosengate pictured instead the form of his own wife bending over her *"Gloire de Dijon"* roses in the rosery, where she generally worked a little before tea now that they were short of gardeners. He saw her, as often he had seen her, raise herself and stand, head to one side, a gloved hand on her slender hip, gazing as it were ironically from under drooped lids at buds which did not come out fast enough. And the word *Caline,* for he was something of a French scholar, shot through his mind: Kathleen—*Caline!* If he found her there when he got in, he would steal up on the grass and—ah! but with great care not to crease her dress or disturb her hair! If only she weren't quite so self-contained, he thought. It's like a cat you can't get near, not really near!

The car, returning faster than it had come down that morning, had already passed the outskirt villas and was breasting the hill to where, among fields and the old trees, Charmleigh lay apart from commoner life. Turning into his drive, Mr. Bosengate thought with a certain surprise, I wonder what she *does* think of! I wonder! He put his gloves and hat down in the outer hall and went into the lavatory to dip his face in cool water and wash it with sweet-smelling soap—delicious revenge on the unclean atmosphere in which he had been stewing so many hours. He came out again into the hall dazed by soap and the mellowed light, and a voice from halfway up the stairs said, "Daddy! Look!" His little daughter was standing up there with one hand on the banisters. She scrambled on to them and came sliding down, her frock up to her eyes, and her Holland knickers to her middle.

Mr. Bosengate said mildly,

"Well, that's elegant!"

"Tea's in the summerhouse. Mummy's waiting. Come on!"

With her hand in his, Mr. Bosengate went on, through the drawing room, long and cool, with sunblinds down, through the billiard room, high and cool, through the conservatory, green and sweet-smelling, out on to the terrace and the upper lawn. He had never felt such sheer exhilarated joy in his home surroundings, so cool, glistening, and green under the July sun; and he said, "Well, Kit, what have you all been doing?"

"I've fed my rabbits and Harry's; and we've been in the attic; Harry got his leg through the skylight."

Mr. Bosengate drew in his breath with a hiss.

"It's all right, Daddy; we got it out again. It's only grazed the skin. And we've been making swabs—I made seventeen—

Mummy made thirty-three, and then she went to the hospital. Did you put many men in prison?"

Mr. Bosengate cleared his throat. The question seemed to him untimely.

"Only two."

"What's it like in prison, Daddy?"

Mr. Bosengate, who had no more knowledge than his little daughter, replied in an absent voice, "Not very nice."

They were passing under a young oak tree, where the path wound round to the rosery and summerhouse. Something shot down and clawed Mr. Bosengate's neck. His little daughter began to hop and suffocate with laughter.

"Oh, Daddy! Aren't you caught! I led you on purpose!"

Looking up, Mr. Bosengate saw his small son lying along a low branch above him—like the leopard he was declaring himself to be (for fear of error), and thought blithely, What an active little chap it is!

"Let me drop on your shoulders, Daddy—like they do on the deer."

"Oh, yes! Do be a deer, Daddy!"

Mr. Bosengate did not see being a deer; his hair had just been brushed. But he entered the rosery buoyantly between his offspring. His wife was standing precisely as he had imagined her, in a pale blue frock open at the neck, with a narrow black band round the waist, and little accordion pleats below. She looked her coolest. Her smile, when she turned her head, hardly seemed to take Mr. Bosengate seriously enough. He placed his lips below one of her half-drooped eyelids. She even smelled of roses. His children began to dance round their mother, and Mr. Bosengate, firmly held between them, was also compelled to do this, until she said, "When you've quite done, let's have tea!"

It was not the greeting he had imagined coming along in the car. Earwigs were plentiful in the summerhouse—used perhaps twice a year, but indispensable to every country residence—and Mr. Bosengate was not sorry for the excuse to get out again. Though all was so pleasant, he felt oddly restless, rather suffocated; and lighting his pipe, began to move about among the roses, blowing tobacco at the greenfly; in wartime one was never quite idle! And suddenly he said, "We're trying a wretched Tommy at the assizes."

His wife looked up from a rose.

"What for?"

"Attempted suicide."

"Why did he?"

"Can't stand the separation from his wife."

She looked at him, gave a low laugh, and said, "Oh dear!"

Mr. Bosengate was puzzled. Why did she laugh? He looked round, saw that the children were gone, took his pipe from his mouth, and approached her.

"You look very pretty," he said. "Give me a kiss!"

His wife bent her body forward from the waist, and pushed her lips out till they touched his mustache. Mr. Bosengate felt a sensation as if he had arisen from breakfast without having eaten marmalade. He mastered it and said, "That jury are a rum lot."

His wife's eyelids flickered. "I wish women sat on juries."

"Why?"

"It would be an experience."

Not the first time she had used that curious expression! Yet her life was far from dull, so far as he could see; with the new interests created by the war and the constant calls on her time made by the perfection of their home life, she had a useful and busy existence. Again the random thought passed through him: But she never tells me anything! And suddenly that lugubrious khaki-clad figure started up among the rose bushes. "We've got a lot to be thankful for!" he said abruptly. "I must go to work!" His wife, raising one eyebrow, smiled. "And I to weep!" Mr. Bosengate laughed—she had a pretty wit! And stroking his comely mustache where it had been kissed, he moved out into the sunshine. All the evening, throughout his labors, not inconsiderable, for this jury business had put him behind time, he was afflicted by that restless pleasure in his surroundings; would break off in mowing the lower lawn to look at the house through the trees; would leave his study and committee papers to cross into the drawing room and sniff its dainty fragrance; paid a special good-night visit to the children having supper in the schoolroom; pottered in and out from his dressing room to admire his wife while she was changing for dinner; dined with his mind perpetually on the next course; talked volubly of the war; and in the billiard room afterward, smoking the pipe which had taken the place of his cigar, could not keep still, but roamed about, now in conservatory, now in the drawing room, where his wife and the governess were still making swabs. It seemed to him that he could not have enough of anything. About eleven o'clock he strolled out—beautiful night, only just dark enough—under the new arrangement with Time—and went down to the little round fountain below the terrace. His wife was playing the piano. Mr. Bosengate looked at the water and the flat, dark water-lily leaves which floated there; looked up at the house, where only narrow chinks of light showed, because of the Lighting Order. The dreamy music drifted out; there was a scent of heliotrope. He moved a few steps back and sat in the children's swing under an old lime tree. Jolly—blissful—in the warm, bloomy dark! Of all hours of the day, this before going to bed was perhaps the pleasantest. He saw the light go up in his wife's bedroom, unscreened for a full minute, and thought, Aha! If I did my duty as a special, I should "strafe" her for that. She came to the window, her figure lighted, hands up to the back of her head, so that her bare arms gleamed. Mr. Bosengate wafted her a kiss, knowing he could not be seen. Lucky chap! he mused; she's a great joy! Up went her arm, down came the blind—the house was dark again. He drew a long breath. Another ten minutes, he thought, then I'll go in and shut up. By Jove! The limes are beginning to smell already! And, the better to take in that acme of his well-being, he tilted the swing, lifted his feet from the ground, and swung himself toward the scented blossoms. He wanted to whelm his senses in their perfume, and closed his eyes. But instead of the domestic vision he expected, the face of the little Welsh soldier, hare-eyed, shadowy, pinched and dark and pitiful, started up with such disturbing vividness that he opened his eyes again at once. Curse! The fellow almost haunted one! Where would he be now—poor little devil! lying in his cell, thinking—thinking of his wife! Feeling suddenly morbid, Mr. Bosengate arrested the swing and stood up. Absurd! All his well-being and mood of warm anticipation had deserted him! A d——d world! he thought. Such a lot of misery!

Why should I have to sit in judgment on that poor beggar, and condemn him? He moved up on to the terrace and walked briskly, to rid himself of this disturbance before going in. That commercial traveler chap, he thought, the rest of those fellows —they see nothing! And, abruptly turning up the three stone steps, he entered the conservatory, locked it, passed into the billiard room, and drank his barley water. One of the pictures was hanging crooked; he went up to put it straight. Still life. Grapes and apples, and lobsters! They struck him as odd for the first time. Why lobsters? The whole picture seemed dead and oily. He turned off the light and went upstairs, passed his wife's door, into his own room, and undressed. Clothed in his pajamas, he opened the door between the rooms. By the light coming from his own he could see her dark head on the pillow. Was she asleep? No—not asleep, certainly. The moment of fruition had come; the crowning of his pride and pleasure in his home. But he continued to stand there. He had suddenly no pride, no pleasure, no desire; nothing but a sort of dull resentment against everything. He turned back, shut the door, and slipping between the heavy curtains and his open window, stood looking out at the night. Full of misery! he thought. Full of d——d misery!

II

Filing into the jury box next morning, Mr. Bosengate collided slightly with a short juryman, whose square figure and square head of stiff yellow-red hair he had only vaguely noticed the day before. The man looked angry, and Mr. Bosengate thought, An ill-bred dog, that!

He sat down quickly, and, to avoid further recognition of his fellows, gazed in front of him. His appearance on Saturdays was always military, by reason of the route march of his Volunteer Corps in the afternoon. Gentleman Fox, who belonged to the corps too, was also looking square; but that commercial traveler on his other side seemed more *louche,* and as if surprised in immorality, than ever; only the proximity of Gentleman Fox on the other side kept Mr. Bosengate from shrinking.

Then he saw the prisoner being brought in, shadowy and dark behind the brightness of his buttons, and he experienced a sort of shock, this figure was so exactly that which had several times started up in his mind. Somehow he had expected a fresh sight of the fellow to dispel and disprove what had been haunting him, had expected to find him just an outside phenomenon, not, as it were, a part of his own life. And he gazed at the carven immobility of the judge's face, trying to steady himself, as a drunken man will, by looking at a light. The regimental doctor, unabashed by the judge's comment on his absence the day before, gave his evidence like a man who had better things to do, and the case for the prosecution was forthwith rounded in by a little speech from counsel. The matter—he said—was clear as daylight. Those who wore His Majesty's uniform, charged with the responsibility and privilege of defending their country, were no more entitled to desert their regiments by taking their own lives than they were entitled to desert in any other way. He asked for a conviction. Mr. Bosengate felt a sympathetic shuffle passing through all feet. The judge was speaking:

"Prisoner, you can either go into the witness box and make your statement on oath, in which you may be cross-examined on it; or you can make your statement there from the dock, in which case you will not be cross-examined. Which do you elect to do?"

"From here, my lord."

Seeing him now full face, and, as it might be, come to life in the effort to convey his feelings, Mr. Bosengate had suddenly a quite different impression of the fellow. It was as if his khaki had fallen off, and he had stepped out of his own shadow, a live and quivering creature. His pinched, clean-shaven face seemed to have an irregular, wilder, hairier look, his large, nervous brown eyes darkened and glowed; he jerked his shoulders, his arms, his whole body, like a man suddenly freed from cramp or a suit of armor. He spoke, too, in a quick, crisp, rather high voice, pinching his consonants a little, sharpening his vowels, like a true Welshman.

"My lord and misters the jury," he said: "I was a hairdresser when the call came on me to join the army. I had a little home and a wife. I never thought what it would be like to be away from them, I surely never did; and I'm ashamed to be speaking it out like this—how it can squeeze and squeeze a man, how it can prey on your mind when you're nervous like I am. 'Tis not everyone that cares for his home—there's a lots o' them never wants to see their wives again. But for me 'tis like being shut up in a cage, it is!" Mr. Bosengate saw daylight between the skinny fingers of the man's hand thrown out with a jerk. "I cannot bear it shut up away from wife and home like what you are in the army. So when I took my razor that morning I was wild—and' I wouldn't be here now but for that man catching my hand. There was no reason in it, I'm willing to confess. It was foolish; but wait till you get feeling like what I was, and see how it draws you. Misters the jury, don't send me back to prison; it is worse still there. If you have wives you will know what it is like for lots of us; only some is more nervous than others. I swear to you, sirs, I could not help it——" Again the little man flung out his hand, his whole thin body shook, and Mr. Bosengate felt the same sensation as when he drove his car over a dog—"Misters the jury, I hope you may never in your lives feel as I've been feeling."

The little man ceased, his eyes shrank back into their sockets, his figure back into its mask of shadowy brown and gleaming buttons, and Mr. Bosengate was conscious that the judge was making a series of remarks; and, very soon, of being seated at a mahogany table in the jury's withdrawing room, hearing the voice of the man with hair like an Irish terrier's saying, "Didn't he talk through his hat, that little blighter!" Conscious, too, of the commercial traveler, still on his left—always on his left!—mopping his brow and muttering, "Phew! It's hot in there today!" when an effluvium, as of an inside accustomed to whisky, came from him. Then the man with the underlip and the three plastered wisps of hair said, "Don't know why we withdrew, Mr. Foreman!"

Mr. Bosengate looked round to where, at the head of the table, Gentleman Fox sat, in defensive gentility and the little white piping to his waistcoat. "I shall be happy to take the sense of the jury," he was saying blandly.

There was a short silence, then the chemist murmured, "I should say he must have what they call claustrophobia."

"Clauster fiddlesticks! The feller's a shirker, that's all. Missed his wife—pretty excuse! Indecent, I call it!"

The speaker was the little wire-haired man; and emotion, deep and angry, stirred in Mr. Bosengate. That ill-bred little cur! He gripped the edge of the table with both hands.

"I think it's d——d natural!" he muttered. But almost before the words had left his lips he felt dismay. What had he said—he, nearly a colonel of Volunteers—endorsing such a want of patriotism! And hearing the commercial traveler murmuring, "'Ear, 'ear!" he reddened violently.

The wire-headed man said roughly, "There's too many of these blighted shirkers, and too much pampering of them."

The turmoil in Mr. Bosengate increased; he remarked in an icy voice, "I agree to no verdict that'll send the man back to prison."

At this a real tremor seemed to go round the table, as if they all saw themselves sitting there through lunchtime. Then the large gray-haired man given to winking, said, "Oh! Come, sir—after what the judge said! Come, sir! What do you say, Mr. Foreman?"

Gentleman Fox—as who should say 'This is excellent value, but I don't wish to press it on you!'—answered, "We are only concerned with the facts. Did he or did he not try to shorten his life?"

"Of course he did—said so himself," Mr. Bosengate heard the wire-haired man snap out, and from the following murmur of assent he alone abstained. Guilty! Well—yes! There was no way out of admitting that, but his feelings revolted against handing "that poor little beggar" over to the tender mercy of his country's law. His whole soul rose in arms against agreeing with that ill-bred little cur and the rest of this job-lot. He had an impulse to get up and walk out, saying, "Settle it your own way. Good morning."

"It seems, sir," Gentleman Fox was saying, "that we're all agreed to guilty, except yourself. If you will allow me, I don't see how you can go behind what the prisoner himself admitted."

Thus brought up to the very guns, Mr. Bosengate, red in the face, thrust his hands deep into the side pockets of his tunic, and, staring straight before him, said, "Very well, on condition we recommend him to mercy."

"What do you say, gentlemen; shall we recommend him to mercy?"

"'Ear 'ear!" burst from the commercial traveler, and from the chemist came the murmur: "No harm in that."

"Well, I think there is. They shoot deserters at the front, and we let this fellow off. I'd hang the cur."

Mr. Bosengate stared at that little wire-haired brute. "Haven't you *any* feeling for others?" he wanted to say. "Can't you see that this poor devil suffers tortures?" But the sheer impossibility of doing this before ten other men brought a slight sweat out on his face and hands; and in agitation he smote the table a blow with his fist. The effect was instantaneous. Everybody looked at the wire-haired man, as if saying, "Yes, you've gone a bit too far there!" The "little brute" stood it for a moment, then muttered surlily, "Well, commend 'im to mercy if you like; I don't care."

"That's right; they never pay any attention to it," said the gray-haired man, winking heartily. And Mr. Bosengate filed back with the others into court.

But when from the jury box his eyes fell once more on the hare-eyed figure in the dock, he had his worst moment yet. Why should this poor wretch suffer so—for no fault, no fault; while he, and these others, and that snapping counsel, and the Caesarlike judge up there, went off to their women and their homes, blithe as bees, and probably never thought of him again? And suddenly he was conscious of the judge's voice:

"You will go back to your regiment and endeavor to serve your country with better spirit. You may thank the jury that you are not sent to prison, and your good fortune that you were not at the front when you tried to commit this cowardly act. You are lucky to be alive."

A policeman pulled the little soldier by the arm; his drab figure, with eyes fixed and lusterless, passed down and away. From his very soul Mr. Bosengate wanted to lean out and say, "Cheer up, cheer up! *I* understand."

It was nearly ten o'clock that evening before he reached home, motoring back from the route march. His physical tiredness was abated, for he had partaken of a snack and a whisky and soda at the hotel but mentally he was in a curious mood. His body felt appeased, his spirit hungry. Tonight he had a yearning, not for his wife's kisses, but for her understanding. He wanted to go to her and say, "I've learnt a lot today—found out things I never thought of. Life's a wonderful thing, Kate, a thing one can't live all to oneself; a thing one shares with everybody, so that when another suffers, one suffers too. It's come to me that what one *has* doesn't matter a bit—it's what one does and how one sympathizes with other people. It came to me in the most extraordinary vivid way, when I was on that jury watching that poor little rat of a soldier in his trap; it's the first time I've ever felt—the—the spirit of Christ, you know. It's a wonderful thing, Kate—wonderful! We haven't been close—really close, you and I, so that we each understand what the other is feeling. It's all in that, you know; understanding—sympathy—it's priceless. When I saw that poor little devil taken down and sent back to his regiment to begin his sorrows all over again—wanting his wife, thinking and thinking of her just as you know I would be thinking and wanting you, I felt what an awful outside sort of life we lead, never telling each other what we really think and feel, never being really close. I daresay that little chap and his wife keep nothing from each other—live each other's lives. That's what *we* ought to do. Let's get to feeling that what really matters is—understanding and loving, and not only just saying it as we all do, those fellows on the jury, and even that poor devil of a judge—what an awful life, judging one's fellow creatures! When I left that poor little Tommy this morning, and ever since, I've longed to get back here quietly to you and tell you about it and make a beginning. There's something wonderful in this, and I want you to feel it as I do, because you mean such a lot to me."

This was what he wanted to say to his wife, not touching or kissing her, just looking into her eyes, watching them soften and glow as they surely must, catching the infection of his new ardor. And he felt unsteady, fearfully unsteady with the desire to say it all as it should be said: swiftly, quietly, with the truth and fervor of his feeling.

The hall was not lit up, for daylight still lingered under the new arrangement. He went toward the drawing room, but from the very door shied off to his study and stood irresolute under the picture of a "Man Catching a Flea" (Dutch school), which had come down to him from his father. The governess would be in there with his wife! He must wait. Essential to go straight to Kathleen and pour it all out, or he would never do it. He felt as nervous as an undergraduate going up for his *viva voce*. This thing was so big, so astoundingly and unexpectedly important. He was suddenly afraid of his wife, afraid of her coolness and her grace, and that something Japanese about her—of all those attributes he had been accustomed to admire; most afraid, as it were, of her attraction. He felt young tonight, almost boyish; would she see that he was not really fifteen years older than herself, and she not really a part of his collection, of all the admirable appointments of his home; but a companion spirit to one who wanted a companion badly? In this agitation of his soul he could keep still no more than he could last night in the agitation of his senses; and he wandered into the dining room. A dainty supper was set out there, sandwiches, and cake, whisky and cigarettes—even an early peach. Mr. Bosengate looked at this peach with sorrow rather than disgust. The perfection of it was of a piece with all that had gone before this new and sudden feeling. Its delicious bloom seemed to heighten his perception of the hedge around him, that hedge of the things he so enjoyed, carefully planted and tended these many years. He passed it by uneaten and went to the window. Out there all was darkening, the fountain, the lime tree, the flower beds, and the fields below, with the Jersey cows who would come to your call; darkening slowly, losing form, blurring into soft blackness, vanishing, but there nonetheless—all there—the hedge of his possessions. He heard the door of the drawing room open, the voices of his wife and the governess in the hall, going up to bed. If only they didn't look in here! If only——! The voices ceased. He was safe now—had but to follow in a few minutes, to make sure of Kathleen alone. He turned round and stared down the length of the dark dining room, over the rosewood table, to where in the mirror above the sideboard at the far end, his figure bathed, a stain, a mere blurred shadow; he made his way down to it along the table edge, and stood before himself as close as he could get. His throat and the roof of his mouth felt dry with nervousness; he put out his finger and touched his face in the glass. You're an ass! he thought. Pull yourself together, and get it over. She will see; of course she will! He swallowed, smoothed his mustache, and walked out. Going up the stairs, he felt his heart beat painfully; but he was in for it now, and marched straight into her room.

Dressed only in a loose blue wrapper, she was brushing her dark hair before the glass. Mr. Bosengate went up to her and stood there silent, looking down. The words he had thought of were like a swarm of bees buzzing in his head yet not one would fly from between his lips. His wife went on brushing her hair under the light which shone on her polished elbows. She looked up at him from beneath one lifted eyebrow.

"Well, dear—tired?"

With a sort of vehemence the single word "No" passed out. A faint, a quizzical smile flitted over her face; she shrugged her shoulders ever so gently. That gesture—he had seen it before! And in desperate desire to make her understand, he put his hand on her lifted arm.

"Kathleen, stop—listen to me!" His fingers tightened in his agitation and eagerness to make his great discovery known. But before he could get out a word he became conscious of that cool round arm, conscious of her eyes half-closed, sliding round at him, of her half-smiling lips, of her neck under the wrapper. And he stammered, "I want—I must—Kathleen, I——"

She lifted her shoulders again in that little shrug. "Yes—I know; all right!"

A wave of heat and shame, and of God knows what came over Mr. Bosengate; he fell on his knees and pressed his forehead to her arm; and he was silent, more silent than the grave. Nothing—nothing came from him but two long sighs. Suddenly he felt her hand stroke his cheek—compassionately, it seemed to him. She made a little movement toward him; her lips met his, and he remembered nothing but that. . . .

In his own room Mr. Bosengate sat at his wide-open window, smoking a cigarette; there was no light. Moths went past, the moon was creeping up. He sat very calm, puffing the smoke out into the night air. Curious thing—life! Curious world! Curious forces in it—making one do the opposite of what one wished; always—always making one do the opposite, it seemed! The furtive light from the creeping moon was getting hold of things down there, stealing in among the boughs of the trees. There's something ironical, he thought, which walks about. Things don't come off as you think they will. I meant, I tried—but one doesn't change like that all of a sudden, it seems. Fact is, life's too big a thing for me! All the same, I'm not the man I was yesterday—not quite! He closed his eyes, and in one of those flashes of vision which come when the senses are at rest, he saw himself as it were far down below—down on the floor of a street narrow as a grave, high as a mountain, a deep dark slit of a street—walking down there, a black midget of a fellow, among other black midgets—his wife, and the little soldier, the judge, and those jury chaps—*fantoches* straight up on their tiny feet, wandering down there in that dark, infinitely tall, and narrow street. Too much for one! he thought. Too high for one—no getting on top of it. We've got to be kind, and help one another, and not expect too much, and not think too much. That's—all! And, squeezing out his cigarette, he took six deep breaths of the night air and got into bed.

The Blushing Beginner and The Bearded Juryman

by:

"O" (THEO MATHEW)

selected by:

GAVIN TURNBULL SIMONDS

I have always enjoyed The Forensic Fables *of my old friend Theo Mathew, and my favorite is probably "The Blushing Beginner and the Bearded Juryman."*

GAVIN TURNBULL SIMONDS

S.S.________________________________

A Solicitor Briefed a Blushing Beginner to Defend a Prisoner at the Assizes. He Assured the Blushing Beginner that there was no Cause for Anxiety as the Prisoner hadn't an Earthly. When the Jury Acquitted the Prisoner the Blushing Beginner could Hardly Believe his Ears. He felt that he had indeed been Wise to Devote so much Time to the Study of the Works of Quintilian on Oratory and the Great Speeches of Such Masters as Cicero and Demosthenes. That his Address to the Jury had Done the Trick he had Little Doubt. For he had Observed that a Juryman with a Black Beard in the Front Row had Paid Close Attention to his Best Points. Which Particular Portion of his Speech had been Most Effective the Blushing Beginner could not be Sure. He Inclined to think it was the Peroration. For when he had Come to the Bit about the Dawn Breaking and the Sun Gilding the Distant Hills the Bearded Juryman had Shewn Considerable Emotion. Thus Meditating, the Blushing Beginner Proceeded from the Court to his Lodgings in High Spirits. On his Way he Observed the Bearded Juryman just Ahead of him. Hurrying Forward, the Blushing Beginner Wished the Bearded Juryman a Good Evening and Engaged him in Conversation. "Could you tell me," he said, "without Divulging any Secret of the Jury box, what it was that Convinced you of the Prisoner's Innocence? Was it my Cross-examination of the Prosecutor? Or the Failure of the Crown to Call Robinson? Or was it, perchance, the Argument which I Put Forward in my Final Speech?" The Bearded Juryman Replied, with Some Warmth, that he didn't Know or Care what the other Mugs Thought, but for his Part he (the Bearded Juryman) didn't See why his Sister's Son should be Sent to Quod even if the Boy *had* Stole a Tenner from the Blinking Blighter who had Done him (the Bearded Juryman) over a Deal Two Years ago. The Bearded Juryman then Expectorated Fiercely and Turned into the "Blue Pig" for Further Refreshment. The Blushing Beginner Gathered from these Remarks that there were Collateral Reasons for the Opinion of the Bearded Juryman which were not Strictly Relevant to the Main Issues in the Case. But he Decided to Treat the Bearded Juryman's Disclosures as Confidential.

MORAL—*Study Quintilian on Oratory.*

The Law and the Profits

by:

OCTAVUS ROY COHEN

selected by:

SAMUEL WILLISTON

Legal reading of cases, statutes, law reviews, and treatises has not left enough time to make me a faithful reader of fiction about law and lawyers. But one story which I recall with delight is Octavus Roy Cohen's "The Law and the Profits."

S.S. SAMUEL WILLISTON

Lawyer Evans Chew was at loggerheads with the universe. He gazed with wrathful and unappreciative eyes from the window of his sanctum on the eighth floor of the Penny Prudential Bank Building. Spring had come; spring, with its sensuous and tantalizing odors of jasmine and violets and barbecued meat; with its fresh green leaves and early vegetables; its siren call to the great open spaces where men can joy ride to their hearts' content.

But in the bosom of one of Birmingham's foremost colored legal luminaries there was no answering lilt. His heart hung heavy beneath the fifth rib, and he was oblivious of the fact that at this particular time of year the majority of humans consider themselves extremely fortunate to be existing. He stared out across the roofs that lined Eighteenth Street, and he muttered anathema upon the cosmos.

Lawyer Chew's pride and pocketbook had both been severely bumped.

The door opened and a young man entered unannounced. Because of the informality of his entrance, the attorney guessed the visitor's identity; but the grunt that emanated from his affluently rounded torso could not possibly have been construed to constitute an enthusiastic welcome.

If Florian Slappey was nonplused, he gave no outward indication. He stepped jauntily across the office and inspected his sartorial perfections in the ample mirror. It was easily apparent that the song of spring had not escaped Mr. Slappey. That gentleman was resplendent in new raiment of pearl gray, edged with white. From floppy Panama to new suède shoes, Florian was a study in masculine perfectivity. What cares he may have possessed had been stored away until the howling advent of another cold gray winter. His voice vibrated cheerily across the room.

"Mawnin', Lawyer Chew. How's business?"

Chew answered without turning: "Terrible!"

Mr. Slappey airily waved a gray-gloved hand.

"What diff'ence do it make? The answer is: None whichsoever. On account, Lawyer Chew, nothin' makes no neverminds on a day like this. Even a fun'ral couldn't make me feel sad, because, Lawyer Chew, if'n I was to see a fun'ral all I could think of would be how slick the flowers would grow over the corpse."

The counselor mouthed something that sounded suspiciously like profanity. Florian smiled broadly.

"Somebody must sho'ly have inwited yo' mother-in-law to visit at yo' house. What the matter is?"

Chew turned. Truth to tell, he was not displeased at the opportunity to air his troubles. His figure—garbed in neatly pressed Prince Albert, snowy vest, and gray trousers—moved ponderously and majestically across the handsomely furnished office. He extended toward his visitor a letter he held in his hand.

"Read that, Florian."

Florian accepted the letter and strolled with it to the window—the one with a southern exposure. There he paused to extract a Turkish cigarette from a near-silver case, tap it lightly on a freshly manicured fingernail, ignite it with a patent lighter, and inhale a single luxurious puff of the heavy smoke. Then he gave his attention to the missive that was typed upon the letterhead of The Sons & Daughters of I Will Arise:

> *Dere Lawyer Chew, Sir:* This is to inform you that your services as Council for this organization has been dispensed with complete from now henceforward and your monthly retainer of

$25 will immediately cease at once. We regrets to do this but is forced along with our trenchment policy. Wishing you best wishes, I am

THE SONS & DAUGHTERS OF I WILL ARISE,
BY ISAAC GETHERS,
GRAND MAGNIFICENT HIGH POTENTATE.

Florian emitted a slow whistle of amazement.

"It ain't so, Lawyer Chew."

"Huh! Maybe you think it ain't!"

Florian slowly recovered his poise and his optimism. After all, on such a day, one simply could not continue to stare at the darkest cloud when the silver lining was in evidence.

"Shuh! What does twenty-five dollars a month mean to a rich feller like you?'

Chew shook his head sadly.

"'Tain't that, Florian—'tain't that, although they ain't never gwine be no time when even such a seemingly insignificant sum like twenty-five dollars per month cash money won't he'p. It is the blow to my pride, Brother Slappey. You visu'lizes befo' you a man completely crushed an' burdened down by his woes. I not on'y has lost my job as their official counsel but also, Florian, I loses the influence which comes fum bein' same an' the business which comes fum hereinbefo'-mentioned influence. The mo' I reflec's an' cogitates upon this outrage, Brother Slappey, the convinceder I becomes that some foul an' arch enemy is wukkin' against me; that some leper in human form——"

Florian's right fist crashed into his left palm.

"Semore Mashby!" he ejaculated violently.

Lawyer Chew nodded.

"You has correc'ly enunciated the cognomen of that viper, Florian. Him is the feller."

"You're dog-gone tootin' he is, Lawyer Chew! Ever sence you won them th'ee cases against him he's been aimin' to git you. An' he's an awful powerful Son & Daughter of I Will Arise."

"He holds a mortgage against their new lodge rooms," said the attorney lugubriously.

"Ain't it the truth? When the Lawd made that cullud man He was shuah in a mean humor."

Chew waxed violent. He unleashed several intensely dramatic gestures.

"An' Mistuh Semore Mashby is gwine be in a mean humor when I finishes up with him. What I done to him in them th'ee cases ain't gwine be a succumstance to what Ise gwine do him fo' fum now hereafter. That po' li'l' skinny, undersized, nickel-nursin', slab-sided, intrust-cha'gin', secon'han' dish of no-good tripe! Ise gwine jar him so hahd it's gwine disturb his ancestors."

"You ain't aimin' to beat him up?"

"Nossuh, I ain't gwine beat him up. Ise gwine git him where it'll hurt wuss'n that carcass of hisn. Ise gwine bust him in the wallet—that's where that ol' skin-flint suffers most."

"Ain't it so?"

"It most posolutely is." The man of legal affairs sighed. "But le's us talk of somethin' else. What is you doin' these days?"

"Nothin'. An' I'm doin' it pretty steady," retorted Florian easily. "'Course I'm losin' a li'l' ev'y day or so down to the Pool & Ginuwine lott'ry. An' campaignin'."

"What's that you elucidates?"

"Ise campaignin'."

"Fo' who?"

"'Tain't a who, it's a which. Ain't you heard 'bout the new campaign?"

Lawyer Chew shook his head.

"I knew The Sons & Daughters of I Will Arise was preparin' to campaign fo' funds to raise that mortgage which Semore Mashby holds, but—"

"Also that the campaign stahted yestiddy," volunteered Florian. "An' at the same time The Gleaming Torchbearers of Divinity let loose a campaign of their own to he'p build a new clubhouse."

"No!"

"Yeah!"

"Then," postulated Lawyer Chew, "all two of 'em is gwine fail. This ain't no time fo' raisin' money nohow, but it jes' nachelly is wuss than no time fo' two lodges to be collectin'."

"Tha's what they thought—which is how come them to git together."

"You say words, Florian Slappey, but they don't impaht no info'mation. Who gotten together?"

"The Sons & Daughters of I Will Arise an' The Gleaming Torchbearers of Divinity. They come together 'cause they realized that wasn't they to do so, neither woul'n't git nowhere."

"Where is they gwine git, now that they has come together?"

"Jes' this far: They has drawed up a 'greement—you would have drawed it yo' ownse'f if you had remained counsel fo' The Sons & Daughters—a 'greement which prescribes that bofe lodges is gwine campaign fo' funds. All what they collec's is to be turned in by the fifteenth of the month, an' then it's all to be counted up. Whichever lodge's teams has turned in the most money gits 60 per cent of the total, an' the other lodge gits 40 per cent. 'Course that don't sound like much, but does it happen that one lodge turns in even one dollar more'n the other one, it gits the 60 per cent just the same, an' the lodge which comes out second sort of gives a big present to its rival."

The attorney nodded comprehendingly.

"I see. 'Tain't sech a bad scheme. Who schum it?"

"Dr. Elijah Atcherson. That ol' feller do suttinly use his head fo' somethin' mo' than a race track fo' a comb."

"He does. An' this campaign ought to go over immense. Was The Gleaming Torchbearers to turn in one thousan' an' one dollars an' The Sons & Daughters one thousan' even, it would make The Sons & Daughters lose a heap of money. Shuh! I reckon them teams is sholy gwine wuk hahd to come out in front."

"You said it, brother. Wuk is the one thing they ain't gwine do nothin' else but. 'Cause one of the mainest features is that neither ain't gwine know what bofe has got until the final countin' up."

Chew shook his head regretfully.

"An' I is out of it all. 'Course, I is still a Son & Daughter, but also I is a Gleaming Torchbearer. I don't hahdly know which I is gwine wuk fo'."

Florian grinned.

"I does. You is gwine wuk fo' The Gleaming Torchbearers. Right now The Sons & Daughters ain't exac'ly the fondest lodge you is of."

On one point at least the two gentlemen were correct: Doctor Atcherson's scheme had fanned to fever heat a rather lukewarm campaign spirit. Each organization had found its spirits waning on receipt of the news that another lodge had simultaneously launched a campaign for funds. As a matter of fact, although each had anticipated having the field to itself, there had been considerable reluctance about starting a drive at this particular time. But just when things seemed destined for failure, this new plan had been set afoot, and now the spirit of competition ran high and militant committees combed the city with highly gratifying results.

Nor was it entirely the desire to win that kept the collectors everlastingly at it; there was the horror of losing by a slight margin. The two lodges were sworn rivals, and though they had slightly interlocking membership, there was yet no love lost between them. And to each the thought of presenting a sizable percentage of its collections to the other was intolerable.

Meanwhile Lawyer Chew's interest in the warfare was decidedly lukewarm. The effect of his recent deposition as counsel for the more influential organization could already be felt in his business. His loss of prestige was enormous—so great, in fact, that he seriously considered proffering his services to The Sons & Daughters free of charge. But that, he figured, would be a decided tactical blunder. He did, however, stifle his pride sufficiently to make a personal call upon Isaac Gethers, Grand Magnificent High Potentate of the order which had until recently boasted Chew as its legal adviser.

Of him the attorney requested definite information.

"We ain't got much money," explained Isaac, "an' what we has got ain't ourn."

"How come it ain't?"

"We owes some mortgage money to Semore Mashby."

Chew made a gesture of disgust.

"That po' mis'able li'l' turkey buzzard! I don't hahdly reckon he had nothin' to do with gittin' me fired fum bein' you' legal representative an' most eruditest adviser, did he?"

"Well, yes," confessed Isaac. "He sort of kinder did."

"I seen his hand all right. They ain't nothin' that feller woul'n't stoop to fo' a dollar. Honest, I b'lieve was he to send flowers to his best friend's fun'ral an' somebody was to offer him more'n he paid for 'em, he'd swipe 'em off the casket an' make a resale."

"Oh, I don't hahdly think Semore is as bad as you has painted him."

"You're right he ain't, Brother Gethers. He's wuss! If he ever happens to die I is sholy gwine to be a most enthusiastic mourner."

"Well, anyway, that ain't neither hither or yon. They ain't nothin' we can do about what we has done. Semore conwinced the members that you was a luxury, an' with them thinkin' thataway an' votin' that you wa'n't to be our lawyer no mo', I reckon they ain't nothin' fo' us to do 'cept reside by their decision."

Chew made a mournful exit. Nor did he derive any particular solace from the visit of a team that was campaigning for The Sons & Daughters of I Will Arise. With a great show of indifference he donated twenty-five dollars to their rapidly swelling fund, reflecting bitterly as he did so that his money would eventually find its way into the capacious pockets of Semore Mashby.

"Him that has gits," he mused unhappily. "An' him that hasn't gits—gits it in the neck."

In the ten days that followed, Lawyer Chew saw little of his friend Florian. It was not until the night before the termination of the drive that they again came in contact with each other. That was at the fortnightly session of the Full House Poker Club. Florian was in fine fettle. Being strictly of the idle—if not of the rich—he had blossomed forth as captain of the team that bade fair to win the trophy offered by The Sons & Daughters for the combination that did the most toward victory.

Too, Florian was exceedingly lucky that night. He filled in between straights with remarkable persistence and seemed to possess uncanny knowledge of the cards in the hands of his rivals. It was altogether a delicious evening from Mr. Slappey's viewpoint; and in line with the recent turn of events in Lawyer Chew's existence, that gentleman was the chief contributor. Somehow the cards that he held, though good, were not good enough. They were enticing; so enticing that he bet them with freedom and confidence, only to discover to his sorrow that someone had him topped. As the evening wore on, Lawyer

Chew became superstitious and refused to play his cards for what they were worth, thus destroying his only chance to recoup.

The session ended on the stroke of one. Florian Slappey, well supplied with money, decided to walk home with the unhappy counselor. They strolled down Avenue F together, Chew bulking large in the moonlight, Florian, twirling a new cane, skipping blithesomely beside him. Mr. Slappey made no effort at conversation. The world was treating him very well, indeed, and he had no particular mind to listen to any one's troubles. But silence was intolerable to Chew.

"How is the drive comin', Florian?"

Mr. Slappey enthused.

"Elegant! Splendiferous! Cou'dn't be better."

"Hmph! Who's gwine win?"

"Us is."

"Who is us?"

"The Sons & Daughters of I Will Arise."

"Who says you is gwine win?"

"I does."

"How do you know?"

"I know—tha's how. An' when a feller knows somethin' it don't make no diff'ence how he knows. It's just enough fo' him to know, ain't it?"

"Yeh, if he knows positive."

"Well, I does." Silence. Finally Florian broke forth confidentially: "If I tell you how much we has got a'ready, Lawyer Chew, will you keep it secret?"

"Positively."

Florian lowered his voice.

"Countin' what we is suttin to collect t'morrow, we has got exac'ly one thousan' fo' hund'ed an' eight dollars an' fifty cents. Semore donated the fifty cents."

Chew uttered an exclamation of surprise.

"Not really?'

"Yep, we sholy has; cash money—or just as good as. Don't you reckon tha's mo'n enough?"

"Suttenly soun's that way to me. I never thought bofe lodges t'gether would raise that much."

"N'r neither I didn't. An', boy, my team has raised more'n

any other team in the lodge, an' us gits a prize. Tha's where li'l' Florian Slappey comes in at. I gits the team prize fo' captainin' the team which collects the most fo' us."

"You kind of has the gittin' habit, ain't you?"

"Yep. An' the on'y time I'll ever stop gittin' is when I has got."

They separated at Florian's boardinghouse. Chew's forehead was puckered. He was exceedingly sad at heart. For the first time in years he had been strictly out of a vital lodge matter and the situation rankled. If only he could be reinstated as counsel for The Sons & Daughters and his position as the legal beacon of Darktown reestablished—— He tossed fitfully for an hour or so after snuggling between the sheets of his twin bed. He dreamed an unpleasant dream wherein he wore the costume of a Greek dancer, while a thing partly resembling a satyr and partly resembling Semore Mashby chased him over hill and dale with a glittering snickersnee. Chew waked in a cold sweat of terror.

"Golly! Seems like I even has got to sleep with that feller!"

He rose early, breakfasted meagerly, and then for a half hour occupied himself with numerous low-voiced telephone calls. But despite that delay he reached his office ahead of time. His stenographer smiled a good morning.

"Folks has been phonin' you ever sence I come in, Lawyer Chew. They is a committee comin' to wait on you."

"Let 'em wait."

"They is bringin' Semore Mashby."

Chew's eyes popped open.

"Says which?"

"They is bringin' Semore Mashby with 'em."

"What is bringin' Semore with who?"

"This heah committee fum The Gleaming Torchbearers of Divinity."

Lawyer Evans Chew sat down suddenly and completely.

"Gal, you utters strange words. What is Semore Mashby doin' with a Gleaming Torchbearers committee? He ain't even a member of that lodge."

"I didn't ask no questions."

"An' Semore is rootin' fo' The Sons & Daughters to win on account he donated fo' bits to their fund."

"Anyway," said the girl with finality, "they is due heah most any minute—or even sooner than that."

Lawyer Chew vanished behind the ground-glass door that bore a gilt sign warning all and sundry that what happened within was private. He was thinking and thinking hard.

"If that six-inch piece of tripe is aimin' to put somethin' else over on me," growled the big man, "they is gwine be mayhem committed inside this office, an' Semore Mashby is gwine be the pusson which gits mayhemed."

He seated himself at the near-mahogany desk and shuffled halfheartedly through the morning's mail. But when a great volume of sound from the outer office informed him that the committee had arrived, he hastily procured several ponderous tomes, spread them out before him, donned his horn-rimmed goggles and assumed a studiousness that he felt not. He did not even raise his eyes when his stenographer opened the door.

"The committee is heah, Lawyer Chew."

"Give 'em seats an' let 'em wait. Ise busy."

He could hear a murmur of impatience and a triumphant gleam appeared in his eyes. He kept them waiting just long enough, then sounded his buzzer. Almost instantly the door opened and the committee filed in. From Dr. Brutus Herring, who headed the committee, to the wizened little Semore Mashby, the visitors were patently ill at ease. Nor did Chew's manner make them any more comfortable.

"Just a minute, you-all, till I finishes what I is wukkin' at."

Finally his task appeared to be completed. He piled some documents neatly on his desk, selected a gold-banded Invincible, shoved his chair back, looped thumbs in the armholes of his white vest, and stared severely at his callers.

"Well?" The word was a booming challenge.

Dr. Herring cleared his throat.

"Lawyer Chew, us is the executive committee fum The Gleaming Torchbearers of Divinity."

"I could see that even if I di'n't know it a'ready."

"We has come to see you—"

"I know that. S'posin' you splain somethin' I is ign'rant of—if any."

"We—er—that is, we has a hunch that just recently you ain't lovin' The Sons & Daughters none, is you?"

The glance of Lawyer Chew and Semore Mashby clashed. Mr. Mashby cringed. Chew's voice trembled with emotion.

"I ain't said I ain't."

"Well, I asts you: Is you is or is you ain't?"

Chew rose and paced the room, a judicial expression upon his countenance.

"S'pose you fellers sit down on brass tacks 'stead of runnin' around the bush."

"We will, we will," promised Herring hastily. "But of course it's understood that what transpires herein is stric'ly confidential."

"Suttinly. Absotively."

"It's this-a-way," explained the spokesman doubtfully: "As you know, they is sev'al members of our lodge which is also members of The Sons & Daughters."

"Correc'."

"An' we has therefo' been keepin' in pretty close touch with how much they has raised in this campaign. The thing closes at six o'clock this evenin', an' we has raised ev'y nickel which is possible to be rose. We figgers that we is about two hund'ed dollars behind The Sons & Daughters, which means that if we finishes that-a-way it'll be just like handin' them a gift."

"An' you ain't cravin' to present The Sons & Daughters with nothin'?"

"You is tootin' now, Brother Chew."

"That's that," muttered the lawyer. "Shoot on!"

Dr. Herring was warming up to his subject. Lawyer Chew appeared to be in a highly receptive mood.

"We done held a meetin' early this mawnin' an' made up our minds we wa'n't gwine give nobody nothin', 'specially them Sons & Daughters of I Will Arise. So we decided to go out an' borry enough money so's we'd be ahaid when the final count-up come."

"Borry it?"

"Tha's what I said. Semore Mashby has agreed to loaned us five hund'ed dollars cash until tomorrow mawnin'. Tha's gwine put us comfuttubly ahaid of them other fellers, an' make it so that us gits sixty per cent of all we has raised and sixty per cent of all they has raised. Then we returns Semore's money, plus a li'l' honorium fo' his kin'ness in loanding it to us."

"H'm! I commences to see. I been kinder wonderin' why Semore Mashby was mixin' up in this. Of course I knowed that however come him to git in, it wa'n't gwine injure his feenancial status none whatever. Now I asts you, how much you is gwine pay Semore fo' the use of his five hund'ed dollars fo' one day?"

"Fifty dollars," proclaimed Doctor Herring.

Semore blushed a guilty lavender.

"A-ha! Ten per cent a day, huh? Tha's pretty salubrious intrus' even fo' you, ain't it, Semore?"

The little man leaped to his feet.

"You done promised that ev'ything you heard in this office was gwine be kep' private."

"An' I keeps my promise. They ain't none of this gwine be tol' to nobody by me. But if I has got my pussonal 'pinion of a feller like you, then Ise entitled to possess same. An' what that is, Semore Mashby, you could have me hung fo' thinkin'."

"That ain't neither heah nor otherwise," interrupted Dr. Herring hastily. "The point is, Lawyer Chew, is you willin' to draw up these papers fo' us?"

Chew smiled slightly.

"Ise the world's champeen contrac' drawer," he said modestly. "Contrac's which Lawyer Chew draws cain't never be busted by nobody no time, never."

He sounded the buzzer for his stenographer, and then for ten minutes his mellifluous voice flowed through the office. As he dictated he paced the room, filling the atmosphere with impressive, magniloquent gestures.

"—and in consideration of the services so rendered said Gleaming Torchbearers of Divinity, the said Semore Mashby shall receive, not later than six P.M. of the sixteenth day of May, Anni Domino 1923, as his fee, the cash money sum of fifty dollars to him in hand paid; and fu'thermore—"

Over in the corner Mr. Mashby had been doing some rapid figuring on the nether side of an ex-envelope. He now untangled himself slowly and rose to his feet, one skinny paw upraised.

"I craves attention," said he.

All eyes focused upon him as he stood in the corner of the

room. A threadbare coat that had originally been black but was now worn to a rich golden brown flapped grotesquely about his attenuated figure; the shoes, overlarge even for his enormous feet, were placed firmly on the floor so as to form a right angle; trousers that had seen their best days threatened any minute to part company with the suspenders that through design and use appeared to represent a flower garden in the dead of winter. Chew bestowed upon him a glance in which there was no brotherly love.

"What you desiahs, Useless?"

"I been thinkin'—"

"Huh! Tha's what you says."

"An' it strikes me it woul'n't be noways fair fo' me to git fifty dollars fo' the use of my money fo' one day. So I reflects that I has a suggestion to make."

Lawyer Chew snorted, but Dr. Herring hastened to pour oil upon the troubled waters.

"Go ahaid, Semore; be as suggestive as you like."

"Seems to me," announced the emaciated money lender, "that this heah ought to be a coop'rative proposition. So I asts Lawyer Chew, if you Gleaming Torchbearers is willin', that he should write that contract to read that I gits fifty per cent of the profits which you makes by usin' my money."

The committeemen gazed blankly at one another. There was a trifle too much mathematics involved. They held a whispered conference and finally announced their willingness. Lawyer Chew resumed his dictation:

"And it is fu'thermore decided and agreed and made a part and parcel of this contract and mutual consideration thereof that the said Semore Mashby shall share equally with the said lodge, The Gleaming Torchbearers of Divinity, in the division of the amount said society obtains by reason of this transaction and what they would have obtained without it." He faced the others. "Is that salisfractory, gemmun?"

They nodded. Chew whirled angrily upon the triumphant Mashby.

"Reckon you figgers you has done somethin', don't you?—gittin' these fellers——"

"You leave me be, Evans Chew. I didn't come heah to git insulted."

"Then," snapped Lawyer Chew, "you has sho'ly got somethin' you wa'n't lookin' fo'."

The contract was typed in triplicate. One copy was placed in the attorney's files, the others—mutually signed—were delivered to the contracting parties, and as they departed Chew discerned a triumphant grin upon the face of his *bête noir*.

Six o'clock had been set as the official end of the drive; the selected meeting place for the finance committees was the lodge rooms of The Sons & Daughters of I Will Arise. By five o'clock the dignitaries of the rival lodges commenced putting in appearance. Florian Slappey was very much in evidence, gloriously garbed, spreading pep upon the landscape.

There, too, was Lawyer Evans Chew. It was quite evident that something had occurred to restore his faith in humanity, for his ebony countenance wore a smile of surpassing contentment. For perhaps twenty minutes he was in conference with Isaac Gethers, Grand Magnificent High Potentate of The Sons & Daughters, and throughout the confab Isaac's head could be seen nodding affirmatively. Immediately thereafter Isaac was seen to buttonhole various members of the executive committee of his lodge and to talk earnestly with them, occasionally pausing to designate the protuberantly triumphant figure of Lawyer Evans Chew.

Something vital was evidently under consideration and whatever it was did not seem to fill the grandiloquent attorney with misery. And then, on the stroke of six, the committees filed importantly into the clubhouse, leaving the excited spectators in buzzing and eager groups. Semore Mashby was nervously present. Semore had glimpsed the beatitude that was Chew's and found naught of reassurance there. He scrupulously avoided the larger man.

Twenty minutes passed—thirty—one hour. And finally Isaac Gethers appeared in the doorway. He beckoned to Lawyer Chew and held whispered conversation with him. There was violent nodding on both sides, then a warm handclasp and mutual slappings upon mutual backs. After which Isaac disappeared within the building.

The crowd hummed expectantly. It had witnessed the bit of byplay and was keenly interested. The more inquisitive ones clustered about Lawyer Chew, but it was Florian Slappey who put the question direct.

"How come you and Isaac Gethers gotten to be sech buddies again?"

Lawyer Chew waved pompously.

"He was just infohming me, brethren, that I has been unanimously reinstated as counsel fo' The Sons & Daughters of I Will Arise, said lodge havin' discovered that it cain't no longer dispense with my vallible services."

A roar of approval rose from those loyal members of The Sons & Daughters who had sincerely disapproved the shaking their confidence in Lawyer Chew had sustained by reason of his brief dethronement. Florian was particularly vociferous in his congratulations, and it was he who sped off to break the news to Semore Mashby. That gentleman received the tidings in dour silence.

"Ain't you got nothin' to say?" demanded Florian.

"Uh-huh—just that."

Florian returned, grinning.

"Ol' Calamity taken it hard," he reported.

Then, side by side, Isaac Gethers and Dr. Brutus Herring, the rival presidents, appeared on the veranda of the clubhouse. With them was the important little figure of Dr. Elijah Atcherson, chairman of the general finance committee. In a voice surprisingly large for his diminutive stature, he announced the results:

"An' so it gives me great pleasure to infohm this heah assembled multitude that The Gleaming Torchbearers of Divinity won the contest, turning in two thousand and six dollars and twenty-five cents. The total collected by The Sons & Daughters of I Will Arise wasn't near up to that, same bein' one thousand four hundred and eight dollars and fifty cents. Under our 'greed arrangement, the winning lodge therefore gits sixty per cent, or two thousand and forty-eight dollars and eighty-five cents and the losin' Sons & Daughters gits one thousand and three hundred and sixty-five dollars and ninety cents. So that no special hardship hasn't been wukked on neither, as the diff'ence 'tween what they raised an' what they got really wasn't ve'y much after all."

The announcement appeared to excite general surprise and approval. The totals were far in excess of what had been expected, and though there was some show of feeling between the rival lodges, the clash of words largely assumed the form of good-natured badinage.

But there was nothing of joy on the faces of the members of the executive committee of The Gleaming Torchbearers of Divinity, who, in the company of Semore Mashby, gathered one hour later at the office of Lawyer Evans Chew.

Chew was in magnificent fettle. He strode up and down the room, puffing happily upon an enormous cigar and belligerently exhaling clouds of the fragrant smoke.

The committee members were shaking their heads sorrowfully. Nobody seemed to understand what it was all about. Victory had brought to them no vestige of triumph. But their unhappiness wasn't a circumstance to the stupendous misery that was reflected upon the face of Semore Mashby.

Lawyer Chew smiled genially upon the assemblage, permitting them to suffer keenly. And when he concluded that all of them—and particularly Semore—had plumbed the nadir of unhappiness he rapped upon the table for order. In his left hand he held the half-smoked cigar, in the other a sheet of paper upon which many figures were inscribed.

"The contest," he announced impressively, "turned out ve'y peculiar an' unexpected; in fact I might almost say startling. Because it now appears that if you gemmun hadn't borried Semore Mashby's five hund'ed dollars the result would have been—speakin' in round figgers an' 'liminating odd dollars an' cents—a victory for you-all in that you had fifteen hund'ed dollars against fourteen hundred for the others." He paused, giving the words time to sink in. Then: "In other words, if you had of left good enough alone you would have got, when the division was made, about seventeen hund'ed dollars as against eleven hund'ed fo' The Sons & Daughters. To elucidate it more clearer, your deal with Mistuh Mashby nets you a dead loss of two hund'ed dollars, while The Sons & Daughters simply gains that amount, same bein' forty per cent of the five hund'ed which you so unneedlessly borried."

His voice droned off. Standing magnificently behind his desk, feet wide apart and solidly planted, white carnation decorating the lapel of his neatly pressed black coat, eyes shining through huge goggles, he surveyed the scene with thorough satisfaction. His audience wallowed in the slough of despond; but, miserable as they were, the shrunken form of Semore Mashby was the one that shrieked ultimate despair.

"The way matters stan' now," pursued Chew, "shows that when you deducts away fum your total the sum of five hund'ed dollars which you has got to return to Semore Mashby, you is left with a little more than fifteen hund'ed dollars; same bein' two hund'ed dollars less than you would of got if you hadn't tried to crook the noble lodge of which I has the honor to be gen'ral counsel.

"Also"—and his voice trembled with triumph—"I regrets to inform Brother Mashby that when he refused to accept the fifty dollars' profit which you gemmun offered him, an' insisted on a percentage, he done hisse'f an awful dirty trick. Because, as you-all c'n see, there ain't no profit."

"An' all I gits back," wailed Semore shrilly, "is my five hund'ed dollars?"

Lawyer Evans Chew favored him with a warm, friendly smile.

"Nossuh, that ain't nearly all you gits. Also you gits a jolt which jars bofe yo' teeth loose. Yo' five hund'ed dollars is what you thinks you gits, Brother Mashby. But thinks you gits ain't is gits. I regrets to infohm you, Semore, that you has made a plumb rotten deal." He produced the contract signed that morning between Semore and The Gleaming Torchbearers. "Accordin' to Paragraph Nine of this contrac', Brother Mashby, same havin' been suggested by you yo' ownse'f, the wordin' prescribes an' provides as follers: Namely, that you shall share equally in the division of the amount which the society obtains by this transaction and what they would have obtained without it.

"Now all that the society obtained by the deal, Semore, was a dead loss of two hund'ed dollars. An' since you has contracted in writin' to share in the diff'ence, you has to stand fo' one-half of that loss, same being one hund'ed dollars!"

The amazing turn of events did not immediately penetrate Semore's consciousness. But when finally it burst upon him that he not only was to get no profit on the deal but that he was also out of pocket one hundred cold, hard dollars, he uttered a shriek that could be heard a block away. He protested that it was a frame-up; that he was the victim of a conspiracy. He denounced Lawyer Evans Chew and all the members of The Gleaming Torchbearers' executive committee. He succeeded in adding materially to his chronic unpopularity. But when he had completed his tirade Dr. Brutus Herring calmly returned to him four hundred dollars of the original five hundred that had been borrowed.

"And," said Dr. Herring with a hint of maliciousness, "we wishes to thank you fo' your gen'rous cont'ibution to our fund, Brother Mashby."

Semore was near to tears. Lawyer Chew gazed benevolently upon him.

"Sort of seems to me, Mistuh Mashby," he said softly, "that this is a case where him who laughs first laughs last."

Semore ignored him. He turned piteously to Dr. Herring.

"They is on'y one thing I craves to know," he mourned. "Who was the person which fust give The Gleaming Torchbearers the idea of borryin' five hund'ed dollars offen me?"

A slow grin decorated Dr. Herring's lips. "That idea?" he retorted gently. "Why, that suggestion come fum Lawyer Evans Chew!"

Boys Will Be Boys

by:

IRVIN S. COBB

selected by:

ROSCOE POUND

The short stories which I have liked particularly were those of Irvin Cobb about a Kentucky rural circuit judge by the name of Priest. They are all good. One which I have always enjoyed is "Boys Will Be Boys," which was selected for The Best Short Stories of 1917.

S.S. ROSCOE POUND

When Judge Priest, on this particular morning, came puffing into his chambers at the courthouse, looking, with his broad beam and in his costume of flappy, loose white ducks, a good deal like an old-fashioned full-rigger with all sails set, his black shadow, Jeff Poindexter, had already finished the job of putting the quarters to rights for the day. The cedar water bucket had been properly replenished; the jagged flange of a fifteen-cent chunk of ice protruded above the rim of the bucket; and alongside, on the appointed nail, hung the gourd dipper that the master always used. The floor had been swept, except, of course, in the corners and underneath things; there were evidences, in streaky scrolls of fine grit particles upon various flat surfaces, that a dusting brush had been more or less sparingly employed. A spray of trumpet flowers, plucked from the vine that grew outside the window, had been draped over the framed steel engraving of President Davis and his Cabinet upon the wall; and on the top of the big square desk in the middle of the room, where a small section of cleared green-blotter space formed an oasis in a dry and arid desert of cluttered law journals and dusty documents, the morning's mail rested in a little heap.

Having placed his old cotton umbrella in a corner, having removed his coat and hung it upon a peg behind the hall door, and having seen to it that a palm-leaf fan was in arm's reach should he require it, the Judge, in his billowy white shirt, sat down at his desk and gave his attention to his letters. There was an invitation from the Hylan B. Gracey Camp of Confederate Veterans of Eddyburg, asking him to deliver the chief oration at the annual reunion, to be held at Mineral Springs on the twelfth day of the following month; an official notice from the clerk of the Court of Appeals concerning the affirmation of a judgment that had been handed down by Judge Priest at the preceding term of his own court; a bill for five pounds of a special brand of smoking tobacco; a notice of a lodge meeting—altogether quite a sizable batch of mail.

At the bottom of the pile he came upon a long envelope addressed to him by his title, instead of by his name, and bearing on its upper right-hand corner several foreign-looking stamps; they were British stamps, he saw on closer examination.

To the best of his recollection it had been a good long time since Judge Priest had had a communication by post from overseas. He adjusted his steel-bowed spectacles, ripped the wrapper with care, and shook out the contents. There appeared to be several inclosures; in fact, there were several—a sheaf of printed forms, a document with seals attached, and a letter that covered two sheets of paper with typewritten lines. To the letter the recipient gave consideration first. Before he reached the end of the opening paragraph he uttered a profound grunt of surprise; his reading of the rest was frequently punctuated by small exclamations, his face meantime puckering up in interested lines. At the conclusion, when he came to the signature, he indulged himself in a soft low whistle. He read the letter all through again, and after that he examined the forms and the document which had accompanied it.

Chuckling under his breath, he wriggled himself free from the snug embrace of his chair arms and waddled out of his own office and down the long, bare, empty hall to the office of Sheriff Giles Birdsong. Within, that competent functionary, Deputy Sheriff Breck Quarles, sat at ease in his shirt sleeves, engaged, with the smaller blade of his pocketknife, in performing upon his fingernails an operation that combined the fine deftness of the manicure with the less delicate art of the farrier. At the sight of the Judge in the open doorway he hastily withdrew from a tabletop, where they rested, a pair of long thin legs, and rose.

"Mornin', Breck," said Judge Priest to the other's salutation. "No, thank you, son. I won't come in; but I've got a little job for you. I wisht, ef you ain't too busy, that you'd step down the street and see ef you can't find Peep O'Day fur me and fetch him back here with you. It won't take you long, will it?"

"No, suh—not very." Mr. Quarles reached for his hat and snuggled his shoulder holster back inside his unbuttoned waistcoat. "He'll most likely be down round Gafford's stable. Whut's Old Peep been doin', Judge—gettin' himself in contempt of court or somethin'?" He grinned, asking the question with the air of one making a little joke.

"No," vouchsafed the Judge, "he ain't done nothin'. But he's about to have somethin' of a highly onusual nature done to him. You jest tell him I'm wishful to see him right away—that'll be sufficient, I reckin."

Without making further explanation, Judge Priest returned to his chambers and for the third time read the letter from foreign parts. Court was not in session, and the hour was early and the weather was hot; nobody interrupted him. Perhaps fifteen minutes passed. Mr. Quarles poked his head in at the door.

"I found him, suh," the deputy stated. "He's outside here in the hall."

"Much obliged to you, son," said Judge Priest. "Send him on in, will you, please?"

The head was withdrawn; its owner lingered out of sight of his Honor, but within earshot. It was hard to figure the presiding judge of the First Judicial District of the State of Kentucky as having business with Peep O'Day; and, though Mr. Quarles was no eavesdropper, still he felt a pardonable curiosity in whatsoever might transpire. As he feigned an absorbed interest in a tax notice, which was pasted on a blackboard just outside the office door, there entered the presence of the Judge a man who seemingly was but a few years younger than the Judge himself—a man who looked to be somewhere between sixty-five and seventy. There is a look that you may have seen in the eyes of ownerless but well-intentioned dogs—dogs that, expecting kicks as their daily portion, are humbly grateful for kind words and stray bones; dogs that are fairly yearning to be adopted by somebody —by anybody—being prepared to give to such a benefactor a most faithful, doglike devotion in return.

This look, which is fairly common among masterless and homeless dogs, is rare among humans; still, once in a while you do find it there too. The man who now timidly shuffled himself across the threshold of Judge Priest's office had such a look out of his eyes. He had a long, simple face, partly inclosed in gray whiskers. Four dollars would have been a sufficient price to pay for the garments he stood in, including the wrecked hat he held in his hands and the broken, misshaped shoes on his feet. A purchaser who gave more than four dollars for the whole in its present state of decrepitude would have been but a poor hand at bargaining.

The man who wore this outfit coughed in an embarrassed fashion and halted, fumbling his ruinous hat in his hands.

"Howdy do?" said Judge Priest heartily. "Come in!"

The other diffidently advanced himself a yard or two.

"Excuse me, suh," he said apologetically; "but this here Breck Quarles he come after me and he said ez how you wanted to see me. 'Twas him ez brung me here, suh."

Faintly underlying the drawl of the speaker was just a suspicion—a mere trace, as you might say—of a labial softness that belongs solely and exclusively to the children and in a diminishing degree to the grandchildren, of native-born sons and daughters of a certain small green isle in the sea. It was not so much a suggestion of a brogue as it was the suggestion of the ghost of a brogue; a brogue almost extinguished, almost obliterated, and yet persisting through the generations—south of Ireland struggling beneath south of Mason and Dixon's Line.

"Yes," said the Judge; "that's right. I do want to see you." The tone was one that he might employ in addressing a bashful child. "Set down there and make yourself at home."

The newcomer obeyed to the extent of perching himself on the extreme forward edge of a chair. His feet shuffled uneasily where they were drawn up against the cross rung of the chair.

The Judge reared well back, studying his visitor over the tops of his glasses with rather a quizzical look. In one hand he balanced the large envelope which had come to him that morning.

"Seems to me I heard somewheres, years back, that your regular Christian name was Paul—is that right?" he asked.

"Shorely is, suh," assented the ragged man, surprised and plainly grateful that one holding a supremely high position in the community should vouchsafe to remember a fact relating to so inconsequent an atom as himself. "But I ain't heared it fur so long I come mighty nigh furgittin' it sometimes, myself. You see, Judge Priest, when I wasn't nothin' but jest a shaver folks started in to callin' me Peep—on account of my last name bein' O'Day, I reckin. They been callin' me so ever since. Fust off, 'twas Little Peep, and then jest plain Peep; and now it's got to be Old Peep. But my real entitled name is Paul, jest like you said, Judge—Paul Felix O'Day."

"Uh-huh! And wasn't your father's name Philip and your mother's name Katherine Dwyer O'Day?"

"To the best of my recollection that's partly so, too, suh. They both of 'em up and died when I was a baby, long before I could remember anything a-tall. But they always told me my paw's name was Phil, or Philip. Only my maw's name wasn't Kath—Kath—wasn't whut you jest now called it, Judge. It was plain Kate."

"Kate or Katherine—it makes no great difference," explained Judge Priest. "I reckin the record is straight this fur. And now think hard and see ef you kin ever remember hearin' of an uncle named Daniel O'Day—your father's brother."

The answer was a shake of the tousled head.

"I don't know nothin' about my people. I only jest know they come over frum some place with a funny name in the Old Country before I was born. The onliest kin I ever had over here was that there no-'count triflin' nephew of mine—Perce Dwyer—him that uster hang round this town. I reckin you call him to mind, Judge?"

The old Judge nodded before continuing:

"All the same, I reckin there ain't no manner of doubt but whut you had an uncle of the name of Daniel. All the evidences would seem to p'int that way. Accordin' to the proofs, this here Uncle Daniel of yours lived in a little town called Kilmare, in

Ireland." He glanced at one of the papers that lay on his desk-top; then added in a casual tone, "Tell me, Peep, whut are you doin' now fur a livin'?"

The object of this examination grinned a faint grin of extenuation.

"Well, suh, I'm knockin' about, doin' the best I kin—which ain't much. I help out round Gafford's liver' stable, and Pete Gafford he lets me sleep in a little room behind the feed room, and his wife she gives me my vittles. Oncet in a while I git a chancet to do odd jobs fur folks round town—cuttin' weeds and splittin' stove wood and packin' in coal, and sech ez that."

"Not much money in it, is there?"

"No, suh; not much. Folks is more prone to offer me old clothes than they are to pay me in cash. Still, I manage to git along. I don't live very fancy; but, then, I don't starve, and that's more'n some kin say."

"Peep, whut was the most money you ever had in your life—at one time?"

Peep scratched with a freckled hand at his thatch of faded whitish hair to stimulate recollection.

"I reckin not more'n six bits at any one time, suh. Seems like I've sorter got the knack of livin' without money."

"Well, Peep, sech bein' the case, whut would you say ef I was to tell you that you're a rich man?"

The answer came slowly:

"I reckin, suh, ef it didn't sound disrepectful, I'd say you was prankin' with me—makin' fun of me, suh."

Judge Priest bent forward in his chair.

"I'm not prankin' with you. It's my pleasant duty to inform you that at this moment you are the rightful owner of eight thousand pounds."

"Pounds of whut, Judge?" The tone expressed a heavy incredulity.

"Why, pounds in money."

Outside, in the hall, with one ear held conveniently near the crack in the door, Deputy Sheriff Quarles gave a violent start and then, at once, was torn between a desire to stay and hear more and an urge to hurry forth and spread the unbelievable tidings. After the briefest of struggles the latter inclination won;

this news was too marvelously good to keep; surely a harbinger and a herald were needed to spread it broadcast.

Mr. Quarles tiptoed rapidly down the hall. When he reached the sidewalk the volunteer bearer of a miraculous tale fairly ran. As for the man who sat facing the Judge, he merely stared in a dull bewilderment.

"Judge," he said at length, "eight thousand pounds of money oughter make a powerful big pile, oughten it?"

"It wouldn't weigh quite that much ef you put it on the scales," explained his Honor painstakingly. "I mean pounds sterlin'—English money. Near ez I kin figger offhand, it comes in our money to somewheres between thirty-five and forty thousand dollars—nearer forty than thirty-five. And it's yours, Peep—every red cent of it."

"Excuse me, suh, and not meanin' to contradict you, or nothin' like that; but I reckin there must be some mistake. Why, Judge, I don't scursely know anybody that's ez wealthy ez all that, let alone anybody that'd give me sech a lot of money."

"Listen, Peep: This here letter I'm holdin' in my hand came to me by today's mail—jest a little spell ago. It's frum Ireland—frum the town of Kilmare, where your people came frum. It was sent to me by a firm of barristers in that town—lawyers we'd call 'em. In this letter they ask me to find you and to tell you what's happened. It seems, from whut they write, that your uncle, by name Daniel O'Day, died not very long ago without issue—that is to say, without leavin' any children of his own, and without makin' any will.

"It appears he had eight thousand pounds saved up. Ever since he died those lawyers and some other folks over there in Ireland have been tryin' to find out who that money should go to. They learnt in some way that your father and your mother settled in this town a mighty long time ago, and that they died here and left one son, which is you. All the rest of the family over there in Ireland have already died out, it seems; that natchelly makes you the next of kin and the heir at law, which means that all your uncle's money comes direct to you.

"So, Peep, you're a wealthy man in your own name. That's the news I had to tell you. Allow me to congratulate you on your good fortune."

The beneficiary rose to his feet, seeming not to see the hand the old Judge had extended across the desktop toward him. On his face, of a sudden, was a queer, eager look. It was as though he foresaw the coming true of long-cherished and heretofore unattainable visions.

"Have you got it here, suh?"

He glanced about him as though expecting to see a bulky bundle. Judge Priest smiled.

"Oh, no; they didn't send it along with the letter—that wouldn't be regular. There's quite a lot of things to be done fust. There'll be some proofs to be got up and sworn to before a man called a British consul; and likely there'll be a lot of papers that you'll have to sign; and then all the papers and the proofs and things will be sent across the ocean. And, after some fees are paid out over there—why, then you'll git your inheritance."

The rapt look faded from the strained face, leaving it downcast. "I'm afeared, then, I won't be able to claim that there money," he said forlornly.

"Why not?"

"Because I don't know how to sign my own name. Raised the way I was, I never got no book learnin'. I can't neither read nor write."

Compassion shadowed the Judge's chubby face; and compassion was in his voice as he made answer:

"You don't need to worry about that part of it. You can make your mark—just a cross mark on the paper, with witnesses present—like this."

He took up a pen, dipped it in the inkwell, and illustrated his meaning.

"Yes, suh; I'm glad it kin be done thataway. I always wisht I knowed how to read big print and spell my own name out. I ast a feller oncet to write my name out fur me in plain letters on a piece of paper. I was aimin' to learn to copy it off; but I showed it to one of the hands at the liver' stable and he busted out laughin'. And then I come to find out this here feller had tricked me fur to make game of me. He hadn't wrote my name out a-tall—he'd wrote some dirty words instid. So after that I give up tryin' to educate myself. That was several years back and I ain't tried sence. Now I reckin I'm too old to learn. . . . I wonder, suh—I wonder ef it'll be very long before that there money gits here and I begin to have the spendin' of it?"

"Makin' plans already?"

"Yes, suh," O'Day answered truthfully; "I am." He was silent for a moment, his eyes on the floor; then timidly he advanced the thought that had come to him. "I reckin, suh, it wouldn't be no more'n fair and proper ef I divided my money with you to pay you back fur all this trouble you're fixin' to take on my account. Would—would half of it be enough? The other half oughter last me fur what uses I'll make of it."

"I know you mean well and I'm much obliged to you fur your offer," stated Judge Priest, smiling a little; "but it wouldn't be fittin' or proper fur me to tech a cent of your money. There'll be some court dues and some lawyers' fees, and sech, to pay over there in Ireland; but after that's settled up everything comes direct to you. It's goin' to be a pleasure to me to help you arrange these here details that you don't understand—a pleasure and not a burden."

He considered the figure before him.

"Now here's another thing, Peep; I judge it's hardly fittin' fur a man of substance to go on livin' the way you've had to live durin' your life. Ef you don't mind my offerin' you a little advice I would suggest that you go right down to Felsburg Brothers when you leave here and git yourself fitted out with some suitable clothin'. And you'd better go to Max Biederman's, too, and order a better pair of shoes fur yourself than them you've got on. Tell 'em I sent you and that I guarantee the payment of your bills. Though I reckin that'll hardly be necessary—when the news of your good luck gits noised round I misdoubt whether there's any firm in our entire city that wouldn't be glad to have you on their books fur a stiddy customer.

"And, also, ef I was you I'd arrange to git me regular board and lodgin's somewheres round town. You see, Peep, comin' into a property entails consider'ble many responsibilities right frum the start."

"Yes, suh," assented the legatee obediently. "I'll do jest ez you say, Judge Priest, about the clothes and the shoes, and all that; but—but, ef you don't mind, I'd like to go on livin' at Gafford's. Peter Gafford's been mighty good to me—him and his wife both; and I wouldn't like fur 'em to think I was gittin' stuck up jest because I've had this here streak of luck come to me. Mebbe, seein' ez how things has changed with me, they'd be willin' to take me in fur a table boarder at their house; but I shorely would hate to give up livin' in that there little room behind the feed room at the liver's stable. I don't know ez I could ever find any place that would seem ez homelike to me ez whut it is."

"Suit yourself about that," said Judge Priest heartily. "I don't know but whut you've got the proper notion about it after all."

"Yes, suh. Them Gaffords have been purty nigh the only real true friends I ever had that I could count on." He hesitated a moment. "I reckin—I reckin, suh, it'll be a right smart while, won't it, before that money gits here frum all the way acrost the ocean?"

"Why, yes; I imagine it will. Was you figurin' on investin' a little of it now?"

"Yes, suh; I was."

"About how much did you think of spendin' fur a beginnin'?"

O'Day squinted his eyes, his lips moving in silent calculation.

"Well, suh," he said at length, "I could use ez much ez a silver dollar. But, of course, sence—"

"That sounds kind of moderate to me," broke in Judge Priest. He shoved a pudgy hand into a pocket of his white trousers. "I reckin this detail kin be arranged. Here, Peep"—he extended his hand—"here's your dollar." Then, as the other drew back, stammering a refusal, he hastily added, "No, no, no; go ahead and take it—it's yours. I'm jest advancin' it to you out of whut'll be comin' to you shortly.

"I'll tell you whut: Until sech time ez you are in position to draw on your own funds you jest drap in here to see me when you're in need of cash, and I'll try to let you have whut you require—in reason. I'll keep a proper reckinin' of whut you git and you kin pay me back ez soon ez your inheritance is put into your hands.

"One thing more," he added as the heir, having thanked him, was making his grateful adieu at the threshold: "Now that you're wealthy, or about to be so, I kind of imagine quite a passel of fellers will suddenly discover themselves strangely and affectionately drawed toward you. You're liable to find out you've always had more true and devoted friends in this community than whut you ever imagined to be the case before.

"Now friendship is a mighty fine thing, takin' it by and large; but it kin be overdone. It's barely possible that some of this here new crop of your well-wishers and admirers will be makin' little business propositions to you—desirin' to have you go partners with 'em in business, or to sell you desirable pieces of real estate; or even to let you loan 'em various sums of money. I wouldn't be surprised but whut a number of sech chances will be comin' your way durin' the next few days, and frum then on. Ef sech should be the case I would suggest to you that, before committin' yourself to anybody or anything, you tell 'em that I'm sort of actin' as your unofficial adviser in money matters, and that they should come to me and outline their little schemes in person. Do you git my general drift?"

"Yes, suh," said Peep. "I won't furgit; and thank you ag'in, Judge, specially fur lettin' me have this dollar ahead of time."

He shambled out with the coin in his hand; and on his face was again the look of one who sees before him the immediate fulfillment of a delectable dream.

With lines of sympathy and amusement crosshatched at the outer corners of his eyelids, Judge Priest, rising and stepping to his door, watched the retreating figure of the town's newest and strangest capitalist disappear down the wide front steps of the courthouse.

Presently he went back to his chair and sat down, tugging at his short chin beard.

"I wonder now," said he, meditatively addressing the emptiness of the room, "I wonder whut a man sixty-odd-year old is goin' to do with the fust whole dollar he ever had in his life!"

It was characteristic of our circuit judge that he should have voiced his curiosity aloud. Talking to himself when he was alone was one of his habits. Also, it was characteristic of him that he had refrained from betraying his inquisitiveness to his late caller. Similar motives of delicacy had kept him from following the other man to watch the sequence.

However, at secondhand, the details very shortly reached him. They were brought by no less a person than Deputy Sheriff

Quarles, who, some twenty minutes or possibly half an hour later, obtruded himself upon Judge Priest's presence.

"Judge," began Mr. Quarles, "you'd never in the world guess whut Old Peep O'Day done with the first piece of money he got his hands on out of that there forty thousand pounds of silver dollars he's come into from his uncle's estate."

The old man slanted a keen glance in Mr. Quarles' direction.

"Tell me, son," he asked softly, "how did you come to hear the glad tidin's so promptly?"

"Me?" said Mr. Quarles innocently. "Why, Judge Priest, the word is all over this part of town by this time. Why, I reckin twenty-five or fifty people must 'a' been watchin' Old Peep to see how he was goin' to act when he come out of this courthouse."

"Well, well, well!" murmured the Judge blandly. "Good news travels almost ez fast sometimes ez whut bad news does—don't it, now? Well, son, I give up the riddle. Tell me jest whut our elderly friend did do with the first installment of his inheritance."

"Well, suh, he turned south here at the gate and went down the street, a-lookin' neither to the right nor the left. He looked to me like a man in a trance, almost. He keeps right on through Legal Row till he comes to Franklin Street, and then he goes up Franklin to B. Weil & Son's confectionery store; and there he turns in. I happened to be followin' 'long behind him, with a few others—with several others, in fact—and we-all sort of slowed up in passin' and looked in at the door; and that's how I come to be in a position to see what happened.

"Old Peep, he marches in jest like I'm tellin' it to you, suh; and Mr. B. Weil comes to wait on him, and he starts in buyin'. He buys hisself a five-cent bag of gumdrops; and a five-cent bag of jelly beans; and a ten-cent bag of mixed candies—kisses and candy mottoes, and sech ez them, you know; and a sack of fresh-roasted peanuts—a big sack, it was, fifteen-cent size; and two prize boxes; and some gingersnaps—ten cents' worth; and a coconut; and half a dozen red bananas; and a half a dozen more of the plain yaller ones. Altogether I figger he spent a even dollar, in fact, I seen him hand Mr. Weil a dollar, and I didn't see him gittin' no change back out of it.

"Then he comes on out of the store, with all these things

stuck in his pockets and stacked up in his arms till he looks sort of like some new kind of a summertime Santy Klaws; and he sets down on a goods box at the edge of the pavement, with his feet in the gutter, and starts in eatin' all them things.

"First, he takes a bite off a yaller banana and then off a red banana, and then a mouthful of peanuts; and then maybe some mixed candies—not sayin' a word to nobody, but jest natchelly eatin' his fool head off. A young chap that's clerkin' in Bagby's grocery, next door, steps up to him and speaks to him, meanin', I suppose, to ast him is it true he's wealthy. And Old Peep, he says to him, 'Please don't come botherin' me now, sonny—I'm busy ketchin' up,' he says; and keeps right on a-munchin' and a-chewin' like all possessed.

"That ain't all of it, neither, Judge—not by a long shot it ain't! Purty soon Old Peep looks round him at the little crowd that's gathered. He didn't seem to pay no heed to the grown-up people standin' there; but he sees a couple of boys about ten years old in the crowd, and he beckons to them to come to him, and he makes room fur them alongside him on the box and divides up his knicknacks with them.

"When I left there to come on back here he had no less'n six kids squatted round him, includin' one little nigger boy; and between 'em all they'd jest finished up the last of the bananas and peanuts and the candy and the gingersnaps, and was fixin' to take turns drinkin' the milk out of the coconut. I s'pose they've got it all cracked out of the shell and et up by now—the coconut, I mean. Judge, you oughter stepped down into Franklin Street and taken a look at the picture whilst there was still time. You never seen sech a funny sight in all your days, I'll bet!"

"I reckin 'twould be too late to be startin' now," said Judge Priest. "I'm right sorry I missed it. . . . Busy ketchin' up, huh? Yes; I reckin he is. . . . Tell me, son, whut did you make out of the way Peep O'Day acted?"

"Why, suh," stated Mr. Quarles, "to my mind, Judge, there ain't no manner of doubt but whut prosperity has went to his head and turned it. He acted to me like a plum' distracted idiot. A grown man with forty thousand pounds of solid money settin' on the side of a gutter eatin' jimcracks with a passel of dirty little boys! Kin you figure it out any other way, Judge—except that his mind is gone?"

"I don't set myself up to be a specialist in mental disorders, son," said Judge Priest softly, "but, sence you ask me the question, I should say, speakin' offhand, that it looks to me more ez ef the heart was the organ that was mainly affected. And possibly"—he added this last with a dry little smile—"and possibly, by now, the stomach also."

Whether or not Mr. Quarles was correct in his psychopathic diagnosis, he certainly had been right when he told Judge Priest that the word was already all over the business district. It had spread fast and was still spreading; it spread to beat the wireless, traveling as it did by that mouth-to-ear method of communication which is so amazingly swift and generally so tremendously incorrect. Persons who could not credit the tale at all nevertheless lost no time in giving to it a yet wider circulation; so that, as though borne on the wind, it moved in every direction, like ripples on a pond; and with each time of retelling the size of the legacy grew.

The *Daily Evening News,* appearing on the streets at 5 P.M., confirmed the tale; though by its account the fortune was reduced to a sum far below the gorgeously exaggerated estimates of most of the earlier narrators. Between breakfast and suppertime Peep O'Day's position in the common estimation of his fellow citizens underwent a radical and revolutionary change. He ceased—automatically, as it were—to be a town character; he became, by universal consent, a town notable, whose every act and every word would thereafter be subjected to close scrutiny and closer analysis.

The next morning the nation at large had opportunity to know of the great good fortune that had befallen Paul Felix O'Day, for the story had been wired to the city papers by the local correspondents of the same; and the press associations had picked up a stickful of the story and sped it broadcast over leased wires. Many who until that day had never heard of the fortunate man, or, indeed, of the place where he lived, at once manifested a concern in his well-being.

Certain firms of investment brokers in New York and Chicago promptly added a new name to what vulgarly they called their "sucker" lists. Dealers in mining stocks, in oil stocks, in all kinds of attractive stocks, showed interest; in circular form samples of the most optimistic and alluring literature the world has ever known were consigned to the post, addressed to Mr. P. F. O'Day, such-and-such a town, such-and-such a state, care of general delivery.

Various lonesome ladies in various lonesome places lost no time in sitting themselves down and inditing congratulatory letters; object matrimony. Some of these were single ladies; others had been widowed, either by death or request. Various other persons of both sexes, residing here, there, and elsewhere in our country, suddenly remembered that they, too, were descended from the O'Days of Ireland, and wrote on forthwith to claim proud and fond relationship with the particular O'Day who had come into money.

It was a remarkable circumstance, which speedily developed, that one man should have so many distant cousins scattered over the Union, and a thing equally noteworthy that practically all these kinspeople, through no fault of their own, should at the present moment be in such straitened circumstances and in such dire need of temporary assistance of a financial nature. Ticker and printer's ink, operating in conjunction, certainly did their work mighty well; even so, several days were to elapse before the news reached one who, of all those who read it, had most cause to feel a profound personal sensation in the intelligence.

This delay, however, was nowise to be blamed upon the tardiness of the newspapers; it was occasioned by the fact that the person referred to was for the moment well out of contact with the active currents of world affairs, he being confined in a workhouse at Evansville, Indiana.

As soon as he had rallied from the shock this individual set about making plans to put himself in direct touch with the inheritor. He had ample time in which to frame and shape his campaign, inasmuch as there remained for him yet to serve nearly eight long and painfully tedious weeks of a three-months' vagrancy sentence. Unlike most of those now manifesting their interest, he did not write a letter; but he dreamed dreams that made him forget the annoyances of a ball and chain fast on his ankle and piles of stubborn stones to be cracked up into fine bits with a heavy hammer.

We are getting ahead of our narrative, though—days ahead of it. The chronological sequence of events properly dates from the morning following the morning when Peep O'Day, having been abruptly translated from the masses of the penniless to the classes of the wealthy, had forthwith embarked upon the gastronomic orgy so graphically detailed by Deputy Sheriff Quarles.

On that next day more eyes probably than had been trained in Peep O'Day's direction in all the unremarked and unremarkable days of his life put together were focused upon him. Persons who theretofore had regarded his existence—if indeed they gave it a thought—as one of the utterly trivial and inconsequential incidents of the cosmic scheme, were moved to speak to him, to clasp his hand, and, in numerous instances, to express a hearty satisfaction over his altered circumstances. To all these, whether they were moved by mere neighborly good will, or perchance were inspired by impulses of selfishness, the old man exhibited a mien of aloofness and embarrassment.

This diffidence or this suspicion—or this whatever it was—protected him from those who might entertain covetous and ulterior designs upon his inheritance even better than though he had been brusque and rude; while those who sought to question him regarding his plans for the future drew from him only mumbled and evasive replies, which left them as deeply in the dark as they had been before. Altogether, in his intercourse with adults he appeared shy and very ill at ease.

It was noted, though, that early in the forenoon he attached to him perhaps half a dozen urchins, of whom the oldest could scarcely have been more than twelve or thirteen years of age; and that these youngsters remained his companions throughout the day. Likewise the events of that day were such as to confirm a majority of the observers in practically the same belief that had been voiced of Mr. Quarles—namely, that whatever scanty brains Peep O'Day might have ever had were now completely addled by the stroke of luck that had befallen him.

In fairness to all—to O'Day and to the town critics who sat in judgment upon his behavior—it should be stated that his conduct at the very outset was not entirely devoid of evidences of sanity. With his troupe of ragged juveniles trailing behind him, he first visited Felsburg Brothers' Emporium to exchange his old and disreputable costume for a wardrobe that, in accordance with Judge Priest's recommendation, he had ordered on the afternoon previous, and which had since been undergoing certain necessary alterations.

With his meager frame incased in new black woolens, and wearing, as an incongruous added touch, the most brilliant of neckties, a necktie of the shade of a pomegranate blossom, he presently issued from Felsburg Brothers' and entered M. Biederman's shoe store, two doors below. Here Mr. Biederman fitted him with shoes, and in addition noted down a further order, which the purchaser did not give until after he had conferred earnestly with the members of his youthful entourage.

Those watching this scene from a distance saw—and perhaps marveled at the sight—that already, between these small boys, on the one part, and this old man, on the other, a perfect understanding appeared to have been established.

After leaving Biederman's, and tagged by his small escorts, O'Day went straight to the courthouse and, upon knocking at the door, was admitted to Judge Priest's private chambers, the boys meantime waiting outside in the hall. When he came forth he showed them something he held in his hand and told them something; whereupon all of them burst into excited and joyous whoops.

It was at that point that O'Day, by the common verdict of most grown-up onlookers, began to betray the vagaries of a disordered intellect. Not that his reason had not been under suspicion already, as a result of his freakish excess in the matter of B. Weil & Son's wares on the preceding day; but the relapse that now followed, as nearly everybody agreed, was even more pronounced, even more symptomatic than the earlier attack of aberration.

In brief, this was what happened: To begin with, Mr. Virgil Overall, who dealt in lands and houses and sold insurance of all the commoner varieties on the side, had stalked O'Day to this point and was lying in wait for him as he came out of the courthouse into the Public Square, being anxious to describe to him some especially desirable bargains, in both improved and unimproved realty; also, Mr. Overall was prepared to book him for life, accident, and health policies on the spot.

So pleased was Mr. Overall at having distanced his professional rivals in the hunt that he dribbled at the mouth. But the warmth of his disappointment and indignation dried up the salivary founts instantly when the prospective patron declined to listen to him at all and, breaking free from Mr. Overall's detaining clasp, hurried on into Legal Row, with his small convoys trotting along ahead and alongside him.

At the door of the Blue Goose Saloon and Short Order Restaurant its proprietor, by name Link Iserman, was lurking, as it were, in ambush. He hailed the approaching O'Day most cordially; he inquired in a warm voice regarding O'Day's health; and then, with a rare burst of generosity, he invited, nay urged, O'Day to step inside and have something on the house—wines, ales, liquors, or cigars; it was all one to Mr. Iserman. The other merely shook his head and, without a word of thanks for the offer, passed on as though bent upon an important mission.

Mark how the proofs were accumulating. The man had disdained the company of men of approximately his own age or thereabout; he had refused an opportunity to partake of refreshment suitable to his years; and now he stepped into the Bon Ton toy store and bought for cash—most inconceivable of acquisitions—a little wagon that was painted bright red and bore on its sides, in curlicued letters, the name Comet.

His next stop was made at Bishop & Bryan's grocery, where, with the aid of his youthful compatriots, he first discriminatingly selected, and then purchased on credit, and finally loaded into the wagon, such purchases as a dozen bottles of soda pop, assorted flavors; cheese, crackers—soda and animal—sponge cakes with weatherproof pink icing on them; fruits of the season; cove oysters; a bottle of pepper sauce; and a quantity of the extra-large-sized bright green cucumber pickles known to the trade as the Fancy Jumbo Brand, Prime Selected.

Presently the astounding spectacle was presented of two small boys, with string bridles on their arms, drawing the wagon through our town and out of it into the country, with Peep O'Day in the role of teamster walking alongside the laden wagon. He was holding the lines in his hands and shouting orders at his team, who showed a colty inclination to shy at objects, to kick up their heels without provocation, and at intervals to try to run away. Eight or ten small boys—for by now the troupe had grown in number and in volume of noise—trailed along, keeping step with their elderly patron and advising him shrilly regarding the management of his refractory span.

As it turned out, the destination of this preposterous procession was Bradshaw's Grove, where the entire party spent the day picknicking in the woods and, as reported by several reliable witnesses, playing games. It was not so strange that holidaying boys should play games; the amazing feature of the performance was that Peep O'Day, a man old enough to be grandfather to any of them, played with them, being by turns an Indian chief, a robber baron, and the driver of a stagecoach attacked by Wild Western desperadoes.

When he returned to town at dusk, drawing his little red wagon behind him, his new suit was rumpled into many wrinkles and marked by dust and grass stains; his flame-colored tie was twisted under one ear; his new straw hat was mashed quite out of shape; and in his eyes was a light that sundry citizens, on meeting him, could only interpret for a spark struck from inner fires of madness.

Days that came after this, on through the midsummer, were, with variations, but repetitions of the day I have just described. Each morning Peep O'Day would go to either the courthouse or Judge Priest's home to turn over to the Judge the unopened mail which had been delivered to him at Gafford's stables; then he would secure from the Judge a loan of money against his inheritance. Generally the amount of his daily borrowing was a dollar; rarely was it so much as two dollars; and only once was it more than two dollars.

By nightfall the sum would have been expended upon perfectly useless and absolutely childish devices. It might be that he would buy toy pistols and paper caps for himself and his following of urchins; or that his whim would lead him to expend all the money in tin flutes. In one case the group he so incongruously headed would be for that one day a gang of make-believe banditti; in another, they would constitute themselves a fife-and-drum corps—with barreltops for the drums—and would march through the streets, where scandalized adults stood in their tracks to watch them go by, they all the while making weird sounds, which with them passed for music.

Or again, the available cash resources would be invested in provender; and then there would be an outing in the woods. Under Peep O'Day's captaincy his chosen band of youngsters picked dewberries; they went swimming together in Guthrie's Gravel Pit, out by the old Fair Grounds, where his spare naked shanks contrasted strongly with their plump freckled legs as all of them splashed through the shallows, making for deep water. Under his leadership they stole watermelons from Mr. Dick Bell's patch, afterward eating their spoils in thickets of grapevines along the banks of Perkins' Creek.

It was felt that mental befuddlement and mortal folly could reach no greater heights—or no lower depths—than on a certain hour of a certain day, along toward the end of August, when O'Day came forth from his quarters in Gafford's stables, wearing a pair of boots that M. Biederman's establishment had turned out to his order and his measure—not such boots as a sensible man might be expected to wear, but boots that were exaggerated and monstrous counterfeits of the red-topped, scroll-fronted, brass-toed, stub-heeled, squeaky-soled bootees that small boys of an earlier generation possessed.

Very proudly and seemingly unconscious of, or, at least, oblivious to, the derisive remarks that the appearance of these new belongings drew from many persons, the owner went clumping about in them, with the rumply legs of his trousers tucked down in them, and ballooning up and out over the tops in folds which overlapped from his knee joints halfway down his attenuated calves.

As Deputy Sheriff Quarles said, the combination was a sight fit to make a horse laugh. It may be that small boys have a lesser sense of humor than horses have, for certainly the boys who were the old man's invariable shadows did not laugh at him, or at his boots either. Between the whiskered senior and his small comrades there existed a freemasonry that made them all sense a thing beyond the ken of most of their elders. Perhaps this was because the elders, being blind in their superior wisdom, saw neither this thing nor the communion that flourished. They saw only the farcical joke. But his Honor, Judge Priest, to cite a conspicuous exception, seemed not to see the lamentable comedy of it.

Indeed, it seemed to some almost as if Judge Priest were aiding and abetting the befogged O'Day in his demented enterprises, his peculiar excursions, and his weird purchases. If he did not actually encourage him in these constant exhibitions of witlessness, certainly there were no evidences available to show that he sought to dissuade O'Day from his strange course.

At the end of a fortnight one citizen, in whom patience had ceased to be a virtue and to whose nature long-continued silence on any public topic was intolerable, felt it his duty to speak to the Judge upon the subject. This gentleman—his name was S. P. Escott—held, with many, that, for the good name of the community, steps should be taken to abate the infantile, futile activities of the besotted legatee.

Afterward Mr. Escott, giving a partial account of the conversation with Judge Priest to certain of his friends, showed unfeigned annoyance at the outcome.

"I claim that old man's not fittin' to be runnin' a court any longer," he stated bitterly. "He's too old and peevish—that's what ails him! For one, I'm certainly not never goin' to vote fur him again. Why, it's gettin' to be ez much ez a man's life is worth to stop that there spiteful old crank in the street and put a civil question to him—that's whut's the matter!"

"What happened, S. P.?" inquired some one.

"Why, here's what happened!" exclaimed the aggrieved Mr. Escott. "I hadn't any more than started in to tell him the whole town was talkin' about the way that daffy Old Peep O'Day was carryin' on, and that somethin' had oughter be done about it, and didn't he think it was beholdin' on him ez circuit judge to do somethin' right away, sech ez havin' O'Day tuck up and tried fur a lunatic, and that I fur one was ready and willin' to testify to the crazy things I'd seen done with my own eyes—when he cut in on me and jest ez good ez told me to my own face that ef I'd quit tendin' to other people's business I'd mebbe have more business of my own to tend to.

"Think of that, gentlemen! A circuit judge bemeanin' a citizen and a taxpayer"—he checked himself slightly—"anyhow, a citizen, thataway! It shows he can't be rational his ownself. Personally I claim Old Priest is failin' mentally—he must be! And ef anybody kin be found to run against him at the next election you gentlemen jest watch and see who gits my vote!"

Having uttered this threat with deep and significant emphasis, Mr. Escott, still muttering, turned and entered the front gate of his boardinghouse. It was not exactly his boardinghouse; his wife ran it. But Mr. Escott lived there and voted from there.

But the apogee of Peep O'Day's carnival of weird vagaries of deportment came at the end of two months—two months in which each day the man furnished cumulative and piled-up material for derisive and jocular comment on the part of a very considerable proportion of his fellow townsmen.

Three occurrences of a widely dissimilar nature, yet all closely interrelated to the main issue, marked the climax of the man's new role in his new career. The first of these was the arrival of his legacy; the second was a one-ring circus; and the third and last was a nephew.

In the form of sundry bills of exchange the estate left by the late Daniel O'Day, of the town of Kilmare, in the island of Ireland, was on a certain afternoon delivered over into Judge Priest's hands, and by him, in turn, handed to the rightful owner, after which sundry indebtednesses, representing the total of the old Judge's day-to-day cash advances to O'Day, were liquidated.

The ceremony of deducting this sum took place at the Planters' Bank, whither the two had journeyed in company from the courthouse. Having, with the aid of the paying teller, instructed O'Day in the technical details requisite to the drawing of personal checks, Judge Priest went home and had his bag packed, and left for Reelfoot Lake to spend a week fishing. As a consequence he missed the remaining two events, following immediately thereafter.

The circus was no great shakes of a circus; no grand, glittering, gorgeous, glorious pageant of education and entertainment, traveling on its own special trains; no vast tented city of world's wonders and world's champions, heralded for weeks and weeks in advance of its coming by dead walls emblazoned with the finest examples of the lithographer's art, and by half-page advertisements in the *Daily Evening News.* On the contrary, it was a shabby little wagon show, which, coming overland on short notice, rolled into town under horse power, and set up its ragged and dusty canvases on the vacant lot across from Yeiser's drugstore.

Compared with the street parade of any of its great and famous rivals, the street parade of this circus was a meager and disappointing thing. Why, there was only one elephant, a dwarfish and debilitated-looking creature, worn mangy and slick on its various angles, like the cover of an old-fashioned haircloth trunk; and obviously most of the closed cages were weather-beaten stake wagons in disguise. Nevertheless, there was a sizable turnout of people for the afternoon's performance. After all, a circus was a circus.

Moreover, this particular circus was marked at the afternoon performance by happenings of a nature most decidedly unusual. At one o'clock the doors were opened; at one-ten the eyes of the proprietor were made glad and his heart was uplifted within him by the sight of a strange procession, drawing nearer and nearer across the scuffed turf of the Common, and heading in the direction of the red ticket wagon.

At the head of the procession marched Peep O'Day—only, of course, the proprietor didn't know it was Peep O'Day—a queer figure in his rumpled black clothes and his red-topped brass-toed boots, and with one hand holding fast to the string of a captive toy balloon. Behind him, in an uneven jostling formation, followed many small boys and some small girls. A census of the ranks would have developed that here were included practically all the juvenile white population who otherwise, through a lack of funds, would have been denied the opportunity to patronize this circus or, in fact, any circus.

Each member of the joyous company was likewise the bearer of a toy balloon—red, yellow, blue, green, or purple, as the case might be. Over the line of heads the taut rubbery globes rode on their tethers, nodding and twisting like so many big irridescent bubbles; and half a block away, at the edge of the lot, a balloon vender, whose entire stock had been disposed of in one splendid transaction, now stood, empty-handed but full-pocketed, marveling at the stroke of luck that enabled him to take an afternoon off and rest his voice.

Out of a seemingly bottomless exchequer Peep O'Day bought tickets of admission for all. But this was only the beginning. Once inside the tent he procured accommodations in the reserved-seat section for himself and those who accompanied him. From such superior points of vantage the whole crew of them witnessed the performance, from the thrilling grand entry, with spangled ladies and gentlemen riding two by two on broad-backed steeds, to the tumbling bout introducing the full strength of the company, which came at the end.

They munched fresh-roasted peanuts and balls of sugar-coated popcorn, slightly rancid, until they munched no longer with zest but merely mechanically. They drank pink lemonade to an extent that threatened absolute depletion of the fluid contents of both barrels in the refreshment stand out in the menagerie tent. They whooped their unbridled approval when the wild Indian chief, after shooting down a stuffed coon with a bow and arrow from somewhere up near the top of the center pole while balancing himself jauntily erect upon the haunches of a coursing white charger, suddenly flung off his feathered headdress, his wig and his fringed leather garments, and revealed himself in pink fleshings as the principal bareback rider.

They screamed in a chorus of delight when the funny old clown, who had been forcibly deprived of three tin flutes in rapid succession, now produced yet a fourth from the seemingly inexhaustible depths of his baggy white pants—a flute with a string and a bent pin attached to it—and, secretly affixing the pin in the tail of the cross ringmaster's coat, was thereafter enabled to toot sharp shrill blasts at frequent intervals, much to the chagrin of the ringmaster, who seemed utterly unable to discover the whereabouts of the instrument dangling behind him.

But no one among them whooped louder or laughed longer than their elderly and bewhiskered friend, who sat among them, paying the bills. As his guests they stayed for the concert; and, following this, they patronized the side show in a body. They had been almost the first upon the scene; assuredly they were the last of the audience to quit it.

Indeed, before they trailed their confrere away from the spot the sun was nearly down; and at scores of supper tables all over the town the tale of poor old Peep O'Day's latest exhibition of freakishness was being retailed, with elaborations, to interested auditors. Estimates of the sum probably expended by him in this crowning extravagance ranged well up into the hundreds of dollars.

As for the object of these speculations, he was destined not to eat any supper at all that night. Something happened that so upset him as to make him forget the meal altogether. It began to happen when he reached the modest home of P. Gafford, adjoining the Gafford stables, on Locust Street, and found sitting on the lowermost step of the porch a young man of untidy and unshaved aspect, who hailed him affectionately as Uncle Paul, and who showed deep annoyance and acute distress upon being rebuffed with chill words.

It is possible that the strain of serving a three months' sentence, on the technical charge of vagrancy, in a workhouse somewhere in Indiana, had affected the young man's nerves. His ankle bones still ached where the ball and chain had been hitched; on his palms the blisters induced by the uncongenial use of a sledge hammer on a rock pile had hardly as yet turned to calluses. So it is only fair to presume that his nervous system felt the stress of his recent confining experiences also.

Almost tearfully he pleaded with Peep O'Day to remember the ties of blood that bound them; repeatedly he pointed out that he was the only known kinsman of the other in all the world, and, therefore, had more reason than any other living being to expect kindness and generosity at his uncle's hands. He spoke socialistically of the advisability of an equal division; failing to make any impression here he mentioned the subject of a loan—at first hopefully, but finally despairingly.

When he was done Peep O'Day, in a perfectly colorless and unsympathetic voice, bade him good-by—not good night but good-by! And, going inside the house, he closed the door behind him, leaving his newly returned relative outside and quite alone.

At this the young man uttered violent language; but, since there was nobody present to hear him, it is likely he found small satisfaction in his profanity, rich though it may have been in metaphor and variety. So presently he betook himself off, going straight to the office in Legal Row of H. B. Sublette, Attorney-at-law.

From the circumstance that he found Mr. Sublette in, though it was long past that gentleman's office hours, and, moreover, found Mr. Sublette waiting in an expectant and attentive attitude, it might have been adduced by one skilled in the trick of putting two and two together that the pair of them had reached a prior understanding sometime during the day; and that the visit of the young man to the Gafford home and his speeches there had all been parts of a scheme planned out at a prior conference.

Be this as it may, so soon as Mr. Sublette had heard his caller's version of the meeting upon the porch he lost no time in taking certain legal steps. That very night, on behalf of his client, denominated in the documents as Percival Dwyer, Esquire, he prepared a petition addressed to the circuit judge of the district, setting forth that, inasmuch as Paul Felix O'Day had by divers acts shown himself to be of unsound mind, now, therefore, came his nephew and next of kin praying that a committee or curator be appointed to take over the estate of the said Paul Felix O'Day, and administer the same in accordance with the orders of the court until such time as the said Paul Felix O'Day should recover his reason, or should pass from this life, and so forth and so on; not to mention whereases in great number and aforesaids abounding throughout the text in the utmost profusion.

On the following morning the papers were filed with Circuit Clerk Milam. That vigilant barrister, Mr. Sublette, brought them in person to the courthouse before nine o'clock, he having the interests of his client at heart and perhaps also visions of a large contingent fee in his mind. No retainer had been paid. The state of Mr. Dwyer's finances—or, rather, the absence of any finances—had precluded the performance of that customary detail; but to Mr. Sublette's experienced mind the prospects of future increment seemed large.

Accordingly he was all for prompt action. Formally he said he wished to go on record as demanding for his principal a speedy hearing of the issue, with a view to preventing the defendant named in the pleadings from dissipating any more of the estate lately bequeathed to him and now fully in his possession—or words to that effect.

Mr. Milam felt justified in getting into communication with Judge Priest over the long-distance phone; and the Judge, cutting short his vacation and leaving uncaught vast numbers of bass and perch in Reelfoot Lake, came home, arriving late that night.

Next morning, having issued divers orders in connection with the impending litigation, he sent a messenger to find Peep O'Day and to direct O'Day to come to the courthouse for a personal interview.

Shortly thereafter a scene that had occurred some two months earlier, with his Honor's private chamber for a setting, was substantially duplicated: there was the same cast of two, the same stage properties, the same atmosphere of untidy tidiness. And, as before, the dialogue was in Judge Priest's hands. He led and his fellow character followed his leads.

"Peep," he was saying, "you understand, don't you, that this here fragrant nephew of yours that's turned up from nowheres in particular is fixin' to git ready to try to prove that you are feeble-minded? And, on top of that, that he's goin' to ask that a committee be app'inted fur you—in other words, that somebody or other shall be named by the court, meanin' me, to take charge of your property and control the spendin' of it frum now on?"

"Yes, suh," stated O'Day. "Pete Gafford he set down with me and made hit all clear to me, yestiddy evenin', after they'd done served the papers on me."

"All right, then. Now I'm goin' to fix the hearin' fur tomorrow mornin' at ten. The other side is askin' fur a quick decision; and I rather figger that they're entitled to it. Is that agreeable to you?"

"Whutever you say, Judge."

"Well, have you retained a lawyer to represent your interests in court? That's the main question that I sent fur you to ast you."

"Do I need a lawyer, Judge?"

"Well, there have been times when I regarded lawyers ez bein' superfluous," stated Judge Priest dryly. "Still, in most cases litigants do have 'em round when the case is bein' heard."

"I don't know ez I need any lawyer to he'p me say whut I've got to say," said O'Day. "Judge, you ain't never ast me no questions about the way I've been carryin' on sence I come into this here money; but I reckin mebbe this is ez good a time ez any to tell you jest why I've been actin' the way I've done. You see, suh—"

"Hold on!" broke in Judge Priest. "Up to now, ez my friend, it would 'a' been perfectly proper fur you to give me your confidences ef you were minded so to do; but now I reckin you'd better not. You see, I'm the judge that's got to decide whether you are a responsible person—whether you're mentally capable of handlin' your own financial affairs, or whether you ain't. So you'd better wait and make your statement in your own behalf to me whilst I'm settin' on the bench. I'll see that you git an opportunity to do so and I'll listen to it; and I'll give it all the consideration it's deservin' of.

"And, on second thought, p'raps it would only be a waste of time and money fur you to go hirin' a lawyer specially to represent you. Under the law it's my duty, in sech a case ez this here one is, to app'int a member of the bar to serve durin' the proceedin's ez your guardian *ad litem*.

"You don't need to be startled," he added, as O'Day flinched at the sound in his ears of these strange and fearsome words. "A guardian *ad litem* is simply a lawyer that tends to your affairs till the case is settled one way or the other. Ef you had a dozen lawyers I'd have to app'int him jest the same. So you don't need to worry about that part of it.

"That's all. You kin go now ef you want to. Only, ef I was you, I wouldn't draw out any more money frum the bank 'twixt now and the time when I make my decision."

All things considered, it was an unusual assemblage that Judge Priest regarded over the top rims of his glasses as he sat facing it in his broad armchair, with the flat top of the bench intervening between him and the gathering. Not often, even in the case of exciting murder trials, had the old courtroom held a larger crowd; certainly never had it held so many boys. Boys, and boys exclusively, filled the back rows of benches downstairs. More boys packed the narrow shelflike balcony that spanned the chamber across its far end—mainly small boys, barefooted, sunburned, freckle-faced, shock-headed boys. And, for boys, they were strangely silent and strangely attentive.

The petitioner sat with his counsel, Mr. Sublette. The petitioner had been newly shaved, and from some mysterious source had been equipped with a neat wardrobe. Plainly he was endeavoring to wear a look of virtue, which was a difficult undertaking, as you would understand had you known the petitioner.

The defending party to the action was seated across the room, touching elbows with old Colonel Farrell, dean of the local bar and its most florid orator.

"The court will designate Colonel Horatio Farrell as guardian *ad litem* for the defendant during these proceedings," Judge Priest had stated a few minutes earlier, using the formal and grammatical language he reserved exclusively for his courtroom.

At once old Colonel Farrell had hitched his chair up alongside O'Day; had asked him several questions in a tone inaudible to those about them; had listened to the whispered answers of O'Day; and then had nodded his huge curly white dome of a head, as though amply satisfied with the responses.

Let us skip the preliminaries. True, they seemed to interest the audience; here, though, they would be tedious reading. Likewise, in touching upon the opening and outlining address of Attorney-at-Law Sublette let us, for the sake of time and space, be very much briefer than Mr. Sublette was. For our present purposes I deem it sufficient to say that in all his professional career Mr. Sublette was never more eloquent, never more forceful, never more vehement in his allegations, and never more convinced—as he himself stated, not once but repeatedly—of his ability to prove the facts he alleged by competent and unbiased testimony. These facts, he pointed out, were common knowledge in the community; nevertheless, he stood prepared to buttress them with the evidence of reputable witnesses, given under oath.

Mr. Sublette, having unwound at length, now wound up. He sat down, perspiring freely and through the perspiration radiating confidence in his contentions, confidence in the result, and, most of all, unbounded confidence in Mr. Sublette.

Now Colonel Farrell was standing up to address the court. Under the cloak of a theatrical presence and a large orotund manner, and behind a Ciceronian command of sonorous language, the colonel carried concealed a shrewd old brain. It was as though a skilled marksman lurked in ambush amid a tangle of luxuriant foliage. In this particular instance, moreover, it is barely possible that the colonel was acting on a cue, privily conveyed to him before the court opened.

"May it please your Honor," he began, "I have just conferred with the defendant here; and, acting in the capacity of his guardian *ad litem,* I have advised him to waive an opening address by counsel. Indeed, the defendant has no counsel. Furthermore, the defendant, also acting upon my advice, will present no witnesses in his own behalf. But, with your Honor's permission, the defendant will now make a personal statement; and thereafter he will rest content, leaving the final arbitrament of the issue to your Honor's discretion."

"I object!" exclaimed Mr. Sublette briskly.

"On what ground does the learned counsel object?" inquired Judge Priest.

"On the grounds that, since the mental competence of this man is concerned—since it is our contention that he is patently and plainly a victim of senility, an individual prematurely in his dotage—any utterances by him will be of no value whatsoever in aiding the conscience and intelligence of the court to arrive at a fair and just conclusion regarding the defendant's mental condition."

Mr. Sublette excelled in the use of big words; there was no doubt about that.

"The objection is overruled," said Judge Priest. He nodded in the direction of O'Day and Colonel Farrell. "The court will hear the defendant. He is not to be interrupted while making his statement. The defendant may proceed."

Without further urging, O'Day stood up, a tall, slab-sided rock of a man, with his long arms dangling at his sides, half facing Judge Priest and half facing his nephew and his nephew's lawyer. Without hesitation he began to speak. And this was what he said:

"There's mebbe some here ez knows about how I was raised and fetched up. My paw and my maw died when I was jest only a baby; so I was brung up out here at the old county porehouse ez a pauper. I can't remember the time when I didn't have to work for my board and keep, and work hard. While other boys was goin' to school and playin' hooky, and goin' in washin' in the creek, and playin' games, and all sech ez that, I had to work. I never done no playin' round in my whole life—not till here jest recently, anyway.

"But I always craved to play round some. I didn't never say nothin' about it to nobody after I growed up, 'cause I figgered it out they wouldn't understand and mebbe'd laugh at me; but all these years, ever sence I left that there porehouse, I've had a hankerin' here inside of me"—he lifted one hand and touched his breast—"I've had a hankerin' to be a boy and do all the things a boy does; to do the things I was chiseled out of doin' whilst I was of a suitable age to be doin' 'em. I call to mind that I uster dream in my sleep about doin' 'em; but the dream never come true—not till jest here lately. It didn't have no chancet to come true—not till then.

"So, when this money come to me so sudden and unbeknownstlike I said to myself that I was goin' to make that there dream come true; and I started out fur to do it. And I done it! And I reckin that's the cause of my bein' here today, accused of bein' feeble-minded. But, even so, I don't regret it none. Ef it was all to do over ag'in, I'd do it jest the very same way.

"Why, I never knowed whut it was, till here two months or so ago, to have my fill of bananas and candy and gingersnaps, and all sech knickknacks ez them. All my life I've been cravin' secretly to own a pair of red-topped boots with brass toes on 'em, like I used to see other boys wearin' in the wintertime when I was out yonder at that porehouse wearin' an old pair of somebody else's cast-off shoes—mebbe a man's shoes, with rags wropped round my feet to keep the snow frum comin' through the cracks in 'em, and to keep 'em from slippin' right spang off my feet. I got three toes frostbit oncet durin' a cold spell, wearin' them kind of shoes. But here the other week I found myself able to buy me some red-top boots with brass toes on 'em. So I had 'em made to order and I'm wearin' 'em now. I wear 'em reg'lar even ef it is summertime. I take a heap of pleasure out of 'em. And, also, all my life long I've been wantin' to go to a circus. But not till three days ago I didn't never git no chancet to go to one.

"That gentleman yonder—Mr. Sublette—he 'lowed jest now that I was leadin' a lot of little boys in this here town into bad habits. He said that I was learnin' 'em nobody knowed whut devilment. And he spoke of my havin' egged 'em on to steal watermelons frum Mister Bell's watermelon patch out here three miles frum town, on the Marshallville gravel road. You-all heared whut he jest now said about that.

"I don't mean no offense and I beg his pardon fur contradictin' him right out before everybody here in the big courthouse; but, mister, you're wrong. I don't lead these here boys astray that I've been runnin' round with. They're mighty nice clean boys, all of 'em. Some of 'em are mighty near ez pore ez whut I uster be; but there ain't no real harm in any of 'em. We git along together fine—me and them. And, without no preachin', nor nothin' like that, I've done my best these weeks we've been frolickin' and projectin' round together to keep 'em frum growin' up to do mean things. I use chawin's tobacco myself; but I've told 'em, I don't know how many times, that ef they chaw it'll stunt 'em in their growth. And I've got several of 'em that was smokin' cigarettes on the sly to promise me they'd quit. So I don't figger ez I've done them boys any real harm by goin' round with 'em. And I believe ef you was to ast 'em they'd all tell you the same, suh.

"Now about them watermelons: Sence this gentleman has brung them watermelons up, I'm goin' to tell you-all the truth about that too."

He cast a quick, furtive look, almost a guilty look, over his shoulder toward the rear of the courtroom before he went on:

"Them watermelons wasn't really stole at all. I seen Mr. Dick Bell beforehand and arranged with him to pay him in full fur whutever damage mout be done. But, you see, I knowed watermelons tasted sweeter to a boy ef he thought he'd hooked 'em out of a patch; so I never let on to my little pardners yonder that I'd the same ez paid Mr. Bell in advance fur the melons we snuck out of his patch and et in the woods. They've all been thinkin' up till now that we really hooked them watermelons. But ef that was wrong I'm sorry fur it.

"Mr. Sublette, you jest now said that I was fritterin' away my property on vain foolishment. Them was the words you used —'fritterin'' and 'vain foolishment.' Mebbe you're right, suh, about the fritterin' part; but ef spendin' money in a certain way gives a man ez much pleasure ez it's give me these last two months, and ef the money is his'n by rights, I figger it can't be so very foolish; though it may 'pear so to some.

"Excusin' these here clothes I've got on and these here boots, which ain't paid fur yet, but is charged up to me on Felsburg Brothers' books and Mr. M. Biederman's books, I didn't spend only a dollar a day, or mebbe two dollars, and once three dollars in a single day out of whut was comin' to me. The Judge here, he let me have that out of his own pocket; and I paid him back. And that was all I did spend till here three days ago when that there circus come to town. I reckin I did spend a right smart then.

"My money had come frum the old country only the day before; so I went to the bank and they writ out one of them pieces of paper which is called a check, and I signed it—with my mark; and they give me the money I wanted—an even two hundred dollars. And part of that there money I used to pay fur circus tickets fur all the little boys and little girls I could find in this town that couldn't 'a' got to the circus no other way. Some of 'em are settin' back there behind you-all now—some of the boys, I mean; I don't see none of the little girls.

"There was several of 'em told me at the time they hadn't never seen a circus—not in their whole lives. Fur that matter, I hadn't, neither; but I didn't want no pore child in this town to grow up to be ez old ez I am without havin' been to at least one circus. So I taken 'em all in and paid all the bills; and when night come there wasn't but 'bout nine dollars left out of the whole two hundred that I'd started out with in the mornin'. But I don't begredge spendin' it. It looked to me like it was money well invested. They all seemed to enjoy it; and I know I done so.

"There may be bigger circuses'n whut that one was; but I don't see how a circus could 'a' been any better than this here one I'm tellin' about, ef it was ten times ez big. I don't regret the investment and I don't aim to lie about it now. Mr. Sublette, I'd do the same thing over ag'in ef the chance should come, lawsuit or no lawsuit. Ef you should win this here case mebbe I wouldn't have no second chance.

"Ef some gentleman is app'inted ez a committee to handle my money it's likely he wouldn't look at the thing the same way I do; and it's likely he wouldn't let me have so much money all in one lump to spend takin' a passel of little shavers that ain't no kin to me to the circus and to the side show, besides lettin' 'em stay fur the grand concert or after show, and all. But I done it once; and I've got it to remember about and think about in my own mind ez long ez I live.

"I'm 'bout finished now. There's jest one thing more I'd like to say, and that is this: Mr. Sublette he said a minute ago that I was in my second childhood. Meanin' no offense, suh, but you was wrong there too. The way I look at it, a man can't be in his second childhood without he's had his first childhood; and I was cheated plum' out of mine. I'm more'n sixty years old, ez near ez I kin figger; but I'm tryin' to be a boy before it's too late."

He paused a moment and looked round him.

"The way I look at it, Judge Priest, suh, and you-all, every man that grows up, no matter how old he may git to be, is entitled to 'a' been a boy oncet in his lifetime. I—I reckin that's all."

He sat down and dropped his eyes upon the floor, as though ashamed that his temerity should have carried him so far. There was a strange little hush filling the courtroom. It was Judge Priest who broke it.

"The court," he said, "has by the words just spoken by this man been sufficiently advised as to the sanity of the man himself. The court cares to hear nothing more from either side on this subject. The petition is dismissed."

Very probably these last words may have been as so much Greek to the juvenile members of the audience; possibly, though, they were made aware of the meaning of them by the look upon the face of nephew Percival Dwyer and the look upon the face of nephew Percival Dwyer's attorney. At any rate, his Honor hardly had uttered the last syllable of his decision before, from the rear of the courtroom and from the gallery above, there arose a shrill, vehement, sincere sound of yelling—exultant, triumphant, and deafening. It continued for upward of a minute before the small disturbers remembered where they were and reduced themselves to a state of comparative quiet.

For reasons best known to himself, Judge Priest, who ordinarily stickled for order and decorum in his courtroom, made no effort to quell the outburst or to have it quelled—not even when a considerable number of the adults present joined in it, having first cleared their throats of a slight huskiness that had come upon them, severally and generally.

Presently the Judge rapped for quiet—and got it. It was apparent that he had more to say; and all there hearkened to hear what it might be.

"I have just this to add," quoth his Honor: "It is the official judgment of this court that the late defendant, being entirely sane, is competent to manage his own affairs after his preferences.

"And it is the private opinion of this court that not only is the late defendant sane but that he is the sanest man in this entire jurisdiction. Mr. Clerk, this court stands adjourned."

Coming down the three short steps from the raised platform of the bench, Judge Priest beckoned to Sheriff Giles Birdsong, who, at the tail of the departing crowd, was shepherding its last exuberant members through the doorway.

"Giles," said Judge Priest in an undertone, when the worthy sheriff had drawn near, "the circuit clerk tells me there's an indictment for malicious mischief ag'in this here Perce Dwyer knockin' round amongst the records somewheres—an indictment the grand jury returned several sessions back, but which was never pressed, owin' to the sudden departure frum our midst of the person in question.

"I wonder ef it would be too much trouble fur you to sort of drap a hint in the ear of the young man or his lawyer that the said indictment is apt to be revived, and that the said Dwyer is liable to be tuck into custody by you and lodged in the county jail some time during the ensuin' forty-eight hours—without he should see his way clear durin' the meantime to get clean out of this city, county and state! Would it?"

"Trouble? No, suh! It won't be no trouble to me," said Mr. Birdsong promptly. "Why, it'll be more of a pleasure, Judge."

And so it was.

Except for one small added and purely incidental circumstance, our narrative is ended. That same afternoon Judge Priest sat on the front porch of his old white house out on Clay Street, waiting for Jeff Poindexter to summon him to supper. Peep O'Day opened the front gate and came up the graveled walk between the twin rows of silver-leaf poplars. The Judge, rising to greet his visitor, met him at the top step.

"Come in," bade the Judge heartily, "and set down a spell and rest your face and hands."

"No, suh; much obliged, but I ain't got only a minute to stay," said O'Day. "I jest come out here, suh, to thank you fur whut you done today on my account in the big courthouse, and—and to make you a little kind of a present."

"It's all right to thank me," said Judge Priest; "but I couldn't accept any reward fur renderin' a decision in accordance with the plain facts."

" 'Tain't no gift of money, or nothin' like that," O'Day hastened to explain. "Really, suh, it don't amount to nothin' at all, scursely. But a little while ago I happened to be in Mr. B. Weil & Sons's store, doin' a little tradin' and I run acrost a new kind of knickknack, which it seemed like to me it was about the best thing I ever tasted in my whole life. So, on the chancet, suh, that you might have a sweet tooth, too, I taken the liberty of bringin' you a sack of 'em and—and—and here they are, suh; three flavors—strawberry, lemon, and vanilly."

Suddenly overcome with confusion, he dislodged a large-sized paper bag from his side coat pocket and thrust it into Judge Priest's hands; then, backing away, he turned and clumped down the graveled path in great and embarrassed haste.

Judge Priest opened the bag and peered down into it.

It contained a sticky, sugary dozen of flattened confections, each molded round a short length of wooden splinter. These sirupy articles, which have since come into quite general use, are known, I believe, as all-day suckers.

When Judge Priest looked up again, Peep O'Day was outside the gate, clumping down the uneven sidewalk of Clay Street with long strides of his booted legs. Half a dozen small boys, who, it was evident, had remained hidden during the ceremony of presentation, now mysteriously appeared and were accompanying the departing donor, half trotting to keep up with him.

Coroner De Luxe

by:

RUEL McDANIEL

selected by:

TOM C. CLARK

For my choice of an exciting story concerning the administration of law, I turn to the tales about Roy Bean, who beyond question cut deeply into the early history of the turbulent Pecos River country of my native Texas.

Some of the Roy Bean saga is true, some is undoubtedly fiction—and the line is hard to draw. More important than this distinction, however, is the obvious moral to the saga: society, however scattered, disorganized, and primitive, intuitively seeks and respects legal authority and legal institutions. Courts of law satisfy the deep-felt needs of every community—even West of the Pecos in a swashbuckling, bygone era.

S.S. TOM C. CLARK

"Judge," a cowboy announced, "we found a dead Mexican down here at the mouth of Pump Canyon. The boss says mebbe yous oughter hold a inquest."

Bean removed his apron, walked from behind the bar to his judge's bench, and there donned a long black alpaca coat. "Certainly, my boy; shore. Show me where."

He had set himself up as law and order west of the Pecos; and he found no little pride in pointing out that no dispensing job, either legal or liquid, within his jurisdiction had stumped him. Inquests seemed to him rather needless things, especially if there were no fees in sight; but if the ranchers wanted them, why, he was the judge who could hold 'em.

The cowboy led him down into the maze of Pump Canyon. Stopping beside an iron-colored boulder, he said, "Here's yore man, Judge; and a fine mess he's in."

Bean made a perfunctory examination of the remains. A bullet hole showed directly in the center of the deceased's forehead. He cleared his throat and declared the inquest officially opened.

"It's the findin' of this court that the Mexican, name unknown, come to his death by bein' shot in the head by an unknown person who was a goldam good shot."

He searched the pockets of the dead man but found nothing; so all he got out of this service was the experience. However, not all inquests were so fruitless.

There was the case of the railroad laborer, for example. News came to Langtry that a workman had fallen off a railroad trestle and killed himself. Bean was asked to hold an inquest.

He proceeded with courtly dignity to the scene of the tragedy. He searched the body of the victim and found a revolver and forty-one dollars in cash.

"It is the duty of this court," he declared, "to confiscate this here concealed weapon, which is a dam' good gun, because it's legally ag'inst the law to carry a gun, especially a dead man.

"And in view of evidence, I find it the court's duty to fine the offender forty-one simoleons for carryin' concealed weapons. And that's my rulin'."

By this time Judge Bean had taken the time to obtain his appointment as justice of the peace, this expedient appearing to be advisable in view of the fact that Val Verde County had been organized out of Pecos, and Langtry was a part of the new county. It was only sixty-seven miles to the new county seat; so the judge felt that things should be a little more in order.

News of this quaint disposition of a dead man and his worldly goods filtered over to Del Rio, Val Verde county seat. There was talk of ousting Bean for irregularities in office. A rancher brought news of this threat back to Bean.

"Hell, they cain't do that!" he expostulated. "It ain't legal. They ain't nobody complainin' except the county attorney and the judge. They're bellyachin' on account of not bein' able to grab that forty-one bucks for theirselves. I tell you, Sam, you got to temper justice with common sense.

"Now take them Del Rio fellers. What would they 'a' done in this case? I'll tell you what. They'd dragged out the matter in a lot of legal terms and ended up by takin' the forty-one dollars and the gun for admin'stration fees; so what's the difference? Me? Well, you know yoreself I give the pore devil a decent burial. Instead of rollin' him in a blanket and throwin' him in a hollow place in a rock and coverin' him with mesquite, why, I hired a hack and hauled him to Langtry. There I hired a preacher, for a *peso,* to orate a decent funeral; then I hired two

Mexicans—well, not exactly hired 'em, because they was my prisoners—to dig a regular grave and bury him like a white man. I'm purty shore the pore devil hisself would 'a' thanked me for it."

Eventually the county attorney did come over to Langtry to investigate the conduct of Bean's court. "You're violating the law by failure to make a report of your proceedings and fees of office," the young barrister told the judge.

"Young man," Roy advised curtly, "this here court is self-supportin'. Whenever it cain't take in enough *dinero* to pay its way, I'll get in touch with you!"

Suicides, accidental deaths, murders, assaults, cattle rustling, horse-thieving, petty disorders, plain drunks, marriages, inquests, divorces, christenings, first aid, and civil suits all came under the elastic jurisdiction of Judge Bean's court. The ranchers soon learned that he was their most powerful ally, and they cooperated to the fullest degree. At his bar of justice they could obtain lightning action; while they went to more formal courts, there might be changes of venue, delays, rehearings, and a dozen other legal tangles to delay the ends of justice. Outlaws feared the crude court as much as the law-abiding citizens appreciated it.

Thus, in spite of the fact that Judge Bean did not conduct his court along orthodox lines, state and district authorities took a passive view, generally, of his methods, because he had established, after a fashion, law beyond the Pecos. That was more than anyone else had dared attempt before.

At first Roy acted as arresting officer, prosecutor, defending attorney, jury, and judge. Thus, he reasoned, he cut down materially the costs of court. Gradually, however, as more settlers and outlaws moved in, business grew and the procedure became somewhat more technical. Although invariably under protest, Judge Bean would permit a defendant to hire an outside lawyer if he insisted long and strong enough. Nevertheless, the "Law West of the Pecos" considered such action a personal affront.

On such an occasion the court was solemnly ready for action. A railroad man, a newcomer in the community and therefore excusable for his audacity, was charged with a grave crime; and he had hired a lawyer from San Antonio to defend him.

The lawyer introduced himself at the outset by objecting to

the whole court procedure. "You have no authority in this case!" he cried.

Judge Roy squinted his cold blue eyes. He thumped one of his guns against the top of the table. "Set down!" he commanded.

"You have no jurisdiction in this case; and I demand constitutional rights and protection for my client."

The "Law West of the Pecos" glared at the young lawyer. "Oscar," he called over to his assistant, who acted as barkeeper and constable during rush hours at either bar. "Come over here. In about eight minutes I expect to find this here prisoner guilty and order you and the boys to take him out and hang him. What'er you intend to do?"

"Take 'im out and hang 'im, of course," Oscar answered without hesitation.

"Supposin'," Judge Roy went on, "I decide you better hang his lawyer, along with him. Then what would you do?"

"Why, hang 'im, judge. It ain't no more trouble to hang two than one."

Bean turned his attention back to the young lawyer. "Ain't that enough jurisdiction for you? Now, young jack-leg, you set down. I'm the Law West of the Pecos. I run my court the way I see fit. An' that's my rulin'."

Penalties imposed in this crude bar of justice ranged all the way from a round of drinks for the house, at the expense of the defendant, to hanging. Judge Bean did not believe in penitentiary sentences. That involved a maze of technicalities into which the state of Texas entered; and he did not care for that. He imposed his own penalties, as his own quaint sense of justice dictated; and he did not wish to impose anything which he could not personally carry out.

This particular defendant's sentence was a hundred-dollar fine, which he paid with an obvious sigh of relief, coming close upon the heels of Judge Roy's demonstration of the court's interpretation of jurisdiction.

"Oscar," Judge Roy said to his lieutenant one morning, "Carter's tryin' to cheat me outer my half of them goats we been raisin' under contract. Take this here sequestration writ, go over there and show it to that double-crossin' coyote and drive my half the goats to my corral."

Roy had entered into an agreement a year before whereby Carter would raise goats from Bean's herd of shares. Now he had contended that Bean's share had died! Roy would have preferred to go over, personally, and escort his goats back under the protection of his two six-guns; but he had set himself up as "Law West of the Pecos." He demanded that other citizens settle their civil differences according to Pecos law; and he proposed to do likewise.

Oscar delivered the goats as ordered. Locked in the Bean corral, the judge then called court to order. "It appears that the stock in question was seized by a duly authorized officer of this court, to wit: Oscar Sweeden. It further appears that the animals was impounded accordin' to law in the complainant's corral for safekeeping. That bein' the status, I hereby dismiss this case. And that's my rulin'."

On occasions, however, he became impatient even of his own rapid-fire justice. An operator of a lunch stand across the street owed him three dollars and seventy-five cents for beer bought six months before. Repeatedly Barkeeper Bean had demanded payment. The debtor continued to put him off.

Finally Roy removed his apron, donned his guns, and walked across the street just at lunchtime. The stand was filled with hungry customers. He unholstered his revolvers and established himself directly in the door of the eating emporium.

"Don't get excited, gents," he explained to the wide-eyed customers. "I'm jest here to collect an old account. You can pay right here, as you leave."

He counted the amount of each customer until he had in hand the three dollars and seventy-five cents due. Then he holstered his guns, thanked the blubbering proprietor, and invited the nervous customers to come over and have drinks on the Jersey Lilly.

The Barrister

by:

A. A. MILNE

selected by:

JOHN J. McCLOY

As an avid fan of the field of legal fiction, I find it not only difficult but impossible to name my number one favorite lawyer story. But certainly one of my favorites is "The Barrister," by A. A. Milne. The only criticism which one can make of the tale is that it comes to an end all too soon.

S.S. JOHN J. McCLOY

The New Bailey was crowded with a gay and fashionable throng. It was a remarkable case of shoplifting. Aurora Delaine, nineteen, was charged with feloniously stealing and conveying certain articles, the property of the Universal Stores: to wit, thirty-five yards of book-muslin, ten pairs of gloves, a sponge, two gimlets, five jars of cold cream, a copy of the *Clergy List,* three hat guards, a mariner's compass, a box of drawing pins, an egg breaker, six blouses, and a cab-man's whistle. The theft had been proved by Albert Jobson, a shopwalker, who gave evidence to the effect that he followed her through the different departments and saw her take the things mentioned in the indictment.

"Just a moment," interrupted the judge. "Who is defending the prisoner?"

There was an unexpected silence. Rupert Carleton, who had dropped idly into court, looked round in sudden excitement. The poor girl had no counsel! What if he—yes, he would seize the chance! He stood up boldly. 'I am, my lord,' he said.

Rupert Carleton was still in the twenties, but he had been a briefless barrister for some years. Yet, though briefs would not come, he had been very far from idle. He had stood for Parliament in both the Conservative and Liberal interests (not to mention his own). He had written half a dozen unproduced plays, and he was engaged to be married. But success in his own profession had been delayed. Now at last was his opportunity.

He pulled his wig down firmly over his ears, took out a pair of pince-nez and rose to cross-examine. It was the cross-examination which is now given as a model in every legal textbook.

"Mr. Jobson," he began suavely, "you say that you saw the accused steal these various articles, and that they were afterward found upon her?"

"Yes."

"I put it to you," said Rupert, and waited intently for the answer, "that that is a pure invention on your part?"

"No."

With an superhuman effort Rupert hid his disappointment. Unexpected as the answer was, he preserved his impassivity.

"I suggest," he tried again, "that you followed her about and concealed this collection of things in her cloak with a view to advertising your winter sale?"

"No. I saw her steal them."

Rupert frowned; the man seemed impervious to the simplest suggestion. With masterly decision he tapped his prince-nez and fell back upon his third line of defense. "You saw her steal them? What you mean is that you saw her take them from the different counters and put them in her bag?"

"Yes."

"With the intention of paying for them in the ordinary way?"

"No."

"Please be very careful. You said in your evidence that the prisoner, when told she would be charged, cried, 'To think that I should have come to this! Will no one save me?' I suggest that she went up to you with her collection of purchases, pulled out her purse, and said, 'What does all this come to? I can't get anyone to serve me.' "

"No."

The obstinacy of some people! Rupert put back his pince-nez in his pocket and brought out another pair. The historic cross-examination continued.

"We will let that pass for the moment," he said. He consulted a sheet of paper and then looked sternly at Mr. Jobson. "Mr. Jobson, how many times have you been married?"

"Once."

"Quite so." He hesitated and then decided to risk it. "I suggest that your wife left you?"

"Yes."

It was a long shot, but once again the bold course had paid. Rupert heaved a sigh of relief.

"Will you tell the gentlemen of the jury," he said, with deadly politeness, "*why* she left you?"

"She died."

A lesser man might have been embarrassed, but Rupert's iron nerve did not fail him.

"Exactly!" he said. "And was that or was that not on the night when you were turned out of the Hampstead Parliament for intoxication?"

"I never was."

"Indeed? Will you cast your mind back to the night of the twenty-fourth of April 1897? What were you doing on that night?"

"I have no idea," said Jobson, after casting his mind back and waiting in vain for some result.

"In that case you cannot swear that you were not being turned out of the Hampstead Parliament——"

"But I never belonged to it."

Rupert leaped at the damaging admission.

"What? You told the court that you lived at Hampstead, and yet you say that you never belonged to the Hampstead Parliament? Is *that* your idea of patriotism?"

"I said I lived at Hackney."

"To the Hackney Parliament, I should say. I am suggesting that you were turned out of the Hackney Parliament for——"

"I don't belong to that either."

"Exactly!" said Rupert triumphantly. "Having been turned out for intoxication?"

"And never did belong."

"Indeed? May I take it, then, that you prefer to spend your evenings in the public house?"

"If you want to know," said Jobson angrily, "I belong to the

Hackney Chess Circle, and that takes up most of my evenings."

Rupert gave a sigh of satisfaction and turned to the jury.

"At *last,* gentlemen, we have got it. I thought we should arrive at the truth in the end, in spite of Mr. Jobson's prevarications." He turned to the witness. "Now, sir," he said sternly, "you have already told the court that you have no idea what you were doing on the night of the twenty-fourth of April, 1897. I put it to you once more that this blankness of memory is due to the fact that you were in a state of intoxication on the premises of the Hackney Chess Circle. Can you swear on your oath that this is not so?"

A murmur of admiration for the relentless way in which the truth had been tracked down ran through the court. Rupert drew himself up and put on both pairs of pince-nez at once.

"Come, sir!" he said, "the jury is waiting."

But it was not Albert Jobson who answered. It was the counsel for the prosecution. "My lord," he said, getting up slowly, "this has come as a complete surprise to me. In the circumstances I must advise my clients to withdraw from the case."

"A very proper decision," said his lordship. "The prisoner is discharged without a stain on her character."

Briefs poured in upon Rupert next day, and he was engaged for all the big Chancery cases. Within a week his six plays were accepted, and within a fornight he had entered Parliament as the miners' Member for Coalville. His marriage took place at the end of the month. The wedding presents were even more numerous and costly than usual, and included thirty-five yards of book muslin, ten pairs of gloves, a sponge, two gimlets, five jars of cold cream, a copy of the *Clergy List,* three hat guards, a mariner's compass, a box of drawing pins, an egg breaker, six blouses, and a cabman's whistle. They were marked quite simply, "From a Grateful Friend."

Tomorrow

by:

WILLIAM FAULKNER

selected by:

ERIC JOHNSTON

Tales of the law, its defense and its enforcement, are generally packed with action and suspense. Because they are, I find stimulation in accounts of lawyers' performances and of the soul-searching problems of judges and jurors, plaintiffs, defendants, witnesses, and even of courthouse loafers. One of my favorite stories of the legal profession and its human drama is William Faulkner's unforgettable "Tomorrow."

ERIC JOHNSTON

S.S.

Uncle Gavin had not always been county attorney. But the time when he had not been was more than twenty years ago and it had lasted for such a short period that only the old men remembered it, and even some of them did not. Because in that time he had had but one case.

He was a young man then, twenty-eight, only a year out of the state-university law school where, at grandfather's instigation, he had gone after his return from Harvard and Heidelberg; and he had taken the case voluntarily, persuaded grandfather to let him handle it alone, which grandfather did, because everyone believed the trial would be a mere formality.

So he tried the case. Years afterward he still said it was the only case, either as a private defender or a public prosecutor, in which he was convinced that right and justice were on his side, that he ever lost. Actually he did not lose it—a mistrial in the fall court term, an acquittal in the following spring term—the defendant a solid, well-to-do farmer, husband and father, too, named Bookwright, from a section called Frenchman's Bend in the remote southeastern corner of the county; the victim a swaggering bravo calling himself Buck Thorpe and called Bucksnort by the other young men whom he had subjugated with his fists during the three years he had been in Frenchman's Bend; kinless, who had appeared overnight from nowhere, a brawler, a gambler, known to be a distiller of illicit whisky and caught once on the road to Memphis with a small drove of stolen cattle, which the owner promptly identified. He had a bill of sale for them, but none in the county knew the name signed to it.

And the story itself was old and unoriginal enough: The country girl of seventeen, her imagination fired by the swagger and the prowess and the daring and the glib tongue; the father who tried to reason with her and got exactly as far as parents usually do in such cases; then the interdiction, the forbidden door, the inevitable elopement at midnight; and at four o'clock the next morning Bookwright waked Will Varner, the justice of the peace and the chief officer of the district, and handed Varner his pistol and said, "I have come to surrender. I killed Thorpe two hours ago." And a neighbor named Quick, who was first on the scene, found the half-drawn pistol in Thorpe's hand; and a week after the brief account was printed in the Memphis papers, a woman appeared in Frenchman's Bend who claimed to be Thorpe's wife, and with a wedding license to prove it, trying to claim what money or property he might have left.

I can remember the surprise that the grand jury even found a true bill; when the clerk read the indictment, the betting was twenty to one that the jury would not be out ten minutes. The district attorney even conducted the case through an assistant, and it did not take an hour to submit all the evidence. Then Uncle Gavin rose, and I remember how he looked at the jury—the eleven farmers and storekeepers and the twelfth man, who was to ruin his case—a farmer, too, a thin man, small, with thin gray hair and that appearance of hill farmers—at once frail and work-worn, yet curiously imperishable—who seem to become old men at fifty and then become invincible to time. Uncle Gavin's voice was quiet, almost monotonous, not ranting as criminal-court trials had taught us to expect; only the words were a little different from the ones he would use in later years. But even then, although he had been talking to them for only a year, he could already talk so that all the people in our country

—the Negroes, the hill people, the rich flatland plantation owners—understood what he said.

"All of us in this country, the South, have been taught from birth a few things which we hold to above all else. One of the first of these—not the best; just one of the first—is that only a life can pay for the life it takes; that the one death is only half complete. If that is so, then we could have saved both these lives by stopping this defendant before he left his house that night; we could have saved at least one of them, even if we had had to take this defendant's life from him in order to stop him. Only we didn't know in time. And that's what I am talking about—not about the dead man and his character and the morality of the act he was engaged in; not about self-defense, whether or not this defendant was justified in forcing the issue to the point of taking life, but about us who are not dead and what we don't know—about all of us, human beings who at bottom want to do right, want not to harm others; human beings with all the complexity of human passions and feelings and beliefs, in the accepting or rejecting of which we had no choice, trying to do the best we can with them or despite them—this defendant, another human being with that same complexity of passions and instincts and beliefs, faced by a problem—the inevitable misery of his child who, with the headstrong folly of youth—again that same old complexity which she, too, did not ask to inherit—was incapable of her own preservation—and solved that problem to the best of his ability and beliefs, asking help of no one, and then abode by his decision and his act."

He sat down. The district attorney's assistant merely rose and bowed to the court and sat down again. The jury went out and I didn't even leave the room. Even the judge didn't retire. And I remember the long breath, something which went through the room when the clock hand above the bench passed the ten-minute mark and then passed the half-hour mark, and the judge beckoned a bailiff and whispered to him, and the bailiff went out and returned and whispered to the judge, and the judge rose and banged his gavel and recessed the court.

I hurried home and ate my dinner and hurried back to town. The office was empty. Even grandfather, who took his nap after dinner, regardless of who hung and who didn't, returned first;

after three o'clock then, and the whole town knew now that Uncle Gavin's jury was hung by one man, eleven to one for acquittal; then Uncle Gavin came in fast, and grandfather said, "Well, Gavin, at least you stopped talking in time to hang just your jury and not your client."

"That's right, sir," Uncle Gavin said. Because he was looking at me with his bright eyes, his thin, quick face, his wild hair already beginning to turn white. "Come here, Chick," he said. "I need you for a minute."

"Ask Judge Frazier to allow you to retract your oration, then let Charley sum up for you," grandfather said. But we were outside then, on the stairs, Uncle Gavin stopping halfway down, so that we stood exactly halfway from anywhere, his hand on my shoulder, his eyes brighter and more intent than ever.

"This is not cricket," he said. "But justice is accomplished lots of times by methods that won't bear looking at. They have moved the jury to the back room in Mrs. Rouncewell's boarding-house. The room right opposite that mulberry tree. If you could get into the back yard without anybody seeing you, and be careful when you climb the tree——"

Nobody saw me. But I could look through the windy mulberry leaves into the room, and see and hear—both—the nine angry and disgusted men sprawled in chairs at the far end of the room; Mr. Holland, the foreman, and another man standing in front of the chair in which the little, worn, dried-out hill man sat. His name was Fentry. I remembered all their names, because Uncle Gavin said that to be a successful lawyer and politician in our country you did not need a silver tongue nor even an intelligence; you needed only an infallible memory for names. But I would have remembered his name anyway, because it was Stonewall Jackson—Stonewall Jackson Fentry.

"Don't you admit that he was running off with Bookwright's seventeen-year-old daughter?" Mr. Holland said. "Don't you admit that he had a pistol in his hand when they found him? Don't you admit that he wasn't hardly buried before that woman turned up and proved she was already his wife? Don't you admit that he was not only no-good but dangerous, and that if it hadn't been Bookwright, sooner or later somebody else would have had to, and that Bookwright was just unlucky?"

"Yes," Fentry said.

"Then what do you want?" Mr. Holland said. "What do you want?"

"I can't help it," Fentry said. "I ain't going to vote Mr. Bookwright free."

And he didn't. And that afternoon Judge Frazier discharged the jury and set the case for retrial in the next term of court; and the next morning Uncle Gavin came for me before I had finished breakfast.

"Tell your mother we might be gone overnight," he said. "Tell her I promise not to let you get either shot, snake-bit, or surfeited with soda pop. . . . Because I've got to know," he said. We were driving fast now, out the northeast road, and his eyes were bright, not baffled, just intent and eager. "He was born and raised and lived all his life out here at the very other end of the county, thirty miles from Frenchman's Bend. He said under oath that he had never even seen Bookwright before, and you can look at him and see that he never had enough time off from hard work to learn how to lie in. I doubt if he ever even heard Bookwright's name before."

We drove until almost noon. We were in the hills now, out of the rich, flat land, among the pine and bracken, the poor soil, the little tilted and barren patches of gaunt corn and cotton which somehow endured, as the people they clothed and fed somehow endured; the roads we followed less than lanes, winding and narrow, rutted and dust choked, the car in second gear half the time. Then we saw the mailbox, the crude lettering: G. A. FENTRY; beyond it, the two-room log house with an open hall, and even I, a boy of twelve, could see that no woman's hand had touched it in a lot of years. We entered the gate.

Then a voice said, "Stop! Stop where you are!" And we hadn't even seen him—an old man, barefoot, with a fierce white bristle of mustache, in patched denim faded almost to the color of skim milk, smaller, thinner even than the son, standing at the edge of the worn gallery, holding a shotgun across his middle and shaking with fury or perhaps with the palsy of age.

"Mr. Fentry——" Uncle Gavin said.

"You've badgered and harried him enough!" the old man said. It was fury; the voice seemed to rise suddenly with a fiercer, an uncontrollable blaze of it: "Get out of here! Get off my land! Go!"

"Come," Uncle Gavin said quietly. And still his eyes were only bright, eager, intent, and grave. We did not drive fast now. The next mailbox was within the mile, and this time the house was even painted, with beds of petunias beside the steps, and the land about it was better, and this time the man rose from the gallery and came down to the gate.

"Howdy, Mr. Stevens," he said. "So Jackson Fentry hung your jury for you."

"Howdy, Mr. Pruitt," Uncle Gavin said. "It looks like he did. Tell me."

And Pruitt told him, even though at that time Uncle Gavin would forget now and then and his language would slip back to Harvard and even to Heidelberg. It was as if people looked at his face and knew that what he asked was not just for his own curiosity or his own selfish using.

"Only ma knows more about it than I do," Pruitt said. "Come up to the gallery."

We followed him to the gallery, where a plump, white-haired old lady in a clean gingham sunbonnet and dress and a clean white apron sat in a low rocking chair, shelling field peas into a wooden bowl. "This is Lawyer Stevens," Pruitt said. "Captain Stevens' son, from town. He wants to know about Jackson Fentry."

So we sat, too, while they told it, the son and the mother talking in rotation.

"That place of theirs," Pruitt said. "You seen some of it from the road. And what you didn't see don't look no better. But his pa and his grandpa worked it, made a living for themselves and raised families and paid their taxes and owed no man. I don't know how they done it, but they did. And Jackson was helping from the time he got big enough to reach up to the plow handles. He never got much bigger than that neither. None of them ever did. I reckon that was why. And Jackson worked it, too, in his time, until he was about twenty-five and already looking forty, asking no odds of nobody, not married and not nothing, him and his pa living alone and doing their own washing and cooking, because how can a man afford to marry when him and his pa have just one pair of shoes between them. If it had been worth-while getting a wife a-tall, since that place had already killed his ma and his grandma both before they were forty years old. Until one night——"

"Nonsense," Mrs. Pruitt said. "When your pa and me married, we didn't even own a roof over our heads. We moved into a rented house, on rented land——"

"All right," Pruitt said. "Until one night he come to me and said how he had got him a sawmilling job down at Frenchman's Bend."

"Frenchman's Bend?" Uncle Gavin said, and now his eyes were much brighter and quicker than just intent. "Yes," he said.

"A day-wage job," Pruitt said. "Not to get rich; just to earn a little extra money maybe, risking a year or two to earn a little extra money, against the life his grandpa led until he died between the plow handles one day, and that his pa would lead until he died in a corn furrow, and then it would be his turn, and not even no son to come and pick him up out of the dirt. And that he had traded with a nigger to help his pa work their place while he was gone, and would I kind of go up there now and then and see that his pa was all right."

"Which you did," Mrs. Pruitt said.

"I went close enough," Pruitt said. "I would get close enough to the field to hear him cussing at the nigger for not moving fast enough and to watch the nigger trying to keep up with him, and to think what a good thing it was Jackson hadn't got two niggers to work the place while he was gone, because if that old man—and he was close to sixty then—had had to spend one full day sitting in a chair in the shade with nothing in his hands to chop or hoe with, he would have died before sundown. So Jackson left. He walked. They didn't have but one mule. They ain't never had but one mule. But it ain't but about thirty miles. He was gone about two and a half years. Then one day——"

"He come home that first Christmas," Mrs. Pruitt said.

"That's right," Pruitt said. "He walked them thirty miles home and spent Christmas Day, and walked them other thirty miles back to the sawmill."

"Whose sawmill?" Uncle Gavin said.

"Quick's," Pruitt said. "Old Man Ben Quick's. It was the second Christmas he never come home. Then, about the beginning of March, about when the river bottom at Frenchman's Bend would be starting to dry out to where you could skid logs through it and you would have thought he would be settled down good to his third year of sawmilling, he come home to stay. He didn't walk this time. He come in a hired buggy. Because he had the goat and the baby."

"Wait," Uncle Gavin said.

"We never knew how he got home," Mrs. Pruitt said. "Because he had been home over a week before we even found out he had the baby."

"Wait," Uncle Gavin said.

They waited, looking at him, Pruitt sitting on the gallery railing and Mrs. Pruitt's fingers still shelling the peas out of the long brittle hulls, looking at Uncle Gavin. His eyes were not exultant now any more than they had been baffled or even very speculative before; they had just got brighter, as if whatever it was behind them had flared up, steady and fiercer, yet still quiet, as if it were going faster than the telling was going.

"Yes," he said. "Tell me."

"And when I finally heard about it and went up there," Mrs. Pruitt said, "that baby wasn't two weeks old. And how he had kept it alive, and just on goat's milk——"

"I don't know if you know it," Pruitt said. "A goat ain't like a cow. You milk a goat every two hours or so. That means all night, too."

"Yes," Mrs. Pruitt said. "He didn't even have diaper cloths. He had some split floursacks the midwife had showed him how to put on. So I made some cloths and I would go up there; he had kept the nigger on to help his pa in the field and he was doing the cooking and washing and nursing that baby, milking the goat to feed it; and I would say, 'Let me take it. At least until he can be weaned. You come stay at my house, too, if you want,' and him just looking at me—little, thin, already wore-out something that never in his whole life had ever set down to a table and et all he could hold—saying, 'I thank you, ma'am. I can make out.' "

"Which was correct," Pruitt said. "I don't know how he was

at sawmilling, and he never had no farm to find out what kind of a farmer he was. But he raised that boy."

"Yes," Mrs. Pruitt said. "And I kept on after him: 'We hadn't even heard you was married,' I said. 'Yessum,' he said. 'We was married last year. When the baby come, she died.' 'Who was she?' I said. 'Was she a Frenchman Bend girl?' 'No'm,' he said. 'She come from downstate.' 'What was her name?' I said. 'Miss Smith,' he said."

"He hadn't even had enough time off from hard work to learn how to lie either," Pruitt said. "But he raised that boy. After their crops were in in the fall, he let the nigger go, and next spring him and the old man done the work like they use to. He had made a kind of satchel, like they say Indians does, to carry the boy in. I would go up there now and then while the ground was still cold and see Jackson and his pa plowing and chopping brush, and that satchel hanging on a fence post and that boy asleep bolt upright in it like it was a feather bed. He learned to walk that spring, and I would stand there at a fence and watch that durn little critter out there in the middle of the furrow, trying his best to keep up with Jackson, until Jackson would stop the plow at the turn row and go back and get him and set him straddle of his neck and take up the plow and go on. In the late summer he could walk pretty good. Jackson made him a little hoe out of a stick and a scrap of shingle, and you could see Jackson chopping in the middle-thigh cotton, but you couldn't see the boy at all; you could just see the cotton shaking where he was."

"Jackson made his clothes," Mrs. Pruitt said. "Stitched them himself, by hand. I made a few garments and took them up there. I never done it but once though. He took them and he thanked me. But you could see it. It was like he even begrudged the earth itself for what that child had to eat to keep alive. And I tried to persuade Jackson to take him to church, have him baptized. 'He's already named,' he said. 'His name is Jackson and Longstreet Fentry. Pa fit under both of them.'"

"He never went nowhere," Pruitt said. "Because where you saw Jackson, you saw that boy. If he had had to steal that boy down there at Frenchman's Bend, he couldn't 'a' hid no closer. It was even the old man that would ride over to Haven Hill store to buy their supplies, and the only time Jackson and that boy was separated as much as one full breath was once a year when Jackson would ride in to Jefferson to pay their taxes, and when I first seen the boy I thought of a setter puppy, until one day I knowed Jackson had gone to pay their taxes and I went up there and the boy was under the bed, not making any fuss, just backed up into the corner, looking out at me. He didn't blink once. He was exactly like a fox or a wolf cub somebody had caught just last night."

We watched him take from his pocket a tin of snuff and tilt a measure of it into the lid and then into his lower lip, tapping the final grain from the lid with delicate deliberation.

"All right," Uncle Gavin said. "Then what?"

"That's all," Pruitt said. "In the next summer him and the boy disappeared."

"Disappeared?" Uncle Gavin said.

"That's right. They were just gone one morning. I didn't know when. And one day I couldn't stand it no longer, I went up there and the house was empty, and I went on to the field where the old man was plowing, and at first I thought the spreader between his plow handles had broke and he had tied a sapling across the handles, until he seen me and snatched the sapling off, and it was that shotgun, and I reckon what he said to me was about what he said to you this morning when you stopped there. Next year he had the nigger helping him again. Then, about five years later, Jackson come back. I don't know when. He was just there one morning. And the nigger was gone again, and him and his pa worked the place like they use to. And one day I couldn't stand it no longer, I went up there and I stood at the fence where he was plowing, until after a while the land he was breaking brought him up to the fence, and still he hadn't never looked at me; he plowed right by me, not ten feet away, still without looking at me, and he turned and come back, and I said, 'Did he die, Jackson?' and then he looked at me. 'The boy,' I said. And he said, 'What boy?' "

They invited us to stay for dinner.

Uncle Gavin thanked them. "We brought a snack with us," he said. "And it's thirty miles to Varner's store, and twenty-two from there to Jefferson. And our roads ain't quite used to automobiles yet."

So it was just sundown when we drove up to Varner's store in Frenchman's Bend Village; again a man rose from the deserted gallery and came down the steps to the car.

It was Isham Quick, the witness who had first reached Thorpe's body—a tall, gangling man in the middle forties, with a dreamy kind of face and near-sighted eyes, until you saw there was something shrewd behind them, even a little quizzical.

"I been waiting for you," he said. "Looks like you made a water haul." He blinked at Uncle Gavin. "That Fentry."

"Yes," Uncle Gavin said. "Why didn't you tell me?"

"I didn't recognize it myself," Quick said. "It wasn't until I heard your jury was hung, and by one man, that I associated them names."

"Names?" Uncle Gavin said. "What na——. Never mind. Just tell it."

So we sat on the gallery of the locked and deserted store while the cicadas shrilled and rattled in the trees and the lightning bugs blinked and drifted above the dusty road, and Quick told it, sprawled on the bench beyond Uncle Gavin, loose-jointed, like he would come all to pieces the first time he moved, talking in a lazy, sardonic voice, like he had all night to tell it in and it would take all night to tell it. But it wasn't that long. It wasn't long enough for what was in it. But Uncle Gavin says it don't take many words to tell the sum of any human experience; that somebody has already done it in eight: He was born, he suffered, and he died.

"It was pap that hired him. But when I found out where he had come from, I knowed he would work, because folks in that country hadn't never had time to learn nothing but hard work. And I knowed he would be honest for the same reason: that there wasn't nothing in his country a man could want bad enough to learn how to steal it. What I seem to have underestimated was his capacity for love. I reckon I figured that, coming from where he come from, he never had none a-tall, and for that same previous reason—that even the comprehension of love had done been lost out of him back down the generations where the first one of them had had to take his final choice between the pursuit of love and the pursuit of keeping on breathing.

"So he come to work, doing the same work and drawing the same pay as the niggers done. Until in the late fall, when the bottom got wet and we got ready to shut down for the winter, I found out he had made a trade with pap to stay on until spring as watchman and caretaker, with three days out to go home Christmas. And he did, and the next year when we started up, he had done learned so much about it and he stuck to it so, that by the middle of summer he was running the whole mill hisself, and by the end of summer pap never went out there no more a-tall and I just went when I felt like it, maybe once a week or so; and by fall pap was even talking about building him a shack to live in in place of that shuck mattress and a old broke-down cookstove in the boiler shed. And he stayed through that winter too. When he went home that Christmas we never even knowed it, when he went or when he come back, because even I hadn't been out there since fall.

"Then one afternoon in February—there had been a mild spell and I reckon I was restless—I rode out there. The first thing I seen was her, and it was the first time I had ever done that—a woman, young, and maybe when she was in her normal health she might have been pretty, too; I don't know. Because she wasn't just thin, she was gaunted. She was sick, more than just starved-looking, even if she was still on her feet, and it wasn't just because she was going to have that baby in a considerable less than another month. And I says, 'Who is that?' and he looked at me and says, 'That's my wife,' and I says, 'Since when? You never had no wife last fall. And that child ain't a month off.' And he says, 'Do you want us to leave?' and I says, 'What do I want you to leave for?' I'm going to tell this from what I know now, what I found out after them two brothers showed up here three years later with their court paper, not from what he ever told me, because he never told nobody nothing."

"All right," Uncle Gavin said. "Tell."

"I don't know where he found her. I don't know if he found her somewhere, or if she just walked into the mill one day or one night and he looked up and seen her, and it was like the fellow says—nobody knows where or when love or lightning either is going to strike, except that it ain't going to strike there twice, because it don't have to. And I don't believe she was hunting for the husband that had deserted her—likely he cut and run soon as she told him about the baby—and I don't believe she was scared or ashamed to go back home just because her brothers and father had tried to keep her from marrying the husband, in the first place. I believe it was just some more of that same kind of black-complected and not extraintelligent and pretty durn ruthless blood pride that them brothers themselves was waving around here for about a hour that day.

"Anyway, there she was, and I reckon she knowed her time was going to be short, and him saying to her, 'Let's get married,' and her saying, 'I can't marry you. I've already got a husband.' And her time come and she was down then, on that shuck mattress, and him feeding her with a spoon, likely, and I reckon she knowed she wouldn't get up from it, and he got the midwife, and the baby was born, and likely her and the midwife both knowed by then she would never get up from that mattress and maybe they even convinced him at last, or maybe she knowed it wouldn't make no difference nohow and said yes, and he taken the mule pap let him keep at the mill and rid seven miles to Preacher Whitfield's and brung Whitfield back about daylight, and Whitfield married them and she died, and him and Whitfield buried her. And that night he come to the house and told pap he was quitting, and left the mule, and I went out to the mill a few days later and he was gone—just the shuck mattress and the stove, and the dishes and skillet mammy let him have, all washed and clean and set on the shelf. And in the third summer from then, them two brothers, them Thorpes——"

"Thorpes," Uncle Gavin said. It wasn't loud. It was getting dark fast now, as it does in our country, and I couldn't see his face at all any more. "Tell," he said.

"Black-complected like she was—the youngest one looked a heap like her—coming up in the surrey, with the deputy or baliff or whatever he was, and the paper all wrote out and stamped and sealed all regular, and I says, 'You can't do this. She come here of her own accord, sick and with nothing, and he taken her in and fed her and nursed her and got help to born that child and a preacher to bury her; and they was even married before she died. The preacher and the midwife both will prove it." And the oldest brother says, 'He couldn't marry her. She already had a husband. We done already attended to him,' And I says, 'All right. He taken that boy when nobody come to claim him. He has raised that boy and clothed and fed him for two years and better.' And the oldest one drawed a money purse half outen his pocket and let it drop back again. 'We aim to do right about that, too—when we have seen the boy,' he says. 'He is our kin. We want him and we aim to have him.' And that wasn't the first time it ever occurred to me that this world ain't run like it ought to be run a heap more times than what it is, and I says, 'It's thirty miles up there. I reckon you all will want to lay over here tonight and rest your horses.' And the oldest one looked at me and says, 'The team ain't tired. We won't stop.' 'Then I'm going with you,' I says. 'You are welcome to come,' he says.

"We drove until midnight. So I thought I would have a chance then, even if I never had nothing to ride. But when we unhitched and laid down on the ground, the oldest brother never laid down. 'I ain't sleepy,' he says. 'I'll set up a while.' So it wasn't no use, and I went to sleep and then the sun was up and it was too late then, and about middle morning we come to that mailbox with the name on it you couldn't miss, and the empty house with nobody in sight or hearing neither, until we heard the ax and went around to the back, and he looked up from the woodpile and seen what I reckon he had been expecting to see every time the sun rose for going on three years now. Because he never even stopped. He said to the little boy, 'Run. Run. Run to the field to grandpap. Run,' and come straight at the oldest brother with the ax already raised and the down-stroke already started, until I managed to catch it by the haft just as the oldest brother grabbed him and we lifted him clean off the ground, holding him, or trying to. 'Stop it, Jackson!' I says. 'Stop it! They got the law!'

"Then a puny something was kicking and clawing me about the legs; it was the little boy, not making a sound, just swarming around me and the brother both, hitting at us as high as he could reach with a piece of wood Fentry had been chopping. 'Catch him and take him on to the surrey,' the oldest one says. So the youngest one caught him; he was almost as hard to hold as Fentry, kicking and plunging even after the youngest one had picked him up, and still not making a sound, and Fentry jerking and lunging like two men until the youngest one and the boy was out of sight. Then he collapsed. It was like all his bones had turned to water, so that me and the oldest brother lowered him down to the chopping block like he never had no bones a-tall, laying back against the wood he had cut, panting, with a little froth of spit at each corner of his mouth. 'It's the law, Jackson,' I says. 'Her husband is still alive.'

"'I know it,' he says. It wasn't much more than whispering. 'I been expecting it. I reckon that's why it taken me so by surprise. I'm all right now.'

"'I'm sorry for it,' the brother says. 'We never found out about none of it until last week. But he is our kin. We want him home. You done well by him. We thank you. His mother thanks you. Here,' he says. He taken the money purse outen his pocket and puts it into Fentry's hand. Then he turned and went away. After a while I heard the carriage turn and go back down the hill. Then I couldn't hear it any more. I don't know whether Fentry ever heard it or not.

"'It's the law, Jackson,' I says. 'But there's two sides to the law. We'll go to town and talk to Captain Stevens. I'll go with you.'

"Then he set up on the chopping block, setting up slow and still. He wasn't panting so hard now and he looked better now, except for his eyes, and they was mostly just dazed-looking. Then he raised the hand that had the money purse in it and started to mop his face with the money purse, like it was a handkerchief; I don't believe he even knowed there was anything in his hand until then, because he taken his hand down and looked at the money purse for maybe five seconds, and then he tossed it—he didn't fling it; he just tossed it like you would a handful of dirt you had been examining to see what it would make—over behind the chopping block and got up and walked across the yard toward the woods, walking straight and not fast, and not looking much bigger than that little boy, and into the woods. 'Jackson,' I says. But he never looked back.

"And I stayed that night at Rufus Pruitt's and borrowed a mule from him; I said I was just looking around, because I didn't feel much like talking to nobody, and the next morning I hitched the mule at that gate and started up the path, and I didn't see old man Fentry on the gallery a-tall at first.

"When I did see him he was moving so fast I didn't even know what he had in his hands until it went 'boom!' and I heard the shot rattling in the leaves overhead and Rufus Pruitt's mule trying his durn best either to break the hitch rein or hang hisself from the gatepost.

"And one day about six months after he had located here to do the balance of his drinking and fighting and sleight-of-hand with other folks' cattle, Bucksnort was on the gallery here, drunk still and running his mouth, and about a half-dozen of the ones he had beat unconscious from time to time by foul means and even by fair on occasion, as such emergencies arose, laughing every time he stopped to draw a fresh breath. And I happened to look up, and Fentry was setting on his mule out there in the road.

"He was just sitting there, with the dust of them thirty miles caking into the mule's sweat, looking at Thorpe. I don't know how long he had been there, not saying nothing, just setting there and looking at Thorpe; then he turned the mule and rid back up the road toward them hills he hadn't ought to never have left. Except maybe it's like the fellow says, and there ain't nowhere you can hide from either lightning or love. And I didn't know why then. I hadn't associated them names. I knowed that Thorpe was familiar to me, but that other business had been twenty years ago and I had forgotten it until I heard about that hung jury of yourn. Of course he wasn't going to vote Bookwright free. . . . It's dark. Let's go to supper."

But it was only twenty-two miles to town now, and we were on the highway now, the gravel; we would be home in an hour and a half, because sometimes we could make thirty and thirty-five miles an hour, and Uncle Gavin said that someday all the main roads in Mississippi would be paved like the streets in Memphis and every family in America would own a car. We were going fast now.

"Of course he wasn't," Uncle Gavin said. "The lowly and

invincible of the earth—to endure and endure and then endure, tomorrow and tomorrow and tomorrow. Of course he wasn't going to vote Bookwright free."

"I would have," I said. "I would have freed him. Because Buck Thorpe was bad. He——"

"No, you wouldn't," Uncle Gavin said. He gripped my knee with one hand even though we were going fast, the yellow light beam level on the yellow road, the bugs swirling down into the light beam and ballooning away. "It wasn't Buck Thorpe, the adult, the man. He would have shot that man as quick as Bookwright did, if he had been in Bookwright's place. It was because somewhere in that debased and brutalized flesh which Bookwright slew there still remained, not the spirit maybe, but at least the memory, of that little boy, that Jackson and Longstreet Fentry, even though the man the boy had become didn't know it, and only Fentry did. And you wouldn't have freed him either. Don't ever forget that. Never."

Triumph of Justice

by:

IRWIN SHAW

selected by:

ESTES KEFAUVER

Without law, there can be no justice; without legal procedure, there can be no law; without lawyers, there can be no procedure, law, or justice. But sometimes, with the help of a lawyer known as a judge, short cuts are possible in achieving a "Triumph of Justice."

S.S. ESTES KEFAUVER

Mike Pilato purposefully threw open the door of Victor's shack. Above him the sign that said, LUNCH, TRUCKMEN WELCOME, shook a little, and the pale shadows its red bulbs threw in the twilight waved over the State Road.

"Victor," Mike said, in Italian.

Victor was leaning on the counter, reading Walter Winchell in a spread-out newspaper. He smiled amiably. "Mike," he said, "I am so glad to see you."

Mike slammed the door. "Three hundred dollars, Victor," he said, standing five feet tall, round and solid as a pumpkin against the door. "You owe me three hundred dollars, Victor, and I am here tonight to collect."

Victor shrugged slightly and closed the paper on Walter Winchell.

"As I've been telling you for the past six months," he said, "business is bad. Business is terrible. I work and I work and at the end . . ." He shrugged again. "Barely enough to feed myself."

Mike's cheeks, farmer-brown, and wrinkled deeply by wind and sun, grew dark with blood. "Victor, you are lying in my face," he said slowly, his voice desperately even. "For six months each time it comes time to collect the rent you tell me, 'Business is bad.' What do I say? I say 'All right, Victor, don't worry, I know how it is.' "

"Frankly, Mike," Victor said sadly, "there has been no improvement this month."

Mike's face grew darker than ever. He pulled harshly at the ends of his iron-gray mustache, his great hands tense and swollen with anger, repressed but terrible. "For six months, Victor," Mike said, "I believed you. Now I no longer believe you."

"Mike," Victor said reproachfully.

"My friends, my relatives," Mike said, "they prove it to me. Your business is wonderful; ten cars an hour stop at your door; you sell cigarettes to every farmer between here and Chicago; on your slot machine alone . . ." Mike waved a short, thick arm at the machine standing invitingly against a wall, its wheels stopped at two cherries and a lemon. Mike swallowed hard, stood breathing heavily, his deep chest rising and falling sharply against his sheepskin coat. "Three hundred dollars!" he shouted. "Six months at fifty dollars! I built this shack with my own hands for you, Victor. I didn't know what kind of a man you were. You were an Italian, I trusted you! Three hundred dollars or get out tomorrow! Finish! That's my last word."

Victor smoothed his newspaper down delicately on the counter, his hands making a dry brushing sound in the empty lunchroom. "You misunderstand," he said gently."

"I misunderstand nothing!" Mike yelled. "You are on my land in my shack and you owe me three hundred dollars . . ."

"I don't owe you anything," Victor said, looking coldly at Mike. "That is what you misunderstand. I have paid you every month, the first day of the month, fifty dollars."

"Victor!" Mike whispered, his hands dropping to his sides. "Victor, what are you saying . . . ?"

"I have paid the rent. Please do not bother me any more." Calmly Victor turned his back on Mike and turned two handles on the coffee urn. Steam, in a thin little plume, hissed up for a moment.

Mike looked at Victor's narrow back, with the shoulder blades jutting far out, making limp wings in the white shirt. There was finality in Victor's pose, boredom, easy certainty. Mike shook his head slowly, pulling hard at his mustache. "My wife," Mike said, to the disdainful back, "she told me not to trust you. My wife knew what she was talking about, Victor." Then, with a last flare of hope, "Victor, do you really mean it when you said you paid me?"

Victor didn't turn around. He flipped another knob on the coffee urn. "I mean it."

Mike lifted his arm, as though to say something, pronounce warning. Then he let it drop and walked out of the shack, leaving the door open. Victor came out from behind the counter, looked at Mike moving off with his little rolling limp down the road and across the cornfield. Victor smiled and closed the door and went back and opened the paper to Walter Winchell.

Mike walked slowly among the cornstalks, his feet crunching unevenly in the October earth. Absently he pulled at his mustache. Dolores, his wife, would have a thing or two to say. "No," she had warned him, "do not build a shack for him. Do not permit him onto your land. He travels with bad men; it will turn out badly. I warn you!" Mike was sure she would not forget this conversation and would repeat it to him word for word when he got home. He limped along unhappily. Farming was better than being a landlord. You put seed into the earth and you knew what was coming out. Corn grew from corn, and the duplicity of Nature was expected and natural. Also no documents were signed in the compact with Nature, no leases and agreements necessary, a man was not at a disadvantage if he couldn't read or write. Mike opened the door to his house and sat down heavily in the parlor, without taking his hat off. Rosa came and jumped on his lap, yelling, "Poppa, Poppa, tonight I want to go to the movies, Poppa, take me to the movies!"

Mike pushed her off. "No movies," he said harshly. Rosa stood in a corner and watched him reproachfully.

The door from the kitchen opened and Mike sighed as he saw his wife coming in, wiping her hands on her apron. She stood in front of Mike, round, short, solid as a plow horse, canny, difficult to deceive.

"Why're you sitting in the parlor?" she asked.

"I feel like sitting in the parlor," Mike said.

"Every night you sit in the kitchen," Dolores said. "Suddenly you change."

"I've decided," Mike said loudly, "that it's about time I made some use of this furniture. After all, I paid for it, I might as well sit in it before I die."

"I know why you're sitting in the parlor," Dolores said.

"Good! You know!"

"You didn't get the money from Victor," Dolores wiped the last bit of batter from her hands. "It's as plain as the shoes on your feet."

"I smell something burning," Mike said.

"Nothing is burning. Am I right or wrong?" Dolores sat in the upright chair opposite Mike. She sat straight, her hands neatly in her lap, her head forward and cocked a little to one side, her eyes staring directly and accusingly into his. "Yes or no?"

"Please attend to your own department," Mike said miserably. "I do the farming and attend to the business details."

"Huh!" Dolores said disdainfully.

"Are you starving?" Mike shouted. "Answer me, are you starving?"

Rosa started to cry because her father was shouting.

"Please, for the love of Jesus," Mike screamed at her, "don't cry!"

Dolores enfolded Rosa in her arms. . . . "Baby, baby," she crooned, "I will not let him harm you."

"Who offered to harm her?" Mike screamed, banging on a table with his fist like a mallet. "Don't lie to her!"

Dolores kissed the top of Rosa's head soothingly. "There, there," she crooned. "There." She looked coldly at Mike. "Well. So he didn't pay."

"He . . ." Mike started loudly. Then he stopped, spoke in a low, reasonable voice. "So. To be frank with you, he didn't pay. That's the truth."

"What did I tell you?" Dolores said as Mike winced. "I repeat the words. 'Do not permit him onto your land. He travels with bad men; it will turn out badly. I warn you!' Did I tell you?"

"You told me," Mike said wearily.

"We will never see that money again," Dolores said, smoothing Rosa's hair. "I have kissed it good-by."

"Please," said Mike. "Return to the kitchen. I am hungry for dinner. I have made plans already to recover the money."

Dolores eyed him suspiciously. "Be careful, Mike," she said. "His friends are gangsters and he plays poker every Saturday night with men who carry guns in their pockets."

"I am going to the law," Mike said. "I'm going to sue Victor for the three hundred dollars."

Dolores started to laugh. She pushed Rosa away and stood up and laughed.

"What's so funny?" Mike asked angrily. "I tell you I'm going to sue a man for money he owes me, you find it funny! Tell me the joke."

Dolores stopped laughing. "Have you got any papers? No! You trust him, he trusts you, no papers. Without papers you're lost in a court. You'll make a fool of yourself. They'll charge you for the lawyers. Please, Mike, go back to your farming."

Mike's face set sternly, his wrinkles harsh in his face with the gray stubble he never managed completely to shave. "I want my dinner, Dolores," he said coldly, and Dolores discreetly moved into the kitchen, saying, "It is not my business, my love; truly, I merely offer advice."

Mike walked back and forth in the parlor, limping, rolling a little from side to side, his eyes on the floor, his hands plunged into the pockets of his denims like holstered weapons, his mouth pursed with thought and determination. After a while he stopped and looked at Rosa, who prepared to weep once more.

"Rosa, baby," he said, sitting down and taking her gently on his lap. "Forgive me."

Rosa snuggled to him. They sat that way in the dimly lit parlor.

"Poppa," Rosa said finally.

"Yes," Mike said.

"Will you take me to the movies tonight, Poppa?"

"All right," Mike said. "I'll take you to the movies."

The next day Mike went into town, dressed in his neat black broadcloth suit and his black soft hat and his high brown shoes.

He came back to the farm like a businessman in the movies, bustly, preoccupied, sober, but satisfied.

"Well?" Dolores asked him, in the kitchen.

He kissed her briskly, kissed Rosa, sat down, took his shoes off, rubbed his feet luxuriously, said paternally to his son who was reading *Esquire* near the window, "That's right, Anthony, study."

"Well?" asked Dolores.

"I saw Dominic in town," Mike said, watching his toes wiggling. "They're having another baby."

"Well," asked Dolores. "The case? The action?"

"All right," Mike said. "What is there for dinner?"

"Veal," Dolores said. "What do you mean 'all right'?"

"I've spoken to Judge Collins. He is filling out the necessary papers for me and he will write me a letter when I am to appear in court. Rosa, have you been a good girl?"

Dolores threw up her hands. "Lawyers. We'll throw away a fortune on lawyers. Good money after bad. We could put in an electric pump with the money."

"Lawyers will cost us nothing." Mike stuffed his pipe elaborately. "I have different plans. Myself. I will take care of the case myself." He lit up, puffed deliberately.

Dolores sat down across the table from him, spoke slowly, carefully. "Remember, Mike," she said. "This is in English. They conduct the court in English."

"I know," said Mike. "I am right. Justice is on my side. Why should I pay a lawyer fifty, seventy-five dollars to collect my own money? There is one time you need lawyers—when you are wrong. I am not wrong. I will be my own lawyer."

"What do you know about the law?" Dolores challenged him.

"I know Victor owes me three hundred dollars." Mike puffed three times, quickly, on his pipe. "That's all I need to know."

"You can hardly speak English, you can't even read or write, nobody will be able to understand you. They'll all laugh at you, Mike."

"Nobody will laugh at me. I can speak English fine."

"When did you learn?" Dolores asked. "Today?"

"Dolores!" Mike shouted. "I tell you my English is all right."

"Say Thursday," Dolores said.

"I don't want to say it," Mike said, banging the table. "I have no interest in saying it."

"Aha," Dolores crowed. "See? He wants to be a lawyer in an American court, he can't even say Thursday."

"I can," Mike said. "Keep quiet, Dolores."

"Say Thursday." Dolores put her head to one side, spoke coquettishly, slyly, like a girl asking her lover to say he loved her.

"Stirday," Mike said, as he always said. "There!"

Dolores laughed, waving her hand. "And he wants to conduct a law case! Holy Mother! They will laugh at you!"

"Let them laugh!" Mike shouted. "I will conduct the case! Now I want to eat dinner! Anthony!" he yelled. "Throw away that trash and come to the table."

On the day of the trial, Mike shaved closely, dressed carefully in his black suit, put his black hat squarely on his head, and with Dolores seated grimly beside him drove early into town in the 1933 family Dodge.

Dolores said nothing all the way into town. Only after the car was parked and they were entering the courthouse, Mike's shoes clattering bravely on the legal marble, did Dolores speak. "Behave yourself," she said. Then she pinched his arm. Mike smiled at her, braced his yokelike shoulders, took off his hat. His rough gray hair sprang up like steel wool when his hat was off, and Mike ran his hand through it as he opened the door to the courtroom. There was a proud, important smile on his face as he sat down next to his wife in the first row and patiently waited for his case to be called.

When Victor came, Mike glared at him, but Victor, after a quick look, riveted his attention on the American flag behind the judge's head.

"See," Mike whispered to Dolores. "I have him frightened. He doesn't dare look at me. Here he will have to tell the truth."

"Sssh!" hissed Dolores. "This is a court of law."

"Michael Pilato," the clerk called, "versus Victor Fraschi."

"Me!" Mike said loudly, standing up.

"Sssh," said Dolores.

Mike put his hat in Dolores' lap, moved lightly to the little gate that separated the spectators from the principals in the proceedings. Politely, with a deep ironic smile, he held the gate open for Victor and his lawyer. Victor passed through without looking up.

"Who's representing you, Mr. Pilato?" the judge asked when they were all seated. "Where's your lawyer?"

Mike stood up and spoke in a clear voice. "I represent myself. I am my lawyer."

"You ought to have a lawyer," the judge said.

"I do not need a lawyer," Mike said loudly. "I am not trying to cheat anybody." There were about forty people in the courtroom and they all laughed. Mike turned and looked at them, puzzled. "What did I say?"

The judge rapped with his gavel and the case was opened. Victor took the stand, while Mike stared, coldly accusing, at him. Victor's lawyer, a young man in a blue pinstripe suit and a starched tan shirt, questioned him. Yes, Victor said, he had paid each month. No, there were no receipts, Mr. Pilato could neither read nor write and they had dispensed with all formalities of that kind. No, he did not understand on what Mr. Pilato based his claim. Mike looked incredulously at Victor, lying under solemn oath, risking Hell for three hundred dollars.

Victor's lawyer stepped down and waved to Mike gracefully. "Your witness."

Mike walked dazedly past the lawyer and up to the witness stand, round, neat, his bull neck, deep red-brown and wrinkled, over his pure white collar, his large scrubbed hands politely but awkwardly held at his sides. He stood in front of Victor, leaning over a little toward him, his face close to Victor's.

"Victor," he said, his voice ringing through the courtroom, "tell the truth, did you pay me the money?"

"Yes," said Victor.

Mike leaned closer to him. "Look in my eye, Victor," Mike said, his voice clear and patient, "and answer me. Did you pay me the money?"

Victor lifted his head and looked unflinchingly into Mike's eyes. "I paid you the money."

Mike leaned even closer. His forehead almost touched Victor's now. "Look me *straight* in the eye, Victor."

Victor looked bravely into Mike's eyes, less than a foot away now.

"Now, Victor," Mike said, his eyes narrowed, cold, the light in them small and flashing and gray, "DID YOU PAY ME THE MONEY?"

Victor breathed deeply. "Yes," he said.

Mike took half a step back, almost staggering, as though he had been hit. He stared incredulously into the perjurer's eyes, as a man might stare at a son who has just admitted he has killed his mother, beyond pity, beyond understanding, outside all the known usage of human life. Mike's face worked harshly as the tides of anger and despair and vengeance rolled up in him.

"You're a goddam liar, Victor!" Mike shouted terribly. He leapt down from the witness platform, seized a heavy oak armchair, raised it murderously above Victor's head.

"Mike, oh, Mike!" Dolores' wail floated above the noise of the courtroom.

"Tell the truth, Victor!" Mike shouted, his face brick red, his teeth white behind his curled lips, almost senseless with rage, for the first time in his life threatening a fellow creature with violence. "Tell it fast!"

He stood, the figure of Justice, armed with the chair, the veins pulsing in his huge wrists, the chair quivering high above Victor's head in his huge gnarled hands, his tremendous arms tight and bulging in their broadcloth sleeves. "Immediately, Victor!"

"Pilato!" shouted the judge. "Put that chair down!"

Victor sat stonily, his eyes lifted in dumb horror to the chair above his head.

"Pilato," the judge shouted, "you can be sent to jail for this!" He banged sternly but helplessly on his desk: "Remember, this is a court of law!"

"Victor?" Mike asked, unmoved, unmoving. "Victor? Immediately, please."

"No," Victor screamed, cringing in his seat, his hands now held in feeble defense before his eyes. "I didn't pay! I didn't!"

"Pilato," screamed the judge, "this is not evidence!"

"You were lying?" Mike said inexorably, the chair still held, axlike, above him.

"Mike, oh, Mike," wailed Dolores.

"It was not my idea," Victor babbled. "As God is my judge,

I didn't think it up. Alfred Lotti, he suggested it, and Johnny Nolan. I am under the influence of corrupt men. Mike, for the love of God, please don't kill me, Mike, it would never have occurred to me myself, forgive me, forgive me . . ."

"Guiness!" the judge called to the court policeman. "Are you going to stand there and let this go on? Why don't you do something?"

"I can shoot him," Guiness said. "Do you want me to shoot the plaintiff?"

"Shut up," the judge said.

Guiness shrugged and turned his head toward the witness stand, smiling a little.

"You were lying?" Mike asked, his voice low, patient.

"I was lying," Victor cried.

Slowly, with magnificent calm, Mike put the chair down neatly in its place. With a wide smile he turned to the judge. "There," he said.

"Do you know any good reason," the judge shouted, "why I shouldn't have you locked up?"

Victor was crying with relief on the witness stand, wiping the tears away with his sleeve.

"There is no possible excuse," the judge said, "for me to admit this confession as evidence. We are a court of law in the state of Illinois, in the United States. We are not conducting the Spanish Inquisition, Mr. Pilato."

"Huh?" Mike asked, cocking his head.

"There are certain rules," the judge went on, quickly, his voice high, "which it is customary to observe. It is not the usual thing, Mr. Pilato," he said harshly, "to arrive at evidence by bodily threatening to brain witnesses with a chair."

"He wouldn't tell the truth," Mike said simply.

"At the very least, Mr. Pilato," the judge said, "you should get thirty days."

"Oh, Mike," wept Dolores.

"Mr. Fraschi," the judge said, "I promise you that you will be protected. That nobody will harm you."

"I did it," sobbed Victor, his hands shaking uncontrollably in a mixture of fear, repentance, religion, joy at delivery from death. "I did it. I will not tell a lie. I'm a weak man and influenced by loafers. I owe him three hundred dollars. Forgive me, Mike, forgive me . . ."

"He will not harm you," the judge said patiently. "I guarantee it. You can tell the truth without any danger. Do you owe Mr. Pilato three hundred dollars?"

"I owe Mr. Pilato three hundred dollars," Victor said, swallowing four times in a row.

The young lawyer put three sheets of paper into his brief case and snapped the lock.

The judge sighed and wiped his brow with a handkerchief as he looked at Mike. "I don't approve of the way you conducted this trial, Mr. Pilato," he said. "It is only because you're a working man who has many duties to attend to on his land that I don't take you and put you away for a month to teach you more respect for the processes of law."

"Yes, sir," Mike said faintly.

"Hereafter," the judge said, "kindly engage an attorney when you appear before me in this court."

"Yes, sir," Mike said.

"Mr. Pilato," the judge said, "it is up to you to decide when and how he is to pay you."

Mike turned and walked back to Victor. Victor shrank into his chair. "Tomorrow morning, Victor," Mike said, waving his finger under Victor's nose, "at eighty-thirty o'clock, I am coming into your store. The money will be there."

"Yes," said Victor.

"Is that all right?" Mike asked the judge.

"Yes," said the judge.

Mike strode over to the young lawyer. "And you," he said, standing with his hands on his hips in front of the young man with the pinstripe suit. "Mr. Lawyer. You knew he didn't pay me. A boy with an education. You should be ashamed of yourself." He turned to the judge, smiled broadly, bowed. "Thank you," he said. "Good morning." Then, triumphantly, smiling broadly, rolling like a sea captain as he walked, he went through the little gate. Dolores was waiting with his hat. He took the hat, put Dolores' arm through his, marched down the aisle, nodding, beaming to the spectators. Someone applauded and by the time he and Dolores got to the door all the spectators were applauding.

He waited until he got outside, in the bright morning sunshine down the steps of the courthouse, before he said anything to Dolores. He put his hat on carefully, turned to her, grinning. "Well," he said, "did you observe what I did?"

"Yes," she said. "I was never so ashamed in my whole life!"

"Dolores!" Mike was shocked. "I got the money. I won the case."

"Acting like that in a court of law!" Dolores started bitterly toward the car. "What are you, a red Indian?"

Dolores got into the car and slammed the door and Mike limped slowly around and got into the other side. He started the car without a word and shaking his head from time to time, drove slowly toward home.

A Wasted Day

by:

RICHARD HARDING DAVIS

selected by:

SAM RAYBURN

One of my favorite stories dealing with law and lawyers is "A Wasted Day," by Richard Harding Davis. Whether it is a favorite because it is a mighty fine story or because it expresses so many of my sentiments, it's hard to say. In any event, it's well worth reading and well worth recommending.

S.S. SAM RAYBURN

When its turn came, the private secretary, somewhat apologetically, laid the letter in front of the Wisest Man in Wall Street.

"From Mrs. Austin, probation officer, Court of General Sessions," he explained. "Wants a letter about Spear. He's been convicted of theft. Comes up for sentence Tuesday."

"Spear?" repeated Arnold Thorndike.

"Young fellow, stenographer, used to do your letters last summer going in and out on the train."

The great man nodded. "I remember. What about him?"

The habitual gloom of the private secretary was lightened by a grin.

"Went on the loose; had with him about five hundred dollars belonging to the firm; he's with Isaacs & Sons now, shoe people on Sixth Avenue. Met a woman and woke up without the money. The next morning he offered to make good, but Isaacs called in a policeman. When they looked into it, they found the boy had been drunk. They tried to withdraw the charge, but he'd been committed. Now, the probation officer is trying to get the judge to suspend sentence. A letter from you, sir, would——"

It was evident the mind of the great man was elsewhere. Young men who, drunk or sober, spent the firm's money on women who disappeared before sunrise did not appeal to him.

Another letter submitted that morning had come from his art agent in Europe. In Florence he had discovered the Correggio he had been sent to find. It was undoubtedly genuine, and he asked to be instructed by cable. The price was forty thousand dollars. With one eye closed, and the other keenly regarding the inkstand, Mr. Thorndike decided to pay the price; and with the facility of long practice dismissed the Correggio, and snapped his mind back to the present.

"Spear had a letter from us when he left, didn't he?" he asked. "What he has developed into, *since* he left us——" he shrugged his shoulders. The secretary withdrew the letter and slipped another in its place.

"Homer Firth, the landscape man," he chanted, "wants permission to use blue flint on the new road, with turf gutters, and to plant silver firs each side. Says it will run to about five thousand dollars a mile."

"No!" protested the great man firmly, "blue flint makes a country place look like a cemetery. Mine looks too much like a cemetery now. Landscape gardeners!" he exclaimed impatiently. "Their only idea is to insult nature. The place was better the day I bought it, when it was running wild; you could pick flowers all the way to the gates." Pleased that it should have recurred to him, the great man smiled. "Why, Spear," he exclaimed, "always took in a bunch of them for his mother. Don't you remember, we used to see him before breakfast wandering around the grounds picking flowers?" Mr. Thorndike nodded briskly. "I like his taking flowers to his mother."

"He *said* it was to his mother," suggested the secretary gloomily.

"Well, he picked the flowers, anyway," laughed Mr. Thorndike. "He didn't pick our pockets. And he had the run of the house in those days. As far as we know," he dictated, "he was satisfactory. Don't say more than that."

The secretary scribbled a mark with his pencil. "And the landscape man?"

"Tell him," commanded Thorndike, "I want a wood road, suitable to a farm; and to let the trees grow where God planted them."

As his car slid downtown on Tuesday morning the mind of

Arnold Thorndike was occupied with such details of daily routine as the purchase of a railroad, the Japanese loan, the new wing to his art gallery, and an attack that morning, in his own newspaper, upon his pet trust. But his busy mind was not too occupied to return the salutes of the traffic policemen who cleared the way for him. Or, by some genius of memory, to recall the fact that it was on this morning young Spear was to be sentenced for theft. It was a charming morning. The spring was at full tide, and the air was sweet and clean. Mr. Thorndike considered whimsically that to send a man to jail with the memory of such a morning clinging to him was adding a year to his sentence. He regretted he had not given the probation officer a stronger letter. He remembered the young man now, and favorably. A shy, silent youth, deft in work, and at other times conscious and embarrassed. But that, on the part of a stenographer, in the presence of the Wisest Man in Wall Street, was not unnatural. On occasions Mr. Thorndike had put even royalty—frayed, impecunious royalty, on the lookout for a loan—at its ease.

The hood of the car was down, and the taste of the air, warmed by the sun, was grateful. It was at this time, a year before, that young Spear picked the spring flowers to take to his mother. A year from now where would young Spear be?

It was characteristic of the great man to act quickly, so quickly that his friends declared he was a slave to impulse. It was these same impulses, leading so invariably to success, that made his enemies call him the Wisest Man. He leaned forward and touched the chauffeur's shoulder. "Stop at the Court of General Sessions," he commanded. What he proposed to do would take but a few minutes. A word, a personal word from him to the district attorney, or the judge, would be enough. He recalled that a Sunday Special had once calculated that the working time of Arnold Thorndike brought him in two hundred dollars a minute. At that rate, keeping Spear out of prison would cost a thousand dollars.

Out of the sunshine Mr. Thorndike stepped into the gloom of an echoing rotunda, shut in on every side, hung by balconies, lit, many stories overhead, by a dirty skylight. The place was damp, the air acrid with the smell of stale tobacco juice, and foul with the presence of many unwashed humans. A policeman, chewing stolidly, nodded toward an elevator shaft, and other policemen nodded him further on to the office of the district attorney. There Arnold Thorndike breathed more freely. He was again among his own people. He could not help but appreciate the dramatic qualities of the situation; that the richest man in Wall Street should appear in person to plead for a humble and weaker brother. He knew he could not escape recognition, his face was too well known, but, he trusted, for the sake of Spear, the reporters would make no display of his visit. With a deprecatory laugh, he explained why he had come. But the outburst of approbation he had anticipated did not follow.

The district attorney ran his finger briskly down a printed card. "Henry Spear," he exclaimed, "that's your man. Part Three, Judge Fallon. Andrews is in that court." He walked to the door of his private office. "Andrews!" he called.

He introduced an alert, broad-shouldered young man of years of much indiscretion and with a charming and inconsequent manner.

"Mr. Thorndike is interested in Henry Spear, coming up for sentence in Part Three this morning. Wants to speak for him. Take him over with you."

The district attorney shook hands quickly, and retreated to his private office. Mr. Andrews took out a cigarette and, as he crossed the floor, lit it.

"Come with me," he commanded. Somewhat puzzled, slightly annoyed, but enjoying withal the novelty of the environment and the curtness of his reception, Mr. Thorndike followed. He decided that, in his ignorance, he had wasted his own time and that of the prosecuting attorney. He should at once have sent in his card to the judge. As he understood it, Mr. Andrews was now conducting him to that dignitary, and, in a moment, he would be free to return to his own affairs, which were the affairs of two continents. But Mr. Andrews led him to an office, bare and small, and offered him a chair, and handed him a morning newspaper. There were people waiting in the room; strange people, only like those Mr. Thorndike had seen on ferry boats. They leaned forward toward young Mr. Andrews, fawning, their eyes wide with apprehension.

Mr. Thorndike refused the newspaper. "I thought I was going to see the judge," he suggested.

"Court doesn't open for a few minutes yet," said the assistant district attorney. "Judge is always late, anyway."

Mr. Thorndike suppressed an exclamation. He wanted to protest, but his clear mind showed him that there was nothing against which, with reason, he could protest. He could not complain because these people were not apparently aware of the sacrifice he was making. He had come among them to perform a kindly act. He recognized that he must not stultify it by a show of irritation. He had precipitated himself into a game of which he did not know the rules. That was all. Next time he would know better. Next time he would send a clerk. But he was not without a sense of humor, and the situation as it now was forced upon him struck him as amusing. He laughed good-naturedly and reached for the desk telephone.

"May I use this?" he asked. He spoke to the Wall Street office. He explained he would be a few minutes late. He directed what should be done if the market opened in a certain way. He gave rapid orders on many different matters, asked to have read to him a cablegram he expected from Petersburg, and one from Vienna.

"They answer each other," was his final instruction. "It looks like peace."

Mr. Andrews with genial patience had remained silent. Now he turned upon his visitors. A Levantine, burly, unshaven, and soiled, towered truculently above him. Young Mr. Andrews with his swivel chair tilted back, his hands clasped behind his head, his cigarette hanging from his lips, regarded the man dispassionately.

"You gotta hell of a nerve to come to see me," he commented cheerfully. To Mr. Thorndike, the form of greeting was novel. So greatly did it differ from the procedure of his own office that he listened with interest.

"Was it you," demanded young Andrews, in a puzzled tone, "or your brother who tried to knife me?" Mr. Thorndike, unaccustomed to cross the pavement to his office unless escorted by bank messengers and plain-clothesmen, felt the room growing rapidly smaller; the figure of the truculent Greek loomed to heroic proportions. The hand of the banker went vaguely to his chin, and from there fell to his pearl pin, which he hastily covered.

"Get out!" said young Andrews, "and don't show your face here——"

The door slammed upon the flying Greek. Young Andrews swung his swivel chair so that, over his shoulder, he could see Mr. Thorndike. "I don't like his face," he explained.

A kindly eyed, sad woman with a basket on her knee smiled upon Andrews with the familiarity of an old acquaintance.

"Is that woman going to get a divorce from my son," she asked, "now that he's in trouble?"

"Now that he's in Sing Sing?" corrected Mr. Andrews. "I *hope* so! She deserves it. That son of yours, Mrs. Bernard," he declared emphatically, "is no good!"

The brutality shocked Mr. Thorndike. For the woman he felt a thrill of sympathy, but at once saw that it was superfluous. From the secure and lofty heights of motherhood, Mrs. Bernard smiled down upon the assistant district attorney as upon a naughty child. She did not even deign a protest. She continued merely to smile. The smile reminded Thorndike of the smile on the face of a mother in a painting by Murillo he had lately presented to the chapel in the college he had given to his native town.

"That son of yours," repeated young Andrews, "is a leech. He's robbed you, robbed his wife. Best thing I ever did for *you* was to send him up the river."

The mother smiled upon him beseechingly.

"Could you give me a pass?" she said.

Young Andrews flung up his hands and appealed to Thorndike.

"Isn't that just like a mother?" he protested. "That son of hers has broken her heart, tramped on her, cheated her, hasn't left her a cent; and she comes to me for a pass, so she can kiss him through the bars! And I'll bet she's got a cake for him in that basket!"

The mother laughed happily; she knew now she would get the pass.

"Mothers," explained Mr. Andrews, from the depth of his

wisdom, "are all like that; your mother, my mother. If you went to jail, your mother would be just like that."

Mr. Thorndike bowed his head politely. He had never considered going to jail, or whether, if he did, his mother would bring him cake in a basket. Apparently there were many aspects and accidents of life not included in his experience.

Young Andrews sprang to his feet, and, with the force of a hose flushing a gutter, swept his soiled visitors into the hall.

"Come on," he called to the Wisest Man, "the court is open."

In the corridors were many people, and with his eyes on the broad shoulders of the assistant district attorney, Thorndike pushed his way through them. The people who blocked his progress were of the class unknown to him. Their looks were anxious, furtive, miserable. They stood in little groups, listening eagerly to a sharp-faced lawyer, or, in sullen despair, eying each other. At a door a tipstaff laid his hand roughly on the arm of Mr. Thorndike.

"That's all right, Joe," called young Mr. Andrews, "he's with *me*." They entered the court and passed down an aisle to a railed enclosure in which were high oak chairs. Again, in his effort to follow, Mr. Thorndike was halted, but the first tipstaff came to his rescue. "All right," he signaled, "he's with Mr. Andrews."

Mr. Andrews pointed to one of the oak chairs. "You sit there," he commanded, "it's reserved for members of the bar, but it's all right. You're with *me*."

Distinctly annoyed, slightly bewildered, the banker sank between the arms of a chair. He felt he had lost his individuality. Andrews had become his sponsor. Because of Andrews he was tolerated. Because Andrews had a pull he was permitted to sit as an equal among police-court lawyers. No longer was he Arnold Thorndike. He was merely the man "with Mr. Andrews."

Then even Andrews abandoned him. "The judge'll be here in a minute, now," said the assistant district attorney, and went inside a railed enclosure in front of the judge's bench. There he greeted another assistant district attorney whose years were those of even greater indiscretion than the years of Mr. Andrews. Seated on the rail, with their hands in their pockets and their backs turned to Mr. Thorndike, they laughed and talked together. The subject of their discourse was one Mike Donlin, as he appeared in vaudeville.

To Mr. Thorndike it was evident that young Andrews had entirely forgotten him. He arose and touched his sleeve. With infinite sarcasm Mr. Thorndike began: "My engagements are not pressing, but——"

A court attendant beat with his palm upon the rail.

"Sit down!" whispered Andrews. "The judge is coming."

Mr. Thorndike sat down.

The court attendant droned loudly words Mr. Thorndike could not distinguish. There was a rustle of silk, and from a door behind him the judge stalked past. He was a young man, the type of the Tammany politician. On his shrewd, alert, Irish-American features was an expression of unnatural gloom. With a smile Mr. Thorndike observed that it was as little suited to the countenance of the young judge as was the robe to his shoulders. Mr. Thorndike was still smiling when young Andrews leaned over the rail.

"Stand up!" he hissed. Mr. Thorndike stood up.

After the court attendant had uttered more unintelligible words, every one sat down; and the financier again moved hurriedly to the rail.

"I would like to speak to him now before he begins," he whispered. "I can't wait."

Mr. Andrews stared in amazement. The banker had not believed the young man could look so serious.

"Speak to him, *now*!" exclaimed the district attorney. "You've got to wait till your man comes up. If you speak to the judge, *now*——" The voice of Andrews faded away in horror.

Not knowing in what way he had offended, but convinced that it was only by the grace of Andrews he had escaped a dungeon, Mr. Thorndike retreated to his armchair.

The clock on the wall showed him that, already, he had given to young Spear one hour and a quarter. The idea was preposterous. No one better than himself knew what his time was really worth. In half an hour there was a board meeting; later he was to hold a post-mortem on a railroad; at every moment questions were being asked by telegraph, by cable, questions that involved the credit of individuals, of firms, of even the country. And the one man who could answer them was risking untold sums only that he might say a good word for an idle apprentice. Inside the railed enclosure a lawyer was reading a typewritten speech. He assured his honor that he must have more time to prepare his case. It was one of immense importance. The name of a most respectable business house was involved, and a sum of no less than nine hundred dollars. Nine hundred dollars! The contrast struck Mr. Thorndike's sense of humor full in the center. Unknowingly, he laughed and found himself as conspicuous as though he had appeared suddenly in his nightclothes. The tipstaffs beat upon the rail, the lawyer he had interrupted uttered an indignant exclamation, Andrews came hurriedly toward him, and the young judge slowly turned his head.

"Those persons," he said, "who cannot respect the dignity of this court will leave it." As he spoke, with his eyes fixed on those of Mr. Thorndike, the latter saw that the young judge had suddenly recognized him. But the fact of his identity did not cause the frown to relax or the rebuke to halt unuttered. In even, icy tones the judge continued: "And it is well they should remember that the law is no respecter of persons and that the dignity of this court will be enforced, no matter who the offender may happen to be."

Andrews slipped into the chair beside Mr. Thorndike and grinned sympathetically.

"Sorry!" he whispered. "Should have warned you. We won't be long now," he added encouragingly. "As soon as this fellow finishes his argument, the judge'll take up the sentences. Your man seems to have other friends; Isaacs & Sons are here, and the typewriter firm who taught him; but what *you* say will help most. It won't be more than a couple of hours now."

"A couple of hours!" Mr. Thorndike raged inwardly. A couple of hours in this place where he had been publicly humiliated. He smiled, a thin, sharklike smile. Those who made it their business to study his expressions, on seeing it, would have fled. Young Andrews, not being acquainted with the moods of the great man, added cheerfully: "By one o'clock, anyway."

Mr. Thorndike began grimly to pull on his gloves. For all he cared now young Spear could go hang. Andrews nudged his elbow.

"See that old lady in the front row?" he whispered. "That's Mrs. Spear. What did I tell you; mothers are all alike. She's not taken her eyes off you since court opened. She knows you're her one best bet."

Impatiently Mr. Thorndike raised his head. He saw a little white-haired woman who stared at him. In her eyes was the same look he had seen in the eyes of men who, at times of panic, fled to him, beseeching, entreating, forcing upon him what was left of the wreck of their fortunes, if only he would save their honor.

"And here come the prisoners," Andrews whispered. "See Spear? Third man from the last." A long line, guarded in front and rear, shuffled into the courtroom, and, as ordered, ranged themselves against the wall. Among them were old men and young boys, well dressed, clever-looking rascals, collarless tramps, fierce-eyed aliens, smooth-shaven, thin-lipped Broadwayards—and Spear.

Spear, his head hanging, with lips white and cheeks ashen, and his eyes heavy with shame.

Mr. Thorndike had risen, and, in farewell, was holding out his hand to Andrews. He turned, and across the courtroom the eyes of the financier and the stenographer met. At the sight of the great man Spear flushed crimson, and then his look of despair slowly disappeared; and into his eyes there came incredulously hope and gratitude. He turned his head suddenly to the wall.

Mr. Thorndike stood irresolute and then sank back into his chair.

The first man in the line was already at the railing, and the questions put to him by the judge were being repeated to him by the other assistant district attorney and a court attendant. His muttered answers were in turn repeated to the judge.

"Says he's married, naturalized citizen, Lutheran Church, diecutter by profession."

The probation officer, her hands filled with papers, bustled forward and whispered.

"Mrs. Austin says," continued the district attorney, "she's

looked into this case and asks to have the man turned over to her. He has a wife and three children; has supported them for five years."

"Is the wife in court?" the judge said.

A thin, washed-out, pretty woman stood up and clasped her hands in front of her.

"Has this man been a good husband to you, madam?" asked the young judge.

The woman broke into vehement assurances. No man could have been a better husband. Would she take him back? Indeed she would take him back. She held out her hands as though she would physically drag her husband from the pillory.

The judge bowed toward the probation officer, and she beckoned the prisoner to her.

Other men followed, and in the fortune of each Mr. Thorndike found himself, to his surprise, taking a personal interest. It was as good as a play. It reminded him of the Sicilians he had seen in London in their little sordid tragedies. Only these actors were appearing in their proper persons in real dramas of a life he did not know, but which appealed to something that had been long untouched, long in disuse. It was an uncomfortable sensation that left him restless because, as he appreciated, it needed expression, an outlet. He found this, partially, in praising, through Andrews, the young judge who had publicly rebuked him. Mr. Thorndike found him astute, sane; his queries intelligent, his comments just. And this probation officer, she, too, was capable, was she not? Smiling at his interest in what to him was an old story, the younger man nodded.

"I like her looks," whispered the great man. "Like her clear eyes and clean skin. She strikes me as able, full of energy, and yet womanly. These men when they come under her charge," he insisted, eagerly, "need money to start again, don't they?" He spoke anxiously. He believed he had found the clue to his restlessness. It was a desire to help; to be of use to these failures who had fallen and who were being lifted to their feet. Andrews looked at him curiously. "Anything you give her," he answered, "would be well invested."

"If you will tell me her name and address?" whispered the banker. He was much given to charity, but it had been perfunctory, it was extended on the advice of his secretary. In helping here he felt a genial glow of personal pleasure. It was much more satisfactory than giving an Old Master to his private chapel.

In the rear of the courtroom there was a scuffle that caused every one to turn and look. A man, who had tried to force his way past the tipstaffs, was being violently ejected, and, as he disappeared, he waved a paper toward Mr. Thorndike. The banker recognized him as his chief clerk. Andrews rose anxiously. "That man wanted to get to you. I'll see what it is. Maybe it's important."

Mr. Thorndike pulled him back.

"Maybe it is," he said dryly. "But I can't see him now, I'm busy."

Slowly the long line of derelicts, of birds of prey, of sorry, weak failures, passed before the seat of judgment. Mr. Thorndike had moved into a chair nearer to the rail, and from time to time made a note upon the back of an envelope. He had forgotten the time or had chosen to disregard it. So great was his interest that he had forgotten the particular derelict he had come to serve, until Spear stood almost at his elbow.

Thorndike turned eagerly to the judge and saw that he was listening to a rotund, gray little man with beady, birdlike eyes who, as he talked, bowed and gesticulated. Behind him stood a younger man, a more modern edition of the other. He also bowed and, behind gold eyeglasses, smiled ingratiatingly.

The judge nodded and, leaning forward, for a few moments fixed his eyes upon the prisoner.

"You are a very fortunate young man," he said. He laid his hand upon a pile of letters. "When you were your own worst enemy, your friends came to help you. These letters speak for you; your employers, whom you robbed, have pleaded with me in your favor. It is urged, in your behalf, that at the time you committed the crime of which you are found guilty, you were intoxicated. In the eyes of the law, that is no excuse. Some men can drink and keep their senses. It appears you cannot. When you drink you are a menace to yourself—and, as is shown by this crime, to the community. Therefore, you must not drink. In view of the good character to which your friends have testified, and on the condition that you do not touch liquor, I will not sentence you to jail, but will place you in charge of the probation officer."

The judge leaned back in his chair and beckoned to Mr. Andrews. It was finished. Spear was free, and from different parts of the courtroom people were moving toward the door. Their numbers showed that the friends of the young man had been many. Mr. Thorndike felt a certain twinge of disappointment. Even though the result relieved and pleased him, he wished, in bringing it about, he had had some part.

He begrudged to Isaacs & Sons the credit of having given Spear his liberty. His morning had been wasted. He had neglected his own interests, and in no way assisted those of Spear. He was moving out of the railed enclosure when Andrews called him by name.

"His Honor," he said impressively, "wishes to speak to you."

The judge leaned over his desk and shook Mr. Thorndike by the hand. Then he made a speech. The speech was about public-spirited citizens who, to the neglect of their own interests, came to assist the ends of justice and fellow creatures in misfortune. He purposely spoke in a loud voice, and everyone stopped to listen.

"The law, Mr. Thorndike, is not vindictive," he said. "It wishes only to be just. Nor can it be swayed by wealth or political or social influences. But when there is good in a man, I, personally, want to know it, and when gentlemen like yourself, of your standing in this city, come here to speak a good word for a man, we would stultify the purpose of justice if we did not listen. I thank you for coming, and I wish more of our citizens were as unselfish and public-spirited."

It was all quite absurd and most embarrassing, but inwardly Mr. Thorndike glowed with pleasure. It was a long time since any one had had the audacity to tell him he had done well. From the friends of Spear there was a ripple of applause, which no tipstaff took it upon himself to suppress, and to the accompaniment of this, Mr. Thorndike walked to the corridor. He was pleased with himself and with his fellow men. He shook hands with Isaacs & Sons and congratulated them upon their public spirit, and the typewriter firm upon their public spirit. And then he saw Spear standing apart regarding him doubtfully.

Spear did not offer his hand, but Mr. Thorndike took it and shook it and said, "I want to meet your mother."

And when Mrs. Spear tried to stop sobbing long enough to tell him how happy she was, and how grateful, he instead told her what a fine son she had, and that he remembered when Spear used to carry flowers to town for her. And she remembered it, too, and thanked him for the flowers. And he told Spear, when Isaacs & Sons went bankrupt, which at the rate they were giving away their money to the Hebrew Hospital would be very soon, Spear must come back to him. And Isaacs & Sons were delighted at the great man's pleasantry and afterward repeated it many times, calling upon each other to bear witness, and Spear felt as though some one had given him a new backbone, and Andrews, who was guiding Thorndike out of the building, was thinking to himself what a great confidence man had been lost when Thorndike became a banker.

The chief clerk and two bank messengers were waiting by the automobile with written calls for help from the office. They pounced upon the banker and almost lifted him into the car.

"There's still time!" panted the chief clerk.

"There is not!" answered Mr. Thorndike. His tone was rebellious, defiant. It carried all the authority of a spoiled child of fortune. "I've wasted most of this day," he declared, "and I intend to waste the rest of it. Andrews," he called, "jump in, and I'll give you a lunch at Sherry's."

The vigilant protector of the public dashed back into the building.

"Wait till I get my hat!" he called.

As the two truants rolled up the avenue the spring sunshine warmed them, the sense of duties neglected added zest to their holiday, and young Mr. Andrews laughed aloud.

Mr. Thorndike raised his eyebrows inquiringly.

"I was wondering," said Andrews, "how much it cost you to keep Spear out of jail?"

"I don't care," said the great man guiltily; "it was worth it."

Doowinkle, Attorney

by:

HARRY KLINGSBERG

selected by:

ERLE STANLEY GARDNER

Harry Klingsberg's "Doowinkle, Attorney" is a story well told. But what I liked most about it is the fact that it portrays an attorney who realizes to the fullest the duty he has not only to his clients but to society; to see that justice is done.

S.S. ERLE STANLEY GARDNER

It was a minute past midnight. The dying old man in the hospital bed breathed brokenly. Bent over him in the hushed room were a staff doctor, a nurse, and Sergeant Ball, of the homicide squad. A police stenographer sat by the bed. For the past hour, during brief conscious spells, the doomed man had managed to speak; now they were waiting for Detective Kelsey, who had sped out to find the man whom James Dobey named as his attacker. They looked up as Kelsey strode in, his hand on a tall young man in his twenties. The officer brought him to the side of the bed. The young man stood frozen with horror.

Detective Kelsey said, "Here's Richard Hunt. Is this the man who stabbed you?"

James Dobey did not speak. His pain-ridden eyes rested on the young man.

From his other side Sergeant Ball repeated, "Is that the man who stabbed you?"

The old man gasped, "Yes, he stabbed me. . . . Dick, how could you? . . . You know I never meant . . . I never would . . ."

A low, shuddering sigh escaped him. His arms sank loosely. James Dobey was dead.

John Doowinkle, slight, bookish assistant district attorney, sat in his cubicle in the prosecutor's section. Like the bleak December day outside, he felt glum and discontented.

Eleven years. And still at this desk. Eleven long years of briefs, appeals, and paperwork for his colleagues. True, now and then he had gone in on small cases, and some had hit the headlines, but the fact remained that after all these years he was still the office factotum; still the desk man. He was tired of it.

The subject had come up for discussion with his wife only last night. In the manner of wives, Martha had pressed him to go to his chief, Graham, and demand that he be made a trial assistant. But John could not bring himself to ask for a promotion.

He turned to his desk with another grievance against Graham. He was lining up the proof against Richard Hunt for the murder of James Dobey; the trial was listed before Judge Rowan only ten days hence. So far Graham had assigned no one to try it, but Doowinkle was positive it would not be himself. This, though Graham knew that it was always his ambition to try a murder case. As it happened it was a simple case; there was a dying declaration and it was open and shut. Still, it was a murder case.

John rose, crossed the room, and began a pretended opening address to a jury:

"Ten years ago, when Richard Hunt was fourteen, James Dobey took him into his home. He raised him and gave him a job in his plant. His reward was murder. We will show you that on the night of November ninth, at ten o'clock, Hunt went up to see the deceased in his library. He left at ten-thirty. Fifteen minutes later Sherman, the old Negro servant, smelling smoke, hastened in and found Dobey on the floor, stabbed near the heart. Burning logs had been dragged from the fireplace to set fire to the room. We will show you that Dobey, with the solemn sense of approaching death, named Hunt as his slayer, an accusation he repeated with his last breath to Hunt's face. . . . Er—good morning, Mr. Graham. Good morning."

"Good morning," smiled Graham. "Political speech?"

"Why, no. Just—ah—practicing something."

"I see. I notice the Hunt case on your desk. Like to go in on it?" He grinned at John's face. "It shouldn't give you any trouble. . . . Oh, a Miss Kane just phoned. Lives near Dobey's house. Said she had some special information about the case. Here's her number. I told her you'd call her. By the way, I heard part of your speech. Sounded all right."

John started to call Martha. No, he wanted to see her face when he told her. This might mean a promotion if he won the case. Maybe it was a test.

He plunged into the file again. *Corpus delicti* and cause of death, clear enough. Weapon, a daggerlike paper knife which had lain on a desk in the library. No fingerprints; the killer wore gloves. To check an outcry, he had clapped a hand over Dobey's mouth—a thread of cotton glove had caught in Dobey's teeth—and after the attack he threw the gloves into the fire; the next morning the police found a section of unburned glove in front of the fireplace, pulled out with the logs. Two associated facts revealed the motive. Hunt quit his job that day without cause. Dobey, during his last hour, had kept gasping that he had not really meant to disinherit him. Seemingly, Hunt's walkout angered Dobey; he threatened, without meaning it, to change his will, whereupon Hunt killed him.

John wondered about Hunt, the inner depravity which made him do such a thing. He had never denied his guilt; he refused to plead, and a plea of not guilty had been entered for him. And yet Dobey must have been fond of him. In his final moment he was loath to name him; according to the stenographer's notes he had to be asked twice before he did so.

The rest of the file was mostly corroboration. Photographs of the library. Statement by Sherman, the old Negro who occupied the third floor of the Dobey house. Hunt's parents, it appeared, had been Dobey's friends; they died in a crash, and Dobey, himself widowed and childless, had fathered him. Data about Dobey's business. He was president-owner of the Dobey Motor Works; at sixty-six he was semiretired and the plant was run by two directors named Walter Sheffer and Paul Conger. There were two other directors: Charles and Robert Moyer,

Dobey's younger half-brothers. Hunt's job had been drawing bids and contracts. By his will, after bequests to Sherman and others, Dobey left an estate worth three hundred thousand dollars equally among Hunt and the four directors, naming Charles Moyer his executor.

John's telephone rang. "Miss Kane? . . . I was about to call you. . . . Suppose we say twelve o'clock?" He hung up, wondering what her information was. She had sounded rather eager. He really had enough evidence to go to trial tomorrow. About all he wanted was to view the murder room, the better to describe it to the jury.

He called Detective Kelsey. An hour later they were at the Dobey house. It was a solid old dwelling near the outskirts of the city, flanked by lawns. Tall trees stood back of the house. The library, on the second floor, had been sealed until the trial and Kelsey opened it with his key. Sherman, still a little dazed by the tragedy, hovered behind them.

John took in the room. Two windows, blinds down, faced the west. Dobey's body had been found in front of the southernmost window. The fireplace, a good-sized one, stood in the south wall. A heavy couch slanted diagonally from the right side of the fireplace into the room. Three or four dead logs and a heap of ashes lay scattered in the angle of the couch. The desk was against the east wall. Near it, a second door led to Dobey's bedroom.

Kelsey said, "Here's how I picture it. Dobey sat on the couch next to the fireplace——"

John remarked, "An odd arrangement for a couch. I noticed it in the photographs."

"Sherman says it used to face the fireplace, but Dobey changed it around last summer and always sat in that corner. . . . That's right, pop?"

Sherman nodded.

"And Hunt sat here. They have this quarrel. Dobey goes to the window and stands with his back to Hunt. Incidentally, he was a small man—weighed about a hundred and twenty. Hunt slips on the gloves, gets the knife, and comes up behind Dobey. He puts his left hand around him and over his mouth and holds him; with his right he reaches across and stabs him.

Dobey fights a little; the knife misses the heart; Dobey sees the face above him. Hunt drops the knife. One glove is bloody from touching the blade and he pitches both gloves in the fire. Then he has another idea. Why not burn all signs of a murder? He grabs hold of that shovel and hauls out the logs. He throws away the shovel and beats it out by that door to the hall."

John studied the hearth. Hunt's attempt to set the room ablaze had failed miserably; he had pulled the logs only two or three feet, and just the thick wool rug and the edge of the couch were charred. John wondered about the quantity of ashes. Seemingly he had stood to one side, blindly raking the hot contents of the fireplace out and away from him. Everything pointed to sudden panic and haste.

He said to Sherman, "You were in bed when you smelled the smoke?"

"Yes, sir. I beat out the logs and call the police." He shook his head. "I still can't believe young Dick do that. He love the old man—he really do."

"I understand he was out until a little before ten?"

"Yes, sir. He phone about six not to wait dinner for him. When he come home I say, 'Mr. Jim keep askin' for you.' He don't answer. He act like somethin' on his mind."

"Afraid to face Dobey after deserting his job," said Kelsey. "When the old man named him I came here to question Sherman. Hunt walked in a minute later. Probably went walking to settle his nerves, came back and saw the house hadn't burned down, and decided to play innocent. I'll say this for him—when he saw Dobey in the hospital he put on the best stunned act I ever saw. Wouldn't talk, though. The next day I found the piece of glove. A cheap pair, no doubt bought for the purpose. He'd determined if Dobey raised hell with him, he'd kill him."

John nodded. It was a clear first-degree case and he meant to say so to the jury.

He found Miss Kane waiting in his office. Her dark, troubled eyes searched John. He had the thought that she was measuring him to put something over on him. She said rapidly, "I'm Ruth Kane. I suppose I should have gone to the police, but

I decided to wait and speak to the prosecutor himself. You see, I saw it happen."

"Really? The actual murder?"

"Yes. You see, I live near the house, and that night I walked by and saw Mr. Dobey at the window. Then I saw a man come behind him and—and stab him. I recognized him. It was Richard Hunt. I saw it quite distinctly. That's good evidence, isn't it?"

"Perfect," agreed John. "Except that the blinds were down at the time and you couldn't possibly have seen it. I'm sorry."

He thought she was going to cry. He watched her go out. There were often these spotlight thirsters in murder cases. Too bad; it seemed even pretty girls could suffer from neuroses.

That night, after dinner, he told Martha about the case. Her manner disconcerted him—she was neither surprised nor enthusiastic. "Incidentally, a young girl tried to tell me she saw the murder." He told her about Miss Kane. "A good thing I noticed the blinds."

Martha said, "She was here. I told her to come back tonight."

When Ruth arrived Martha said dryly, "I think you two have met. . . . Don't be afraid of him. Tell him why you did it."

Ruth burst out, "I wanted you to put me on the stand so I could ruin your case for you, and Dick would be acquitted. He didn't do it. He's innocent!"

John was silent. She said, calmer now, "He was going to his draft board the next day and ask to be inducted. He wanted to do it months ago, but Mr. Dobey wouldn't let him. He was a lonely old man and, well, a little selfish, and Dick was all he had. He had Dick deferred twice because the plant did war work, and Dick hated that. Finally he decided if he quit they'd have to put him in the Army and Mr. Dobey would be proud. We spent the evening together and he went home to tell him. Then he came back. He was all upset. He said Uncle Jim—that's what he called him—was very angry, even said he would disinherit him if he went. Dick knew he didn't mean it, but even if he did—He didn't kill him. He loved Mr. Dobey! Next day, in jail, he said I must never see him again or speak to the police—if I did he would plead guilty. I said

I'd send him a lawyer. He refused. Finally he said all right, but he wouldn't have anything to say to him. I couldn't understand why he acted like that. Later I remembered——"

She hesitated. "I suppose you won't believe me. About twenty minutes after Dick came back the phone rang. He was near it and answered it. He said, 'Yes, it's me.' Then he said, 'Shut up or she what? Who are you?' He hung up and said, 'Some nut thinks he's funny.'" Ruth paused. "Don't you see? That man ordered him to shut up with a threat to me. When Dick saw Mr. Dobey in the hospital he understood what he meant. That's why he won't defend himself. How do they know he's guilty? Nobody saw him do it."

"That's not so. Mr. Dobey saw him. Do you realize he named him?"

"Couldn't he be wrong? Couldn't he have thought it was Dick?"

"I don't see how. He said you could get him a lawyer. Why don't you?"

"I saw two lawyers. They said in the face of Mr. Dobey's statement the best they could hope for was a life sentence. Then I thought up my scheme. I see now how wild it was. After I left you I decided to speak to you again. I looked up where you lived. I'm not afraid of the threat. Even if Dick says he's guilty you mustn't believe him. You mustn't!"

When she had gone, John turned to Martha.

"And by what intuition did it dawn on you that her boy friend is innocent?"

She said, "Maybe I'm not so anxious to send somebody to the chair."

"But Martha, be reasonable. If Hunt didn't stab him, somebody did right after he left. Dobey would certainly have heard him go out of the room——"

"What's the matter?"

"I—I just got a different picture of the murder."

She smiled. "I hoped you would. I told her to come back tomorrow night."

In the morning John telephoned Detective Kelsey. "I'd like to ask you about Dobey's last statement. After you came back with Hunt, which side of his bed did you go to? . . . Was Sergeant Ball on the other side? . . . I see. Thank you."

He hung up. So Dobey could have been wrong, after all. Other signs led away from Hunt. Old Sherman still couldn't believe he did it. And his manner in the hospital. Maybe his stunned act was genuine. A man who stood ready to abandon his inheritance to join the armed service would hardly commit murder for it.

His silence wasn't so fantastic as it sounded. Shaken by Dobey's death, unnerved by his accusation, the threat had worked on his mind and all he could think of was Ruth's safety.

But if Hunt didn't kill Dobey, who did? John went through the file again. With the powerful case against Hunt, the questioning of the four inheriting directors had been only routine. Sheffer said that on the night of the murder he worked at the plant until ten and drove to his home in the suburbs, stopping at a diner for a sandwich. Charles Moyer saw a picture at the Strand, a neighborhood house. Robert Moyer was home alone. These two men were bachelors and lived together ten blocks from Dobey. Nor was Conger's alibi better. He said he was home with his wife, which might simply mean he could get her to swear to it.

John picked up the file and walked to Graham's office.

He began, "About this Hunt case. I'm not sure he's guilty. You see, I think Dobey was partly deaf. When Kelsey brought Hunt to the hospital he came to Dobey's right side and asked him to identify Hunt as the man who stabbed him. Dobey didn't answer."

"Maybe he hated to do it."

"But he'd already named him, and when Ball, who was on his other side, spoke to him, he answered at once. Also, he fixed his couch so that when he sat in his usual place his right—or bad side—would be away from the room."

"All right. Dobey was deaf in his right ear. So?"

"Well, when Dobey went to the window he turned his deaf side to the room. He may not have heard Hunt go out. The real killer could have come from the bedroom. In putting his hand over Dobey's mouth he may have covered his eyes and shut off his vision. Dobey, having just quarreled with Hunt, and thinking he was still in the room——"

"Nonsense. Dobey named him. He must have seen him."

"He didn't say so," argued John. "Dying declarations can be wrong. They're not sacred."

"They still beat theory. How did the killer get in?"

"Well, I noticed the house has a rear entrance and back stairs. If you look at this photograph, there's a set of keys on Dobey's desk. People keep keys in pockets or drawers. The murderer may have stolen them on a visit to Dobey and dropped them on the desk before grabbing the knife. Dobey probably didn't go out much and wouldn't have missed them."

Graham snorted, "He could have this—he may have that. I never heard so much guesswork. If Hunt didn't do it, why doesn't he say so?"

He listened impatiently. "Protecting his girl, eh? Haven't heard that one for years. Quitting to get drafted is a good touch too. Anything else?"

"Well, I was thinking of the fireplace. If the idea was to burn down the house, why weren't the logs pushed farther into the room? Why wasn't something set on fire? Why all the ashes? You can't start a fire with those."

"He bungled the job. Well, now you've acquitted Hunt. Got anybody to convict?"

John reddened. "Each of those directors had a motive for killing Dobey. They all inherited sixty thousand dollars from him, and if Hunt is convicted they'll divide his share. If you examine their alibis, any of them might have done it."

"Except that Dobey didn't name them. I'm sorry, John. I'm not convinced at all. But if that's the way you feel you'd better leave the case with me. I'll try it myself."

That night John told Ruth what happened. "You must get Dick a lawyer at once."

Martha said, "She spoke to two lawyers. You heard what they said."

"There are other lawyers. . . . Now, Martha, don't look at me like that. You know I never handled a case like this. Besides, I'd have to resign——"

"Is that what worries you? Don't you think you'll get along?

I want you to resign. It would show Graham. Who'll defend that boy if you don't?"

Ruth stood in front of him. "Won't you do it? Won't you?"

"He's stubborn," said Martha. "Give him time."

An hour later, when Ruth had left, John sat grimly. He had agreed to resign to defend a man he never met; a man who wouldn't cooperate. And against Graham himself. He had just eight days to do it. He certainly hadn't foreseen anything like this yesterday.

"Well," he told himself, "I wanted to try a murder case!"

Graham said gravely, "It's perfectly all right, John. See you in court."

John took the bus to the county prison. His first thrill of fighting for a man's life faded as he sized up the odds against him. Denial and oratory would never win this case. He would have to find the real murderer and produce him to the jury.

The prisoner was brought in. John introduced himself, explaining that Ruth had sent him. Hunt's eyes flickered faintly.

"I've nothing to say, now or on the stand. If you put me on I'll say I did it."

"I understand. Will you tell me this? Was Mr. Dobey partly deaf?"

"I don't know. Lately he acted like it. Why?"

"Haven't you ever wondered why he accused you?" He explained, watching the relief in the other's eyes. He had evidently been torn by the thought that Dobey named him deliberately. "One more thing. That phone call. Was the voice disguised? What did he say?"

"Oh. Did she remember that? He said, 'Shut up or she goes too.' Maybe it was disguised. I know one thing. It wasn't Paul Conger—" He jumped up. "I said enough!"

"Dick," John spoke soothingly, "you can say anything you want. Can't you see his threat was just a bluff? Harming Ruth wouldn't do him any good."

"No? If I talk she'll have to take the stand, won't she? He'd want to stop that, wouldn't he? Besides, you can't help me. Nobody can. Uncle Jim said it was me. What jury would take my word against that?"

"I thought it wiser not to argue with him," John told Martha. "He must know Conger well enough to feel he'd have recognized his voice. It shows he suspects the directors."

Martha said, "And so do you."

"Who else would know his way in the house? Or where to phone Dick? Whichever one it was, he must have been greedy for money or he'd have waited until Dobey died. And since the estate can't be settled for months, you'll find he's already pledged or sold his legacy."

He went on. "Coming back to the murder, it gives every appearance of being timed to throw suspicion on Dick. Yet he couldn't have foreseen that Dick would be with Dobey. I think he meant to kill Dobey in his bedroom, maybe by strangling him, but seized the opportunity to pin it on Dick. It would put another fifteen thousand dollars in his pocket. But I can't understand why he took the chance to phone Dick. He'd left Dobey for dead. Dick would be blamed. Everything was fine. As a director his voice couldn't have been unknown to Dick. True, Dick didn't recognize it, but he might have. Why did he take the risk?"

"Maybe everything wasn't so fine."

John nodded. "That could be it. Maybe he made a damaging slip and he was afraid the police would discover it. Risk or no risk, if he could silence Dick the case would end with him. Something else keeps bothering me. What happened at the fireplace? They say it was a bungled attempt to burn down the house. But would even a bungler keep raking ashes after the logs, especially when he was in a hurry? That has a meaning of its own. The only other answer is that he was searching for something. But what? I can't figure it out."

The next day John hired a detective agency and began a probe of the directors. The business, he found, had incorporated rather recently—June, 1940. Sheffer, now president, had been with Dobey thirty years. Conger, in charge of production, had been with him nineteen years. The two Moyers were in their early fifties. They were not active in the company, coming only to board meetings. Charles, the older, had a tire business up to early 1940; Robert worked for him. Ruth added her own impressions; she met them all at a party in the plant.

Sheffer was abrupt, Conger retiring. Of the two Moyers she recalled Charles best, an affable man. Robert struck her as surly. Conger and Dick, she told John, worked together a lot in the plant. It all didn't add up to much.

John was pleased at the change in Ruth. Just helping with the case made her more cheerful. Thinking of her safety, John urged her to hire a bodyguard. She flatly refused. Martha had a suggestion: she move in with them until the trial.

One night they all went to the Dobey house. To the surprised Sherman, John explained his new stature in the case. "Was Mr. Dobey hard of hearing?"

Sherman said thoughtfully, "Could be he was. Could be."

They stood in Dobey's bedroom. *Here,* John thought, *the killer waited for his victim; here he escaped later.* The room opened to the center hall. They went down the rear stairs to the lawn behind the house. It sloped to a narrow dark street. He always, Sherman said, locked the back door at night. Three people had keys: himself, Dick, and Dobey.

"But Mr. Jim never use them. I say to the police, 'This is funny. He always keep these keys inside the desk. Now they on top.' They think he put them there."

John nodded. That much of his guesswork was right. "Who visited him?"

"Mostly Mr. Sheffer to talk business with him, on account Mr. Jim stop going to the plant. His brothers come once a week, except the time lately when Mr. Charles have the flu." His voice faltered. "A paper come today. Do I have to go on that stand against that boy? I never believe he do it." John saw tears spring to Ruth's eyes.

"It wasn't Conger," said John on their way home. "He didn't visit Dobey, and Dick was sure it wasn't his voice. We'll find out who it was."

But as the trial neared, his confidence fell. He looked up gloomily one evening from the reports of the detective agency. "There's nothing to single out any of them, no signs of sudden wealth or special use of money lately. I saw Charles Moyer today and asked him to show me his records as executor of the estate. He said he had no right to do that without a court order. But even if one of them did cash his legacy, how will I prove that he killed Dobey?"

He paced the room. "I've nothing to seize on. I still can't grasp everything that happened in that library. Why did he search the fireplace? Look. He stabs Dobey. He throws them in the fire—" John stood.

"Well!" he exclaimed. "It took me long enough!"

District Attorney Graham dismissed his last witness. "Commonwealth rests."

The courtroom stirred slightly. The reporters looked bored. Yesterday, when the trial opened, they had headlined that counsel for the accused would be a former prosecutor, who had resigned to defend him, but he had simply sat for two days and let the proof pile over his client. They watched Doowinkle as he rose. Did he have anything?

John glanced at Dick Hunt. He had come in with his head up, even smiling at Ruth in a front row with Martha, and he had shown life when two directors took the stand against him: Sheffer that he quit his job, Charles Moyer to explain Dobey's will. Both times he had stiffened angrily. But Dobey's last statement, used by Graham as his final gun, had plunged him into blackness again.

"Members of the jury, dying declarations, like all human actions, are subject to error. This defendant did not murder James Dobey. Before this trial is over, I hope to show you the man who did."

Graham objected, "Why not now? Why prolong the case?"

Judge Rowan said briefly, "We will rule on the testimony as it is offered. Proceed."

John called, "Daniel Sherman."

The old Negro walked slowly to the stand.

"Mr. Sherman, you told us you have known the defendant for ten years. During that time how did he behave to the deceased?"

"Always kind and affectionate. I never believe that boy lift a finger to him."

"Objection! I move that be stricken out."

"Strike it out. . . . No opinions, please. Simply answer the questions."

John examined the witness, expanding on his previous testimony for the Commonwealth. He and Dobey were alone in the house that night, Sherman said; the cook always left at eight. Dobey usually went to bed at eleven. Over Graham's objection, he described the house: the rear entrance and back stairs. John brought out the changed position of Dobey's keys.

"Now, Mr. Sherman, was there much of a blaze when you entered the library?"

"No, sir. The logs almost die out. More smoke than flame in that room."

"What time did you make the fire that night?"

"About eight o'clock. A little before ten Mr. Jim ask me to build it up again, on account he wait for Dick. I make a good roaring fire—he like it that way."

"And when was the last time you cleaned the fireplace?"

Judge Rowan asked doubtfully, "Is that material?"

"Very. . . . Do you remember?"

"Let me see. This was Monday night. . . . I clean out that fireplace on Saturday."

Between then and the murder, Sherman went on to testify, nobody visited Dobey; and since then the room had been locked to all but the police. John said, "Cross-examine."

"No questions."

"I call Walter Sheffer." The new company head strode to the box. Spectators, remembering John's opening statement, watched intently.

"You telephoned Dobey the night he died and told him that Dick had left his job?"

"It wasn't why I called. He happened to mention that Dick hadn't come home. I said, 'He's probably thinking up a story. He quit and gave me no reason.' "

"Perhaps he felt he owed his first explanation to Mr. Dobey?"

"Perhaps. He made none to me."

Had Dobey, John asked, ever complained to him about Dick? . . . He had not, Sheffer said. Actually they treated each other with affection? . . . It seemed so. What was Dick's manner at the plant? . . . Quiet; not quarrelsome.

Over repeated objections, John drew some facts about the business. Why had Dobey incorporated it? He felt old, Sheffer said, and wanted to make sure it would go on. And, John suggested, to provide for his brothers? That might have been part of it. The Moyers were paid just for coming to the meetings? Yes; fifty dollars each, weekly.

"Did you and the other directors know you would inherit equally from Dobey?"

"We did. He told us so."

"That's all. Cross-examine."

Graham said dryly, "Apparently this wasn't the culprit. No questions."

"I call Robert Moyer."

Curious eyes followed the younger half-brother to the stand. John studied him as he took the oath. Ruth had judged him correctly: he was jowly and sullen. The witness, openly perturbed, said he was fifty-one, two years younger than Charles. They visited Dobey on Thursday night before he died and listened to a round-table program in the living room.

"Did either you or Charles go up stairs alone during the evening?"

"Do you expect me to remember that? Maybe we did."

"Did you know Dobey kept a set of keys in his desk?"

The witness bristled up. "I went there to see him, not to spy in his desk."

"By the way, I understand Charles had an attack of flu recently?"

"It was the beginning of October. He was in bed a couple of weeks."

"I will now ask what you did the night of the murder. . . . Why are you nervous?"

"I'm not nervous. I listened to the radio. After the eleven-o'clock news I went up to bed. A few minutes later I heard Charles come in."

John looked at him a moment. "That's all. Cross-examine."

"No questions." Graham remarked, "The great disclosure has yet to come."

John wheeled, "I call Charles Moyer."

Something in his tone sent a current through the court. Even

Dick felt it. He sat up and stared at John. Charles Moyer, amid whispers, moved to the stand. He was taller than Robert; quick-eyed, assured. He smiled genially as he sat down. The court waited.

"Mr. Moyer, do you wish me to inform you of your constitutional rights?"

Moyer's eyes tightened a little. "You needn't bother. I know them."

"Then I will ask you: Did you kill James Dobey?"

"I will answer you. I did not."

John addressed the bench. "Your honor, I plead surprise at his answer and ask leave to cross-examine him."

The courtroom stilled. The witness' smile gradually froze.

Graham shot up. "I object! This man was my witness and I am responsible for his integrity. Is he charging him with the crime? If so, let's have the proof."

Judge Rowan turned to John. "You expected him to say he killed him?"

"I did. Since he chose to speak, I assumed he had decided to confess. As he has not done so, I do not wish to be bound by his testimony. I renew my request."

"I oppose it! It is a common device in capital cases to throw dust in the eyes of the jury by reckless charges against innocent people. It is for your honor's discretion."

The jurist said slowly, "My discretion is more fancied than real. He was asked if he committed the crime. His denial being adverse to the accused, he becomes, by close definition, a hostile witness. I am obliged to grant the request."

John stepped toward the stand. "Mr. Moyer, what did you do the night of the murder?"

"The police know what I did. I saw a picture at the Strand. And I can prove it. It was a detective mystery called *The Red Shadow*. A café owner named Lawton was killed." He described the story in detail. "Are you satisfied?"

"Why didn't you volunteer the plot to the police? Because you didn't know it then?"

"Not at all. They didn't ask for it."

"And you realized if they had asked for it you'd have been

sunk, so you repaired your alibi by seeing the picture later in another theater?"

"I tell you I saw it that night. The owner will vouch that I went in. I spoke to him."

"Will he vouch that you remained until the end of the show?"

"How can he? He didn't sit with me and I assume he didn't watch me."

"I spoke to him also and they let out that night at eleven. According to Robert, you got home about eleven-twenty. Did it take you twenty minutes to walk five blocks?"

"Well, I stopped in the drugstore for a soda."

"But you told the police you came straight home from the theater. Why do you introduce the drugstore now—to account for those twenty minutes? By the way, are you fond of detective pictures—is that where you picked up the expression, 'Shut up or she goes next'?"

The witness eyed him. "I don't know what you're talking about."

"Mr. Moyer, I suggest that you did stop in a drugstore to phone this defendant——"

"I deny that. I told you what I did."

"And delayed your return home until Robert went to bed because you had just committed a murder and your nerves might betray you. Is that true?"

"It's false! Absolutely false!"

John paused to look at him. His confident mask still held, but the strain of his secret had begun to crack it a little. His eyes darted hatred at John.

"Mr. Moyer, did you steal Dobey's keys on the Thursday night visit, or before?"

"I never stole them. I didn't know where he kept them."

"Let us see what you did know. Of course you knew the house—by using the rear entrance and stairs you could get to Dobey's bedroom?"

"No. I paid no attention to the house."

"And that he and Sherman went to bed early? And that the defendant usually went out in the evening, and where a telephone call would find him?"

"I did not. I hadn't the least interest in the defendant."

"Perhaps you feel Mr. Dobey shouldn't have made a ward of him? Speaking of Mr. Dobey, what was your attitude to him? Were you grateful to him for taking care of you?"

Moyer sneered, "Nobody has to take care of me. If you mean the directorship, that was just temporary."

"You have other plans for yourself? Why did you give up your tire business?"

"Because I foresaw the rubber shortage. I paid off my creditors and got out."

"You foresaw it in April, 1940, two years before it happened? Would it interest you to know that I spoke to Dobey's bankers and they told me he put up the money for your creditors because you were insolvent? And that he did this at least twice before?"

Moyer scowled. "What if he did? I happened to be unlucky."

"Meaning he was luckier in making his fortune and you hated him for it?"

Graham said, "Don't answer that. . . . Your Honor, I feel the time has come to intervene. He has hurled all sorts of charges at this man, but he has proved nothing except a trifling discrepancy in his statement to the police."

Judge Rowan nodded. "Mr. Doowinkle, have you any other questions aside from his actions on the night of the murder?"

"I have. He is the executor of Dobey's will. He did not employ counsel. He refused to let me see his records. I subpoenaed them and wish to know if they are here. I want to know if he raised money by pledging his legacy."

"Objection! Incompetent and irrelevant."

"If your honor please, my purpose is to indicate a motive for the murder."

"I understand your purpose. Suppose he did borrow on his legacy? Many people do so without having murdered the testator. Your status here is to defend the accused. I will not allow you to do so by unsupported innuendo against others. You may have an exception."

A slow hush settled over the court. The reporters watched John. On the stand the witness smiled easily again.

"Mr. Moyer, what did you wear that night?"

"Do you want an inventory? Hat, suit, shoes——"

"I am interested in gloves—cotton gloves which would leave no prints on doors or furniture and could easily be destroyed. Did you wear those?"

"No. I wore no gloves."

John stood before him. "I notice a sapphire ring on your left hand in a gold setting. May I see it? Take it off, please. . . . Did you wear this?"

The witness jolted with sudden fright. He gripped his chair.

"Please answer my question. Did you wear this ring?"

"Yes. I've worn it for years." He was white.

John said slowly, "Here is your ring. . . . Mr. Moyer, my guess is that you left the theater a little after ten. You walked to the Dobey house, a matter of seven or eight minutes, and stood behind the house until lights on the third floor indicated that Sherman was in his room. You let yourself in with keys stolen from the deceased——"

"No! It's a lie!" He jumped tremblingly to his feet.

"You waited, murder in your heart, in Dobey's bedroom. You overheard his scene with Dick Hunt. You conceived the idea of branding Dick with the crime. Dick left and you went in." John pointed to the exhibit table. "You seized that knife. You stabbed Dobey. You dropped the knife. One glove was bloody and you threw both gloves in the fire——"

"More lies! Your Honor, I appeal for protection!"

Judge Rowan spoke to John. "I cannot stop you from pursuing this line. I will simply point out your responsibility as an officer of the court. You wish to proceed?"

"I do, sir. . . . You threw them in the fire, but your recent illness had made you lose weight and your ring came off in the glove and went into the flame. You pulled the fire apart in a desperate attempt to recover your ring. You failed. The room filled with smoke. You feared Sherman would enter, and escaped the way you came. Is that true?"

"All lies! You will answer for this!"

John said quietly, "There is a way to find out. . . . Your Honor, I ask an adjournment to permit the district attorney to have the fireplace searched."

"I protest! You'll find nothing!" Charles Moyer reeled slowly. John turned from him. "You'll be home tonight, Dick."

"John, you saved that boy and I bow to you." Graham eyed the blackened ring in his hand. The gold band had melted to a nugget, but the stone was intact. "I see how you guessed about the ring. He was obviously looking for something he missed after throwing in his gloves, and about the only thing that could have gone in with them was his ring. Of course he bought another like it to avoid questions. What made you go after Charles? Because he'd been sick and you figured he lost weight?"

John nodded. "Things began to point to him. He was the only director who wore a ring. He was plainly covering up something about the estate. What worried me was whether he found the ring. I felt he hadn't or he wouldn't have phoned Dick, and when I saw the one he had on I was sure of it. It didn't look as if he'd worn it for years."

Sergeant Ball walked in. "We found these papers in his room."

"Let's have them. . . . You were right. He pawned his legacy with loan sharks for thirty thousand dollars. . . . H'm. Been trying to get rich quick out of the war. Started a bootleg tire ring. That's why he wanted money in a hurry. That's all, sergeant. . . . John, you can come back as trial assistant if you want to. Do you want to?"

"Well, I'd like to think it over—discuss it at home——"

"You mean you had a taste of independence and liked it. Well, I'll help you by withdrawing the offer. I'm thinking of those two kids when they realized he was free. The lawyer's true place is in front of the railing, guarding the weak and correcting the prosecutor's mistakes." He grinned. "John Doowinkle, attorney-at-law. See you in court!"

Coroner's Inquest

by:

MARC CONNELLY

selected by:

OSCAR HAMMERSTEIN, 2d

There will probably never be a coroner's inquest like this one. And if there is, the report to the legal profession will not be graced with the pen of a Marc Connelly. The story is an O. Henry award winner and worthy of O. Henry at his best.

S.S. OSCAR HAMMERSTEIN, 2d

"What is your name?"

"Frank Wineguard."

"Where do you live?"

"A hundred and eighty-five West Fifty-fifth Street."

"What is your business?"

"I'm stage manager for *Hello, America*."

"You were the employer of James Dawle?"

"In a way. We both worked for Mr. Bender, the producer, but I have charge backstage."

"Did you know Theodore Robel?"

"Yes, sir."

"Was he in your company, too?"

"No, sir. I met him when we started rehearsals. That was about three months ago, in June. We sent out a call for midgets and he and Jimmy showed up together, with a lot of others. Robel was too big for us. I didn't see him again until we broke into their room Tuesday."

"You discovered their bodies?"

"Yes, sir. Mrs. Pike, there, was with me."

"You found them both dead?"

"Yes, sir."

"How did you happen to be over in Jersey City?"

"Well, I'd called up his house at curtain time Monday night when I found Jimmy hadn't shown up for the performance. Mrs. Pike told me they were both out, and I asked her to have either Jimmy or Robel call me when they came in. Then Mrs. Pike called me Tuesday morning and said she tried to get into the room but she'd found the door was bolted. She said all her other roomers were out and she was alone and scared.

"I'd kind of suspected something might be wrong. So I said to wait and I'd come over. Then I took the tube over and got there about noon. Then we went up and I broke down the door."

"Did you see this knife there?"

"Yes, sir. It was on the floor, about a foot from Jimmy."

"You say you suspected something was wrong. What do you mean by that?"

"I mean I felt something might have happened to Jimmy. Nothing like this, of course. But I knew he'd been feeling very depressed lately, and I knew Robel wasn't helping to cheer him up any."

"You mean they had had quarrels?"

"No, sir. They just both had the blues, Robel had had them for a long time. Robel was Jimmy's brother-in-law. He'd married Jimmy's sister—she was a midget, too—about five years ago, but she died a year or so later. Jimmy had been living with them and after the sister died he and Robel took a room in Mrs. Pike's house together."

"How did you learn this?"

"Jimmy and I were pretty friendly at the theater. He was a nice little fellow and seemed grateful that I'd given him his job. We'd only needed one midget for an Oriental scene in the second act and the agencies had sent about fifteen. Mr. Gehring, the director, told me to pick one of them as he was busy and I picked Jimmy because he was the littlest.

"After I got to know him he told me how glad he was I'd given him the job. He hadn't worked for nearly a year. He wasn't little enough to be a featured midget with circuses or in museums so he had to take whatever came along. Anyway, we got to be friendly and he used to tell me about his brother-in-law and all."

"He never suggested that there might be ill feeling between him and his brother-in-law?"

"No, sir. I don't imagine he'd ever had any words at all with Robel. As a matter of fact from what I could gather I guess Jimmy had quite a lot of affection for him and he certainly did everything he could to help him. Robel was a lot worse off than Jimmy. Robel hadn't worked for a couple of years and Jimmy practically supported him. He used to tell me how Robel had been sunk ever since he got his late growth."

"His what?"

"His late growth. I heard it happens among midgets often, but Jimmy told me about it first. Usually a midget will stay as long as he lives at whatever height he reaches when he's fourteen or fifteen, but every now and then one of them starts growing again just before he's thirty, and he can grow a foot or even more in a couple of years. Then he stops growing for good. But of course he don't look so much like a midget any more.

"That's what had happened to Robel about three years ago. Of course he had trouble getting jobs and it hit him pretty hard.

"From what Jimmy told me and from what Mrs. Pike says, I guess he used to talk about it all the time. Robel used to come over and see his agent in New York twice a week, but there was never anything for him. Then he'd go back to Jersey City. Most of the week he lived alone because after the show started Jimmy often stayed in New York with a cousin or somebody that lived uptown.

"Lately Robel hadn't been coming over to New York at all. But every Saturday night Jimmy would go over to Jersey City and stay till Monday with him, trying to cheer him up. Every Sunday they'd take a walk and go to a movie. I guess as they walked along the street Robel realized most the difference in their heights. And I guess that's really why they're both dead now."

"How do you mean?"

"Well, as I told you, Jimmy would try to sympathize with Robel and cheer him up. He and Robel both realized that Jimmy was working and supporting them and that Jimmy would probably keep right on working, according to the ordinary breaks of the game, while Robel would always be too big. It simply preyed on Robel's mind.

"And then three weeks ago Monday Jimmy thought he saw the ax fall.

"I was standing outside the stage door—it was about seven-thirty—and Jimmy came down the alley. He looked down in the mouth, which I thought was strange seeing that he usually used to come in swinging his little cane and looking pretty cheerful. I said, 'How are you feeling, Jimmy?' and he said, 'I don't feel so good, Mr. Wineguard.' So I said, 'Why, what's the matter, Jimmy?' I could see there really was something the matter with him by this time."

" 'I'm getting scared,' he said, and I says, 'Why?'

" 'I'm starting to grow again,' he says. He said it the way you'd say you found out you had some disease that was going to kill you in a week. He looked like he was shivering.

" 'Why, you're crazy, Jimmy,' I says. 'You ain't growing.'

" 'Yes, I am,' he says. 'I'm thirty-one and it's that late growth like my brother-in-law has. My father had it, but his people had money, so it didn't make much difference to him. It's different with me, I've got to keep working.'

"He went on like that for a while and then I tried to kid him out of it.

" 'You look all right to me,' I said. 'How tall have you been all along?'

" 'Thirty-seven inches,' he says. So I says, 'Come on into the prop room and I'll measure you.'

"He backed away from me. 'No,' he says, 'I don't want to know how much it is.' Then he went up to the dressing room before I could argue with him.

"All week he looked awful sunk. When he showed up the next Monday evening he looked almost white.

"I grabbed him as he was starting upstairs to make up.

" 'Come on out of it,' I says. I thought he'd make a break and try to get away from me, but he didn't. He just sort of smiled as if I didn't understand. Finally he says, 'It ain't any use, Mr. Wineguard.'

" 'Listen,' I says, 'you've been over with that brother-in-law of yours, haven't you?' He said yes, he had. 'Well,' I says, 'that's what's bothering you. From what you tell me about him he's talked about his own tough luck so much that he's given you the willies, too. Stay away from him the end of this week.'

"He stood there for a second without saying anything. Then he says, 'That wouldn't do any good. He's all alone over there and he needs company. Anyway, it's all up with me, I guess. I've grown nearly two inches already.'

"I looked at him. He was pretty pathetic, but outside of that there wasn't any change in him as far as I could see.

"I says, 'Have you been measured?' He said he hadn't. Then I said, "Then how do you know? Your clothes fit you all right, except your pants, and as a matter of fact they seem a little longer."

" 'I fixed my suspenders and let them down a lot farther,' he says. 'Besides they were always a little big for me.'

" 'Let's make sure,' I says. 'I'll get a yardstick and we'll make absolutely sure.'

"But I guess he was too scared to face things. He wouldn't do it.

"He managed to dodge me all week. Then, last Saturday night, I ran into him as I was leaving the theater. I asked him if he felt any better.

" 'I feel all right,' he says. He really looked scared to death.

" 'That's the last time I saw him before I went over to Jersey City after Mrs. Pike phoned me Tuesday morning."

"Patrolman Gorlitz has testified that the bodies were in opposite ends of the room when he arrived. They were in that position when you forced open the door?"

"Yes, sir."

"The medical examiner has testified that they were both dead of knife wounds, apparently from the same knife. Would you assume the knife had fallen from Dawle's hand as he fell?"

"Yes, sir."

"Has it been your purpose to suggest that both men were driven to despondency by a fear of lack of employment for Dawle, and that they might have committed suicide?"

"No, sir. I don't think anything of the kind."

"What do you mean?"

"Well, when Mrs. Pike and I went in the room and I got a look at the knife, I said to Mrs. Pike that that was a funny kind of a knife for them to have in the room. You can see it's a kind of a butcher knife. Then Mrs. Pike told me it was one that she's missed from her kitchen a few weeks before. She'd never thought either Robel or Jimmy had taken it. It struck me as funny Robel or Jimmy had stolen it, too. Then I put two and two together and found out what really happened. Have you got the little broken cane that was lying on the bed?"

"Is this it?"

"Yes, sir. Well, I'd never been convinced by Jimmy that he was really growing. So when Mrs. Pike told me about the knife I started figuring. I figured that about five minutes before that knife came into play Jimmy must have found it, probably by accident."

"Why by accident?"

"Because Robel had gone a little crazy, I guess. He'd stolen it and kept it hidden from Jimmy. And when Jimmy found it he wondered what Robel had been doing with it. Then Robel wouldn't tell him and Jimmy found out for himself. Or maybe Robel did tell him. Anyway, Jimmy looked at the cane. It was the one he always carried. He saw where, when Jimmy wasn't looking, Robel had been cutting little pieces off the end of it."

The Devil and Daniel Webster

by:

STEPHEN VINCENT BENÉT

selected by:

ELMER RICE

Certainly a classic of our time—and a story much enjoyed—is Stephen Vincent Benét's "The Devil and Daniel Webster." It has been made into a movie and has been presented over the radio and on television, but it is still best as a great short story—a great lawyer short story.

ELMER RICE

S.S.____

It's a story they tell in the border country, where Massachusetts joins Vermont and New Hampshire.

Yes, Dan'l Webster's dead—or, at least, they buried him. But every time there's a thunderstorm around Marshfield, they say you can hear his rolling voice in the hollows of the sky. And they say that if you go to his grave and speak loud and clear, "Dan'l Webster—Dan'l Webster!" the ground'll begin to shiver and the trees begin to shake. And after a while you'll hear a deep voice saying, "Neighbor, how stands the Union?" Then you better answer the Union stands as she stood, rock-bottomed and copper-sheathed, one and indivisible, or he's liable to rear right out of the ground. At least, that's what I was told when I was a youngster.

You see, for a while, he was the biggest man in the country. He never got to be president, but he was the biggest man. There were thousands that trusted in him right next to God Almighty, and they told stories about him that were like the stories of patriarchs and such. They said, when he stood up to speak, stars and stripes came right out in the sky, and once he spoke against a river and made it sink into the ground. They said, when he walked the woods with his fishing rod, Killall, the trout would jump out of the streams right into his pockets, for they knew it was no use putting up a fight against him; and, when he argued a case, he could turn on the harps of the blessed and the shaking of the earth underground. That was the kind of man he was, and his big farm up at Marshfield was suitable to him. The chickens he raised were all white meat down through the drumsticks, the cows were tended like children, and the big ram he called Goliath had horns with a curl like a morning-glory vine and could butt through an iron door. But Dan'l wasn't one of your gentlemen farmers; he knew all the ways of the land, and he'd be up by candlelight to see that the chores got done. A man with a mouth like a mastiff, a brow like a mountain, and eyes like burning anthracite—that was Dan'l Webster in his prime. And the biggest case he argued never got written down in the books, for he argued it against the devil, nip and tuck and no holds barred. And this is the way I used to hear it told.

There was a man named Jabez Stone, lived at Cross Corners, New Hampshire. He wasn't a bad man to start with, but he was an unlucky man. If he planted corn, he got borers; if he planted potatoes, he got blight. He had good-enough land, but it didn't prosper him; he had a decent wife and children, but the more children he had, the less there was to feed them. If stones cropped up in his neighbor's field, boulders boiled up in his; if he had a horse with the spavins, he'd trade it for one with the staggers and give something extra. There's some folks bound to be like that, apparently. But one day Jabez Stone got sick of the whole business.

"He'd been plowing that morning and he'd just broke the plowshare on a rock that he could have sworn hadn't been there yesterday. And, as he stood looking at the plowshare, the off horse began to cough—that ropy kind of cough that means sickness and horse doctors. There were two children down with the measles, his wife was ailing, and he had a whitlow on his thumb. It was about the last straw for Jabez Stone. "I vow," he said, and he looked around him kind of desperate—"I vow it's enough to make a man want to sell his soul to the devil! And I would, too, for two cents!"

Then he felt a kind of queerness come over him at having said what he'd said; though, naturally, being a New Hampshireman, he wouldn't take it back. But, all the same, when it got to be evening and, as far as he could see, no notice had been taken, he felt relieved in his mind, for he was a religious man. But notice is always taken, sooner or later, just like the Good Book says. And, sure enough, next day, about suppertime, a soft-spoken, dark-dressed stranger drove up in a handsome buggy and asked for Jabez Stone.

Well, Jabez told his family it was a lawyer, come to see him about a legacy. But he knew who it was. He didn't like the looks of the stranger, nor the way he smiled with his teeth. They were white teeth, and plentiful—some say they were filed to a point, but I wouldn't vouch for that. And he didn't like it when the dog took one look at the stranger and ran away howling, with his tail between his legs. But having passed his word, more or less, he stuck to it, and they went out behind the barn and made their bargain. Jabez Stone had to prick his finger to sign, and the stranger lent him a silver pin. The wound healed clean, but it left a little white scar.

After that, all of a sudden, things began to pick up and prosper for Jabez Stone. His cows got fat and his horses sleek, his crops were the envy of the neighborhood, and lightning might strike all over the valley, but it wouldn't strike his barn. Pretty soon, he was one of the prosperous people of the county; they asked him to stand for selectman, and he stood for it; there began to be talk of running him for state senate. All in all, you might say the Stone family was as happy and contented as cats in a dairy. And so they were, except for Jabez Stone.

He'd been contented enough, the first few years. It's a great thing when bad luck turns; it drives most other things out of your head. True, every now and then, especially in rainy weather, the little white scar on his finger would give him a twinge. And once a year, punctual as clockwork, the stranger with the handsome buggy would come driving by. But the sixth year, the stranger lighted, and, after that, his peace was over for Jabez Stone.

The stranger came up through the lower field, switching his boots with a cane—they were handsome black boots, but Jabez Stone never liked the look of them, particularly the toes. And, after he'd passed the time of day, he said, "Well, Mr. Stone, you're a hummer! It's a very pretty property you've got here, Mr. Stone."

"Well, some might favor it and others might not," said Jabez Stone, for he was a New Hampshireman.

"Oh, no need to decry your industry!" said the stranger, very easy, showing his teeth in a smile. "After all, we know what's been done, and it's been according to contract and specifications. So when—ahem—the mortgage falls due next year, you shouldn't have any regrets."

"Speaking of that mortgage, mister," said Jabez Stone, and he looked around for help to the earth and the sky, "I'm beginning to have one or two doubts about it."

"Doubts?" said the stranger, not quite so pleasantly.

"Why, yes," said Jabez Stone. "This being the U.S.A. and me always having been a religious man." He cleared his throat and got bolder. "Yes, sir," he said, "I'm beginning to have considerable doubts as to that mortgage holding in court."

"There's courts and courts," said the stranger, clicking his teeth. "Still, we might as well have a look at the original document." And he hauled out a big black pocketbook, full of papers. "Sherwin, Slater, Stevens, Stone," he muttered. "I, Jabez Stone, for a term of seven years—Oh, it's quite in order, I think."

But Jabez Stone wasn't listening, for he saw something else flutter out of the black pocketbook. It was something that looked like a moth, but it wasn't a moth. And as Jabez Stone stared at it, it seemed to speak to him in a small sort of piping voice, terrible small and thin, but terrible human. "Neighbor Stone!" it squeaked. "Neighbor Stone! Help me! For God's sake, help me!"

But before Jabez Stone could stir hand or foot, the stranger whipped out a big bandanna handkerchief, caught the creature in it, just like a butterfly, and started tying up the ends of the bandanna.

"Sorry for the interruption," he said. "As I was saying——"

But Jabez Stone was shaking all over like a scared horse.

"That's Miser Stevens' voice!" he said, in a croak. "And you've got him in your handkerchief!"

The stranger looked a little embarrassed.

"Yes, I really should have transferred him to the collecting box," he said with a simper, "but there were some rather unusual specimens there and I didn't want them crowded. Well, well, these little contretemps will occur."

"I don't know what you mean by contertan," said Jabez Stone, "but that was Miser Stevens' voice! And he ain't dead! You can't tell me he is! He was just as spry and mean as a woodchuck, Tuesday!"

"In the midst of life——" said the stranger, kind of pious. "Listen!" Then a bell began to toll in the valley and Jabez Stone listened, with the sweat running down his face. For he knew it was tolled for Miser Stevens and that he was dead.

"These long-standing accounts," said the stranger with a sigh; "one really hates to close them. But business is business."

He still had the bandanna in his hand, and Jabez Stone felt sick as he saw the cloth struggle and flutter.

"Are they all as small as that?" he asked hoarsely.

"Small?" said the stranger, "Oh, I see what you mean. Why, they vary." He measured Jabez Stone with his eyes, and his teeth showed. "Don't worry, Mr. Stone," he said. "You'll go with a very good grade. I wouldn't trust you outside the collecting box. Now, a man like Dan'l Webster, of course—well, we'd have to build a special box for him, and even at that, I imagine the wingspread would astonish you. But, in your case, as I was saying——"

"Put that handkerchief away!" said Jabez Stone, and he began to beg and to pray. But the best he could get at the end was a three years' extension, with conditions.

But till you make a bargain like that, you've got no idea of how fast four years can run. By the last months of those years, Jabez Stone's known all over the state and there's talk of running him for governor—and it's dust and ashes in his mouth. For every day, when he gets up, he thinks, "There's one more night gone," and every night when he lies down, he thinks of the black pocketbook and the soul of Miser Stevens, and it makes him sick at heart. Till, finally, he can't bear it any longer, and, in the last days of the last year, he hitches up his horse and drives off to seek Dan'l Webster. For Dan'l was born in New Hampshire, only a few miles from Cross Corners, and it's well known that he has a particular soft spot for old neighbors.

It was early in the morning when he got to Marshfield, but Dan'l was up already, talking Latin to the farm hands and wrestling with the ram, Goliath, and trying out a new trotter and working up speeches to make against John C. Calhoun. But when he heard a New Hampshireman had come to see him, he dropped everything else he was doing, for that was Dan'l's way. He gave Jabez Stone a breakfast that five men couldn't eat, went into the living history of every man and woman in Cross Corners, and finally asked him how he could serve him.

Jabez Stone allowed that it was a kind of mortgage case.

"Well, I haven't pleaded a mortgage case in a long time, and I don't generally plead now, except before the Supreme Court," said Dan'l, "but if I can, I'll help you."

"Then I've got hope for the first time in ten years," said Jabez Stone, and told him the details.

Dan'l walked up and down as he listened, hands behind his back, now and then asking a question, now and then plunging his eyes at the floor, as if they'd bore through it like gimlets. When Jabez Stone had finished, Dan'l puffed out his cheeks and blew. Then he turned to Jabez Stone and a smile broke over his face like the sunrise over Monadnock.

"You've certainly given yourself the devil's own row to hoe, Neighbor Stone," he said, "but I'll take your case."

"You'll take it?" said Jabez Stone, hardly daring to believe.

"Yes," said Dan'l Webster. "I've got about seventy-five other things to do and the Missouri Compromise to straighten out, but I'll take your case. For if two New Hampshiremen aren't a match for the devil, we might as well give the country back to the Indians." Then he shook Jabez Stone by the hand and said, "Did you come down here in a hurry?"

"Well, I admit I made time," said Jabez Stone.

"You'll go back faster," said Dan'l Webster, and he told 'em to hitch up Constitution and Constellation to the carriage. They were matched grays with one white forefoot, and they stepped like greased lightning.

Well, I won't describe how excited and pleased the whole Stone family was to have the great Dan'l Webster for a guest, when they finally got there. Jabez Stone had lost his hat on the way, blown off when they overtook a wind, but he didn't take much account of that. But after supper he sent the family off to bed, for he had most particular business with Mr. Webster. Mrs. Stone wanted them to sit in the front parlor, but Dan'l Webster knew front parlors and said he preferred the kitchen. So it was there they sat, waiting for the stranger, with a jug on the table between them and a bright fire on the hearth—the stranger being scheduled to show up on the stroke of midnight, according to specifications.

Well, most men wouldn't have asked for better company than Dan'l Webster and a jug. But with every tick of the clock Jabez Stone got sadder and sadder. His eyes roved round, and though he sampled the jug you could see he couldn't taste it. Finally, on the stroke of eleven-thirty o'clock he reached over and grabbed Dan'l Webster by the arm.

"Mr. Webster, Mr. Webster!" he said, and his voice was shaking with fear and a desperate courage. "For God's sake, Mr. Webster, harness your horses and get away from this place while you can!"

"You've brought me a long way, neighbor, to tell me you don't like my company," said Dan'l Webster, quite peaceable, pulling at the jug.

"Miserable wretch that I am!" groaned Jabez Stone. "I've brought you a devilish way, and now I see my folly. Let him take me if he wills. I don't hanker after it, I must say, but I can stand it. But you're the Union's stay and New Hampshire's pride! He musn't get you, Mr. Webster! He musn't get you!"

Dan'l Webster looked at the distracted man, all gray and shaking in the firelight, and laid a hand on his shoulder.

"I'm obliged to you, Neighbor Stone," he said gently. "It's kindly thought of. But there's a jug on thé table and a case in hand. And I never left a jug or a case half finished in my life."

And just at that moment there was a sharp rap on the door.

"Ah," said Dan'l Webster, very coolly, "I thought your clock was a trifle slow, Neighbor Stone." He stepped to the door and opened it. "Come in!" he said.

The stranger came in—very dark and tall he looked in the firelight. He was carrying a box under his arm—a black, japanned box with little air holes in the lid. At the sight of the box, Jabez Stone gave a low cry and shrank into a corner of the room.

"Mr. Webster, I presume," said the stranger, very polite, but with his eyes glowing like a fox's deep in the woods.

"Attorney of record for Jabez Stone," said Dan'l Webster, but his eyes were glowing too. "Might I ask your name?"

"I've gone by a good many," said the stranger carelessly. "Perhaps Scratch will do for the evening. I'm often called that in these regions."

Then he sat down at the table and poured himself a drink from the jug. The liquor was cold in the jug, but it came steaming into the glass.

"And now," said the stranger, smiling and showing his teeth, "I shall call upon you, as a law-abiding citizen, to assist me in taking possession of my property."

Well, with that the argument began—and it went hot and heavy. At first, Jabez Stone had a flicker of hope, but when he saw Dan'l Webster being forced back at point after point, he just scrunched in his corner, with his eyes on that japanned box. For there wasn't any doubt as to the deed or the signature—that was the worst of it. Dan'l Webster twisted and turned and thumped his fist on the table, but he couldn't get away from that. He offered to compromise the case; the stranger wouldn't hear of it. He pointed out the property had increased in value, and state senators ought to be worth more; the stranger stuck to the letter of the law. He was a great lawyer, Dan'l Webster, but we know who's the King of Lawyers, as the Good Book tells us, and it seemed as if, for the first time, Dan'l Webster had met his match.

Finally, the stranger yawned a little. "Your spirited efforts on behalf of your client do you credit, Mr. Webster," he said, "but if you have no more arguments to adduce, I'm rather pressed for time"—and Jabez Stone shuddered.

Dan'l Webster's brow looked dark as a thundercloud.

"Pressed or not, you shall not have this man!" he thundered. "Mr. Stone is an American citizen, and no American citizen may be forced into the service of a foreign prince. We fought England for that in '12 and we'll fight all hell for it again!"

"Foreign?" said the stranger. "And who calls me a foreigner?"

"Well, I never yet heard of the dev—of your claiming American citizenship," said Dan'l Webster with surprise.

"And who with better right?" said the stranger, with one of his terrible smiles. "When the first wrong was done to the first Indian, I was there. When the first slaver put out for the Congo, I stood on her deck. Am I not in your books and stories and beliefs, from the first settlements on? Am I not spoken of, still, in every church in New England? 'Tis true the North claims me for a Southerner and the South for a Northerner, but I am neither. I am merely an honest American like yourself—and of the best descent—for, to tell the truth, Mr. Webster, though I don't like to boast of it, my name is older in this country than yours."

"Aha!" said Dan'l Webster, with the veins standing out in his forehead. "Then I stand on the Constitution! I demand a trial for my client!"

"The case is hardly one for an ordinary court," said the stranger, his eyes flickering. "And, indeed, the lateness of the hour——"

"Let it be any court you choose, so it is an American judge and an American jury!" said Dan'l Webster in his pride. "Let it be the quick or the dead; I'll abide the issue!"

"You have said it," said the stranger, and pointed his finger at the door. And with that, and all of a sudden, there was a rushing of wind outside and a noise of footsteps. They came, clear and distinct, through the night. And yet, they were not like the footsteps of living men.

"In God's name, who comes by so late?" cried Jabez Stone, in an ague of fear.

"The jury Mr. Webster demands," said the stranger, sipping at his boiling glass. "You must pardon the rough appearance of one or two; they will have come a long way."

And with that the fire burned blue and the door blew open and twelve men entered, one by one.

If Jabez Stone had been sick with terror before, he was blind with terror now. For there was Walter Butler, the loyalist, who spread fire and horror through the Mohawk Valley in the times of the Revolution; and there was Simon Girty, the renegade, who saw white men burned at the stake and whooped with the Indians to see them burn. His eyes were green, like a catamount's, and the stains on his hunting shirt did not come from the blood of the deer. King Philip was there, wild and proud as he had been in life, with the great gash in his head that gave him his death wound, and cruel Governor Dale, who broke men on the wheel. There was Morton of Merry Mount, who so vexed the Plymouth Colony, with his flushed, loose, handsome face and his hate of the godly. There was Teach, the bloody pirate, with his black beard curling on his breast. The Reverend John Smeet, with his strangler's hands and his Geneva gown, walked as daintily as he had to the gallows. The red print of the rope was still around his neck, but he carried a perfumed handkerchief in one hand. One and all, they came into the room with the fires of hell still upon them, and the stranger named their names and their deeds as they came, till the tale of twelve was told. Yet the stranger had told the truth—they had all played a part in America.

"Are you satisfied with the jury, Mr. Webster?" said the stranger mockingly, when they had taken their places.

The sweat stood upon Dan'l Webster's brow, but his voice was clear.

"Quite satisfied," he said. "Though I miss General Arnold from the company."

"Benedict Arnold is engaged upon other business," said the stranger, with a glower. "Ah, you asked for a justice, I believe."

He pointed his finger once more, and a tall man, soberly clad in Puritan garb, with the burning gaze of the fanatic, stalked into the room and took his judge's place.

"Justice Hathorne is a jurist of experience," said the stranger. "He presided at certain witch trials once held in Salem. There were others who repented of the business later, but not he."

"Repent of such notable wonders and undertakings?" said the stern old justice. "Nay, hang them—hang them all!" And he muttered to himself in a way that struck ice into the soul of Jabez Stone.

Then the trial began, and, as you might expect, it didn't look anyways good for the defense. And Jabez Stone didn't make much of a witness in his own behalf. He took one look at Simon Girty and screeched, and they had to put him back in his corner in a kind of swoon.

It didn't halt the trial, though; the trial went on, as trials do.

Dan'l Webster had faced some hard juries and hanging judges in his time, but this was the hardest he'd ever faced, and he knew it. They sat there with a kind of glitter in their eyes, and the stranger's smooth voice went on and on. Every time he'd raise an objection, it'd be "Objection sustained," but whenever Dan'l objected, it'd be "Objection denied." Well, you couldn't expect fair play from a fellow like this Mr. Scratch.

It got to Dan'l in the end, and he began to heat, like iron in the forge. When he got up to speak he was going to flay that stranger with every trick known to the law, and the judge and jury too. He didn't care if it was contempt of court or what would happen to him for it. He didn't care any more what happened to Jabez Stone. He just got madder and madder, thinking of what he'd say. And yet, curiously enough, the more he thought about it, the less he was able to arrange his speech in his mind.

Till, finally, it was time for him to get up on his feet, and he did so, all ready to bust out with lightnings and denunciations. But before he started he looked over the judge and jury for a moment, such being his custom. And he noticed the glitter in their eyes was twice as strong as before, and they all leaned forward. Like hounds just before they get the fox, they looked, and the blue mist of evil in the room thickened as he watched them. Then he saw what he'd been about to do, and he wiped his forehead, as a man might who's just escaped falling into a pit in the dark.

For it was him they'd come for, not only Jabez Stone. He read it in the glitter of their eyes and in the way the stranger hid his mouth with one hand. And if he fought them with their own weapons, he'd fall into their power; he knew that, though he couldn't have told you how. It was his own anger and horror that burned in their eyes; and he'd have to wipe that out or the case was lost. He stood there for a moment, his black eyes burning like anthracite. And then he began to speak.

He started off in a low voice, though you could hear every word. They say he could call on the harps of the blessed when he chose. And this was just as simple and easy as a man could talk. But he didn't start out by condemning or reviling. He was talking about the things that make a country a country, and a man a man.

And he began with the simple things that everybody's known and felt—the freshness of a fine morning when you're young, and the taste of food when you're hungry, and the new day that's every day when you're a child. He took them up and he turned them in his hands. They were good things for any man. But without freedom, they sickened. And when he talked of those enslaved, and the sorrows of slavery, his voice got like a big bell. He talked of the early days of America and the men who had made those days. It wasn't a spread-eagle speech, but he made you see it. He admitted all the wrong that had ever been done. But he showed how, out of the wrong and the right, the suffering and the starvations, something new had come. And everybody had played a part in it, even the traitors.

Then he turned to Jabez Stone and showed him as he was—an ordinary man who'd had hard luck and wanted to change it. And, because he'd wanted to change it, now he was going to be punished for all eternity. And yet there was good in Jabez Stone, and he showed that good. He was hard and mean, in some ways, but he was a man. There was sadness in being a man, but it was a proud thing too. And he showed what the pride of it was till you couldn't help feeling it. Yes, even in hell, if a man was a man, you'd know it. And he wasn't pleading for any one person any more, though his voice rang like an organ. He was telling the story and the failures and the endless journey of mankind. They got tricked and trapped and bamboozled, but it was a great journey. And no demon that was ever foaled could know the inwardness of it—it took a man to do that.

The fire began to die on the hearth and the wind before morning to blow. The light was getting gray in the room when Dan'l Webster finished. And his words came back at the end to New Hampshire ground, and the one spot of land that each man loves and clings to. He painted a picture of that, and to each one of that jury he spoke of things long forgotten. For his voice could search the heart, and that was his gift and his strength. And to one, his voice was like the forest and its secrecy, and to another like the sea and the storms of the sea; and one heard the cry of his lost nation in it, and another saw a little harmless scene he hadn't remembered for years. But each saw something. And when Dan'l Webster finished he didn't know whether or not he'd saved Jabez Stone. But he knew he'd done a miracle. For the glitter was gone from the eyes of judge and jury, and, for the moment, they were men again, and knew they were men.

"The defense rests," said Dan'l Webster, and stood there like a mountain. His ears were still ringing with his speech, and he didn't hear anything else till he heard Judge Hathorne say, "The jury will retire to consider its verdict."

Walter Butler rose in his place and his face had a dark, gay pride on it.

"The jury has considered its verdict," he said, and looked the stranger full in the eye. "We find for the defendant, Jabez Stone."

With that, the smile left the stranger's face, but Walter Butler did not flinch.

"Perhaps 'tis not strictly in accordance with the evidence," he said, "but even the damned may salute the eloquence of Mr. Webster."

With that, the long crow of a rooster split the gray morning sky, and judge and jury were gone from the room like a puff of smoke and as if they had never been there. The stranger turned to Dan'l Webster, smiling wryly.

"Major Butler was always a bold man," he said. "I had not thought him quite so bold. Nevertheless, my congratulations, as between two gentlemen."

"I'll have that paper first, if you please," said Dan'l Webster, and he took it and tore it into four pieces. It was queerly warm to the touch. "And now," he said, "I'll have you!" and his hand came down like a bear trap on the stranger's arm. For he knew that once you bested anybody like Mr. Scratch in fair fight, his power on you was gone. And he could see that Mr. Scratch knew it too.

The stranger twisted and wriggled, but he couldn't get out of that grip. "Come, come, Mr. Webster," he said, smiling palely. "This sort of thing is ridic—ouch!—is ridiculous. If you're worried about the costs of the case, naturally, I'd be glad to pay——"

"And so you shall!" said Dan'l Webster, shaking him till his teeth rattled. "For you'll sit right down at that table and draw up a document, promising never to bother Jabez Stone nor his heirs or assigns nor any other New Hampshireman till doomsday! For any hades we want to raise in this state, we can raise ourselves, without assistance from strangers."

"Ouch!" said the stranger. "Ouch! Well, they never did run very big to the barrel, but—ouch!—I agree!"

So he sat down and drew up the document. But Dan'l Webster kept his hand on his coat collar all the time.

"And, now, may I go?" said the stranger, quite humble, when Dan'l'd seen the document was in proper and legal form.

"Go?" said Dan'l, giving him another shake. "I'm still trying to figure out what I'll do with you. For you've settled the costs of the case, but you haven't settled with me. I think I'll take you back to Marshfield," he said, kind of reflective. "I've got a ram there named Goliath that can butt through an iron door. I'd kind of like to turn you loose in his field and see what he'd do."

Well, with that the stranger began to beg and to plead. And he begged and he pled so humble that finally Dan'l, who was naturally kindhearted, agreed to let him go. The stranger seemed terrible grateful for that and said, just to show they were friends, he'd tell Dan'l fortune before leaving. So Dan'l agreed to that, though he didn't take much stock in fortunetellers ordinarily. But, naturally, the stranger was a little different.

Well, he pried and he peered at the lines in Dan'l's hands. And he told him one thing and another that was quite remarkable. But they were all in the past.

"Yes, all that's true, and it happened," said Dan'l Webster. "But what's to come in the future?"

The stranger grinned, kind of happily, and shook his head.

"The future's not as you think it," he said. "It's dark. You have a great ambition, Mr. Webster."

"I have," said Dan'l firmly, for everybody knew he wanted to be president.

"It seems almost within your grasp," said the stranger, "but you will not attain it. Lesser men will be made president and you will be passed over."

"And, if I am, I'll still be Daniel Webster," said Dan'l. "Say on."

"You have two strong sons," said the stranger, shaking his

head. "You look to found a line. But each will die in war and neither reach greatness."

"Live or die, they are still my sons," said Dan'l Webster. "Say on."

"You have made great speeches," said the stranger. "You will make more."

"Ah," said Dan'l Webster.

"But the last great speech you make will turn many of your own against you," said the stranger. "They will call you Ichabod; they will call you by other names. Even in New England, some will say you have turned your coat and sold your country, and their voices will be loud against you till you die."

"So it is an honest speech, it does not matter what men say," said Dan'l Webster. Then he looked at the stranger and their glances locked.

"One question," he said. "I have fought for the Union all my life. Will I see that fight won against those who would tear it apart?"

"Not while you live," said the stranger, grimly, "but it will be won. And after you are dead, there are thousands who will fight for your cause, because of words that you spoke."

"Why, then, you long-barreled, slab-sided, lantern-jawed, fortunetelling note shaver!" said Dan'l Webster, with a great roar of laughter, "be off with you to your own place before I put my mark on you! For, by the thirteen original colonies, I'd go to the Pit itself to save the Union!"

And with that he drew back his foot for a kick that would have stunned a horse. It was only the tip of his shoe that caught the stranger, but he went flying out of the door with his collecting box under his arm.

"And now," said Dan'l Webster, seeing Jabez Stone beginning to rouse from his swoon, "let's see what's left in the jug, for it's dry work talking all night. I hope there's pie for breakfast, Neighbor Stone."

But they say that whenever the devil comes near Marshfield, even now, he gives it a wide berth. And he hasn't been seen in the state of New Hampshire from that day to this. I'm not talking about Massachusetts or Vermont.

All the Little Jokers

by:

JAMES REID PARKER

selected by:

WILLIAM J. DONOVAN

James Reid Parker's stories about the mythical firm of "Forbes, Hathaway, Bryan, and Devore" are stories which I have always enjoyed. Although written in recent years, they are already classics in the field of lawyer fiction. It is difficult to say which one is my favorite, but certainly one of the best is "All the Little Jokers."

S.S. WILLIAM J. DONOVAN

Keoghan was just as pleased that it was Mr. Forbes, and not one of the others, who wanted to see him. In a way Mr. Forbes' brusqueness was preferable to the labyrinthine rhetoric that certain senior partners—notably Mr. Devore—were fond of inflicting on the younger lawyers. Walking into Mr. Forbes' office, Keoghan found his superior, who was about to leave for the week end, making a frantic effort to clear his desk. Mr. Forbes was so busy slapping papers around and banging desk drawers that he failed to see Keoghan standing there. Presently the junior said tactfully, "Miss Helm said you wanted to see me, Mr. Forbes."

"Yes, yes. I did. I do. Sit down. Tell me something. Have you ever heard of a soft drink called John Willow's Tonic?"

Keoghan stared at him in astonishment. "You mean they still *make* it?" he said. "I haven't run across that name in years. They used to sell Willow's Tonic in all the country stores in Maine when I was a kid. We drank gallons of it every summer."

Mr. Forbes shook his head sadly. "I wish someone would tell me why Americans go out of their way to drink sweetened dishwater," he said, in a manner becoming to one who lived in a dignified house near the Metropolitan Museum, with antique silver paper peeling genteelly off the dining-room walls, and good brandy after dinner. "Miracle they don't all die of kidney trouble!"

Keoghan started to grin, but changed his mind. Miss Helm appeared in the doorway. She said that it was ten minutes past twelve, and that if Mr. Forbes was still planning to have his phenobarbital prescription filled in Grand Central, he'd better hurry.

"I know, I know. I'm keeping my eye on the time," he said, and Miss Helm departed, looking extremely doubtful. "My reason for mentioning Willow's Tonic is that the people who make it, the North American Beverage Company, may very possibly have a case for us in the near future. I learned about their predicament last night at a dinner party. Let me give you a rough idea of the situation, and then ask you what chance you think North American Beverage would have if its executives should decide to go on the warpath."

Keoghan brightened. Under circumstances such as this he always felt as if he were in a theater, waiting for the curtain to go up. Irritating though his job frequently was, it still had the power to charm him on occasion.

"North American Beverage is an unusually large bottling and distributing outfit, it seems," Mr. Forbes said with satisfaction. "Its headquarters are in Boston. In 1930 it bought out the Willow Bottling Works, a Portland firm that had always made just the one product, John Willow's Tonic. The Willow Bottling Works had been started in a small way in 1896 by this man John Willow, and it did fairly well. When the founder sold out, he got a good price. The North American Beverage people had more success with the stuff, of course, because they could sell it in a wider New England territory than just the Portland area. Now here's where the trouble starts. This John Willow is living. Some men here in New York put up the necessary backing and persuaded him to lend his name to a new firm, John Willow, Incorporated. After making him president at an attractive salary, they're putting out a soft drink that's substantially the same —it's just been launched—and the label has his picture on it."

"I'm beginning to understand," Keoghan said. "This sounds interesting."

"What they've done," Mr. Forbes said, "is to call it 'The Old John Willow.' Their lawyer—he's some lone wolf I've never even heard of—told them this was within the law. They've put 'John Willow' in big letters on the label, and 'The Old' in little letters just above it. From what I hear, it might be argued that they've purposely made the lettering more or less old-fashioned, to resemble the label on the original bottle."

"That's what I'd call inviting trouble," Keoghan said.

"It would seem so, wouldn't it?" said Mr. Forbes. "Now suppose the case comes our way, and the North American Beverage people ask us to seek an injunction. Assuming that you've heard all the basic facts, what would you say, offhand? Would you say that regardless of whether a man has a right to use his own name and picture, there's been a deliberate violation of a purchased trade-mark and that the new company, John Willow, Incorporated, is proposing to set up unfair competition? Personally, I'm inclined to feel that the evidence trends in that direction."

"It does a lot more than *trend* there," Keoghan said, unable to control his exuberance. "It makes a perfect landing. I'd say an injunction was practically in the bag."

Mr. Forbes seemed hurt.

"That's the trouble with you younger men," he complained. "You always think everything's going to be so damned easy! When you've practiced as long as I have, you'll realize that all the little jokers in a case like this aren't on the surface. I admit to being reasonably hopeful of the outcome if we get the case—mind you, I say *if* we get it—but I see no reason to believe that the actual work will be child's play, as you seem to think."

Miss Helm came in and said with some asperity, "You have exactly twenty minutes to get to Grand Central, Mr. Forbes." The senior partner made a feverish dash for his hat and valise. He took just enough time to say accusingly, "Probably miss my train!" and fled.

Keoghan made no plans for his Saturday afternoon, beyond a vague intention of going home to New Rochelle and doing a little work in his garden. Now he felt sufficiently tempted, as a result of Mr. Forbes' recital, to stay on the premises a little longer and to see whether he could dig up something that might clarify the status of the North American Beverage Company, just for the fun of it. Then, too, he was stimulated by the knowledge that F. H. B. & D. approved of such displays of initiative. He had only a limited reference collection at home, and on the whole it was something of a luxury to be able to browse around the office library uninterrupted. Keoghan sent the last available messenger out for sandwiches and a coffee frosted, and settled down in the handsome, walnut-paneled retreat to ponder the case Mr. Forbes had outlined. At the top of a ruled yellow pad, he idly printed the legend *"North Am. Bev. Co.* v. *Willow,"* and, setting this aside for the time being, chose an assortment of digests from the shelves and plunged into them with determination. Given such a meager background, he of course could not prepare a memorandum of law, but at least he might contrive what, in his office, was known as a "baby memorandum."

He was glad that Forbes, Hathaway, Bryan & Devore and the North American Beverage Company, if they got together, would undoubtedly take immediate action, thereby precluding any possibility of the defense dragging in laches. Let a thing like this go for only a brief period, and the attorneys for the offending firm were practically certain to counter with an argument that the plaintiffs should have voiced his objections sooner.

On the other hand, it disturbed Keoghan to note that thus far John Willow, Inc., presumably had not encroached on the North American Beverage Company's territory, which, or so Mr. Forbes had implied, was limited to the New England states. If the defense chose to dramatize this point, and Keoghan was disposed to fear that equity might allow it, perhaps one could say, "The court must not forget that North American Beverage is expanding continuously. It claims a right to market John Willow's Tonic anywhere in the United States without the interference of unfair competition, and asks for a free hand to do so as rapidly as its ever-growing facilities will permit."

These pretty heroics were all very well in their way, Keoghan decided with a sigh, but they weren't getting him any further with his baby memo, which would have to be a businesslike affair, richly documented with precedents. He took a cigarette from a crumpled package in his vest pocket and idly smoothed the wrinkled outside paper. The phrase, "a mellowed blend of fine Virginia and Turkish tobaccos," caught his eye, and in some absurd way this seemed to have some bearing on the case, although he could determine no basis for the association. However, the line clung irritatingly in the back of his mind as he worked. He had had enough experience with the devious workings of his own mind to feel sure that there was some significance to this, but for the life of him he didn't know what it was.

Then, quite unexpectedly, he came across something very promising in one of the digests. Equity, he learned, would restrain an unreasonable use of secret chemical formulas and manufacturing processes. Suppose a chemical analysis of the two brands should reveal that old Mr. Willow had duplicated his tonic too exactly? Or even to an appreciable extent? Mr. Forbes had said that the two products were substantially the same. Humming "Tiger Rag" in a jubilant monotone, Keoghan scribbled *"Haskins* v. *Ryan* (71 N.J.Eq. 575); *Little* v. *Gollus* (38 N.Y.S. 487)" on his pad. He was recalled abruptly to less fascinating matters by a voice saying in a tone of indescribable boredom, "All outta tongue. Gotcha tuna fish."

"Thanks, Ralph," Keoghan said. "That's all right."

"Yeah," the youth said, coming to life just long enough to achieve a humorous leer. "Brain food."

Keoghan went back to work, mechanically consuming frosted coffee and tuna fish while he hunted for precedents with which to vanquish John Willow, Inc. In reality, he was almost as interested in vanquishing Mr. Forbes by proving that *North American Beverage Co.* v. *Willow,* in the hands of a talented junior, was no problem at all, but thus far, at any rate, Mr. Forbes' prediction that the case would not be too easy seemed moderately justified. It would be a simple enough matter to prove that there had been an infringement of trade-mark, but Keoghan knew perfectly well that this alone would not be enough. John Willow, Inc., would be able to go right on marketing the product with a shrewdly redesigned label if Forbes, Hathaway, Bryan & Devore's victory were limited to this single point. Unfair competition was the important angle. The longer a solution eluded Geoghan, the more Mr. Forbes' little homily about jokers and child's play annoyed him. It was so disheartening to be proved wrong. And what concrete research had Mr.

Forbes done? None at all. Keoghan fumbled for another cigarette. "A mellow blend of Virginia and Turkish tobaccos." Now was that just a catch phrase? he wondered. If you added half a Virginia Round, or something like that, to half a Melachrino, would you be getting the same thing, and, if so, would it cost you more or less? Keoghan, in a waspish mood as far as the business world in general was concerned, became more hostile than ever toward the Original John. "Old goat!" he muttered. "Ought to be ashamed of himself!" He struck a match and then, without lighting his cigarette at all, extinguished the flame and said, "My God! I *remember*!"

Association of ideas was an amazing thing, Keoghan was forced to conclude. He tracked down his quarry in the comprehensive reports, and then ransacked the library shelves until he found the complete story. He checked the outstanding points, which pleased him so much that he performed, without any marked ability but with great enthusiasm, a few dance steps. This, like his humming of "Tiger Rag," was symptomatic. Keoghan sat down at the table again, this time with *American Tobacco Co.* v. *Miltiades Melachrino, Inc.,* in front of him, and rapidly covered several sheets of the yellow paper with notes. No small part of his satisfaction lay in the fact that every stroke of his pencil made Mr. Forbes look increasingly silly.

In 1905, Mr. Melachrino had come to the United States and, with very little money, had started to manufacture cigarettes. After securing further capital, he had established the firm of M. Melachrino & Co. and had succeeded in building a sound and profitable business. By 1912 he had been able to sell his assets—formula, trade-marks, labels, good will, and so on—for two million dollars. Moreover, he had become president of M. Melachrino & Co., Inc., the new corporation, which had gone on manufacturing the same product. Thirteen years later the American Tobacco Company had purchased the firm, and Mr. Melachrino, no longer owner or part-owner of M. Melachrino & Co., Inc., had felt free to create a wholly new company, Miltiades Melachrino, Inc. The paper of his new cigarette, like that of the old one, bore his name and the packaging of the two brands was on the whole similar. Suing for an injunction, the American Tobacco Company triumphed nicely. The judge held that Miltiades Melachrino could continue to make cigarettes and even use his name in connection with them, but effectively balanced the scales by deciding that the defendant should be restrained—at this point Keoghan happily copies the decision of Knox J., *verbatim*—"from describing itself as the original manufacturer of Melachrino cigarettes, and from so using the word "Melachrino" as to give the appearance, and create the impression, that it is now manufacturing and marketing Melachrino cigarettes."

The result of all this was that Keoghan caught the three fifty-five to New Rochelle and was able to do quite a lot of work in his garden before dinner, after all.

Contrary to his expectations, he was unable to brandish his discovery before Mr. Forbes on Monday because Mr. Forbes didn't come into the office at all that day, but on Tuesday Keoghan went into the holy of holies and announced modestly, "I've been looking into the North American Beverage situation to see just where they'd stand, and frankly I think they're going to be able to take old Mr. Willow by the neck and throw him down the back stairs."

Mr. Forbes seemed lamentably unimpressed by this good news. "I hope," he said, frowning, "that with good luck we'll be able to avert any such catastrophe." He studied the bewildered Keoghan for a moment and then said, "Yesterday I stretched my week end to include a flying trip to Boston, where I pulled a few wires to find out just what North American Beverage's attitude is. I learned that they have been shrewd enough to retain Breed, Pear, Whittemore & Breed to handle the matter, and that an injunction is to be sought immediately. Perhaps I needn't explain that Breed, Pear is quite capable of seeing it through without our assistance."

Keoghan was thoroughly confused. "In that case the job was all washed up, as far as we're concerned, isn't it?" he said, with a gesture that expressed the futility of his effort.

"Not at all," Mr. Forbes said with dignity. "At least, I hope not. It merely means that we're back where we were on Saturday, or rather on Friday night, after I first learned about the problem from Mr. Willow."

"Mr. Willow!" Keoghan said. "But I thought you'd been

talking with someone who was closely associated with North American Beverage!"

Mr. Forbes smiled. "Oh, no," he said. "I was wholly unacquainted with that end of it. My informant was Mr. Willow. We met at the H. Truman Naylors', where we both were dinner guests."

"Mother of God!" Keoghan said involuntarily.

"I shall now get in touch with the Willow corporation and see whether we can arrange to handle the defense. I believe I told you on Saturday that they've been working with an independent attorney. The man must be a fool! As I took the precaution of warning Mr. Willow the other evening, the poor fellow will probably need associate counsel. In the light of recent developments, I shall endeavor to make my point much clearer. There's really no reason why we shouldn't get *something* out of all this."

Keoghan had begun to feel dizzy.

"Perhaps you'll be able to devise a successful brief for us —who knows?" said Mr. Forbes.

Keoghan was Irish enough to take this on the chin. "Who knows?" he said weakly.

Unable to add anything in the least constructive to this remark, he departed.

Parcel of Land

by:

CORNELIA OTIS SKINNER

selected by:

LLOYD PAUL STRYKER

Cornelia Otis Skinner's recital of experiences in taking title to a piece of real estate makes a most entertaining tale. The description of the session with the lawyers on the closing of title is not only striking in its accuracy but at the same time filled with real humor. This is a story I have enjoyed very much and one which belongs in any comprehensive anthology of lawyer stories.

LLOYD PAUL STRYKER

S.S.

It is always enlightening to learn that one's preconceptions of everyday transactions are completely erroneous. Take, for example, the purchase of a piece of real estate. For a number of years my husband and I and our family have spent our summers in the country, in a rented house which we recently decided to buy. Our landlord was willing to sell, he lived nearby, the price for the house and land had been agreed upon, and mine was the innocent fantasy that all there remained for me to do was to sign a document, hand over a check, and set up a smart little black sign bearing our name in gold letters at the entrance gate. But it turns out that this is not the way one goes about it. The house is a good fifty miles out on Long Island, so was the gentleman from whom I (my husband and I agreed that the purchase was to be in my name) was buying it, and so was I. Therefore the formal purchase had to be effected in Wall Street.

It was a shock to learn that property deeds, like divorce papers, have to be handled by lawyers. It was a continuation of the shock when my phone rang and a lady with a brisk voice informed me that she was the secretary to Mr. X, my real-estate lawyer (it was the first I knew I had one, my husband having started the ball rolling), and would I please be at Mr. X's office Wednesday morning at nine-thirty for the "closing"? I asked her politely if the appointment couldn't possibly be put off an hour, to which she replied politely that it couldn't possibly be. Apparently, deed signings, like operations, have to take place in the early morning. I stayed at our apartment in town Tuesday night, had a light dinner, and got to bed early, but some pals showed up from Chicago and took me out on what they laughingly called the town, and Wednesday morning, after a savage alarm clock had brought me back to reluctant consciousness, I lay for a space wondering miserably what good the property could be to me now, with the possible exception of that little plot in the pine grove.

By dint of considerable fortitude and black coffee, I trembled into some clothes, selecting the soberest in my wardrobe. It was raining, so I put on rubbers and took the only umbrella to be found in the hall closet—a large, cotton, man's affair. These items, I hoped, helped to create an aspect of substantial respectability. Bravely I emerged, found my way to the nearest subway station, and managed to board a downtown train.

Wall Street always frightens me, and lawyers' offices frighten me even more. When I enter them, I find myself wanting to say to the girl at the reception desk, "Please tell them I've come to make a complete confession." It was worse than usual this time because Mr. X, my newly acquired real-estate lawyer, was a member of one of those impressive firms with a name like Threadwell, Hayes, Plunkett, Farmer & Sinus, whose outer office was only a degree less imposing than the entrance vestibule of the White House. Paneled walls formed a cream-colored background for candelabra which might have come out of Mount Vernon, and there was a black marble floor on which I should have skidded sickeningly if it hadn't been for my rubbers.

The reception young lady, who operated an Early Colonial switchboard, inquired if she might do something for me. When I'm particularly overawed I'm apt to go nervously folksy, and I heard myself babbling something like how did she do and yes indeed she *could* help me—I'd bought a house, that is I hadn't quite bought it, because I had come in now to buy it, although the house itself was fifty miles out on Long Island. The young woman brought me to a merciful stop by saying she guessed I wanted to see Mr. X and what was the name, please. After a little thought, I told her, and she plugged in Mr. X and told him I was there. The effect of this information to Mr. X was food for speculation, for after imparting it, the girl listened for several suspensive seconds, murmured a laconic "I see, sir," unplugged the connection, and, with a look which implied that she certainly knew all about me, asked if I'd be kind enough to wait. I said I'd be kind enough to and pulled out one of six Sheraton chairs grouped around a polished table. It made a rasping noise and the girl turned to look.

The table was strewn with reading matter for the edification of waiting clients—the *Tribune,* some *Time* magazines, a *Life,* and the latest edition of *Fortune,* a publication which impresses me very much because I can't understand it. I didn't try to read, partly because I had left my glasses at home and partly because the way I was feeling I wasn't sure I still knew how to. I just sat still, except for one unfortunate moment when, in spite of all efforts to stifle it, I emitted a lone, loud hiccough. The young lady again turned. I turned, too, hoping to see someone behind me on whom I might throw the guilt. The only thing behind me was a steel engraving of Thomas Jefferson, and the sight made me sigh over the sorry depths to which American womanhood has sunk since the days of the lions. I continued to wait, and for a time everything was very hushed.

Then a distant door opened and two men advanced along a corridor, conversing in low tones on a subject which appeared to be not only secret but of grave import to the State. One of them, who wore a dark raincoat and carried a bowler, was obviously a Titan in the world of finance, and the cares of his position showed in the distinguished furrows on his strong face. The other, having neither hat nor raincoat, was obviously a member of the firm, and, as the two drew near, with a start of joy I recognized him as a close friend and neighbor whose sentiments for me I had hitherto fatuously believed to be those of admiration, not untinged with a certain amount of conservative prurience. Certain that he would be overjoyed to see me, I leapt to my overshod feet and rushed over to him with outstretched hand and said cheerily, "Hello, darling!" He looked at me blankly, while the captain of industry turned to him with an expression that clearly said, "Do you know this woman, or shall I ring for the guard?" For a moment I thought my friend was having his little joke, but I was reckoning in ignorance of the way of a lawyer in his lair. He paused for a considerable time before he allowed a cold glint of recognition to come into his eye, then gave me a stiff bow and the smile an elderly uncle manages to force when a small child has just slapped a mud pie on his white flannels, muttered a staid "How do you do?" and continued his ambulatory conference with his impressive client. I slunk back onto my Sheraton chair and opened *Fortune*. Before me was an article illustrated with graphs which looked to me like the fever chart of my own state of debility. I put *Fortune* down.

After a time a bright-looking young man appeared and, with some hesitancy, asked if I were Mrs. Y. Apologetically I said I was. He was quite a presentable young man, and I rather wanted to explain that this was a bit early in the morning for me and to please not think I always looked this way. I vaguely hoped he might be Mr. X, my real-estate lawyer, but he informed me that he was a Mr. Whitby and that he'd come to take me to Mr. X. Apparently Mr. Whitby was a sort of intern around the place. Trying bravely to rise above my rubbers and umbrella, I followed him down a corridor, up a palatial stairway, and along another corridor to the open door of Mr. X's office. Mr. X was a distinguished-looking gentleman. He greeted me with a solemn, "How do you do, Mrs. Y. I'm Mr. X," and, not to be outdone in matters of legal etiquette, I answered, "How do you do, Mr. X. I'm Mrs. Y." With great courtesy he asked me to be seated, indicating a line of heavy chairs drawn up around the kind of massive table at which one imagines peace treaties are negotiated. I chose a place down at the end, in a position that was definitely below the salt. Mr. X's manner was so politely solemn that I wanted gently to remind him that I had come about buying the house, not reading the will, but before I could say anything, another gentleman entered, carrying a brief case. He approached Mr. X and, in a tone of deep bereavement, announced that he was

Mr. Beddoes, attorney for the seller. This surprised me and quite hurt my feelings. Why should the seller, whom I regarded as an old and true friend, require an attorney? Didn't he trust me? Maybe he did, but it was obvious Mr. Beddoes didn't. After being formally introduced, he gave me a look of considerable doubt, gathered his brief case to his bosom, and betook himself to the farther end of the Dumbarton Oaks conference board.

Another gentleman with a brief case walked in and informed Mr. X that he was Mr. Fenner, closer for the title corporation. I had no idea what a closer was, but I gathered by Mr. Fenner's bearing that he must be mighty important. He bowed distantly to me and also took a seat at the far end of the table. Mr. Fenner was followed by Mr. Coogan, who said he was from the office of Henry Rafferty. I never did find out who Mr. Rafferty was. There then arrived a Mr. Davison, who said that he had come to acknowledge the mortgage. I hadn't realized there was to be a mortgage until Mr. Davison showed up to acknowledge it. The word has a sound of doom for me, and I had a premonitory picture of our little family being turned out of the old homestead on the eve of the final payment.

The seller, my landlord, then appeared, and it was somewhat cheering to note that the gentleman at the far end of the table greeted him as they had me—politely, but definitely as a suspect. He modestly took the chair beside me, and for a time we exchanged shy snatches of conversation in the subdued manner of parishioners waiting for service to start. A few further individuals made their appearances—some ladies who I gathered were secretaries, a little gray man whose identity was a mystery to the end, and an unhappy-looking office boy who handed Mr. X a rolled-up something which looked like an enormous diploma. It proved to be the blueprint of the property that was to be mine, and Mr. X opened it out on the table, asking if I would please verify it as being "a correct map of your intended parcel of land." I have never understood maps, and without my glasses I couldn't even make out the white lines, but I rose and leaned over the blueprint, carefully scrutinizing, trying my best to look like General MacArthur planning a campaign. Mr. X nodded to one of the secretaries, who started reading off a quaint and completely incomprehensible description of the boundaries of the place. Instead of "left by the Jones' cornfield," which is what I would have said, she rattled off a lot of stuff about north so many degrees so many seconds, which struck me as peculiar. What struck me as not only peculiar but definitely depressing was the list of landmarks they had picked out to define my boundaries: "Southeast by three decayed trees," and "West around stagnant swamp," and even "Due north past large manure pile." My neighbor, the seller, shifted his feet uneasily. I began to wonder if I weren't buying a tract of land on Riker's Island.

Then began an extended period of signing things. Mr. Beddoes produced a document to which, he explained, reading from a lesser document, "forty-four dollars in revenue stamps must be affixed and canceled upon acceptance of the deed and payment therefor." Mr. Fenner, after examining the first document with an air of mixed respect and suspicion, passed it on to Mr. X, who announced it to be in order and handed it on to me, asking me please to read it and sign it. Even if I had had my glasses, it is doubtful if I would have been able to read, much less understand, it. Shyly I asked what it was. In shocked astonishment Mr. X said, "The deed," and I said, "Oh, the deed," and signed. As I did so, someone—I think it was Mr. Coogan—said, and it's all I remember him saying ever, "The deed contains no covenants except the one required by the lien law," to which I murmured that that was indeed comforting, as I certainly didn't want any covenants. The deed was followed by the statement of closing figures and adjustments, which had to do with a village tax and a town tax. Wondering why there should be both, I asked if the elders of our country hamlet hadn't made up their minds yet whether we were a town or a village. I guess Mr. X didn't know, because all he said was "If you'd just sign here, please——" He then handed me two documents which he said were affidavits in regard to my citizenship. Not without some slight indignation, I asked if there were anything wrong with my citizenship, and Mr. X, with an indulgent smile, explained, "One is to induce the title company to issue a policy to insure your title fee, and the other is to induce the title company to insure the mortgage." Expressing the hope that the title company would prove to be easily induced, I signed both papers. As I did, I heard someone say that something—I didn't get just what—was in escrow. Now, "in escrow" is a phrase which for years I've been intending to take a day off and look up; it always gives me a mental picture of some kind of deep-freeze apparatus in the nethermost subbasement of a bank. Everybody seemed relieved that, wherever it is, the property was in it, and I felt relieved too, somehow.

I was next asked to make out a certain number of checks, not in payment for the house but for such interesting items as appraisal fees, a credit report, and tax accrual. Then there was Mr. Coogan to be taken care of. He had turned out to be a very pleasant gentleman but seemed hardly to have contributed fifty dollars' worth to the occasion. These items disposed of, Mr. Fenner, in a nervous voice, asked the seller if he was ready to surrender the lease (which is what my husband and I had had on the property all along). The seller said he was, and did, and that last bit of drama closed the closing. Mr. X smiled like a minister who has just tied the knot, and informed me that I now owned the house and land. At what moment during the formalities they came into my possession, I shall never know. Everybody shook hands with everybody but me, and I hastened to the Pennsylvania Station. I wanted to see my land. I was afraid it had grown into the Louisiana Purchase.

A local took me back to our little station, and when I got out I hailed Mr. Moore, our town's taximan, and started for my property with palpitating heart. I was almost afraid to look as we turned in at the gate, but I needn't have been. The house wasn't Chenonceaux and the land looked just the same. The hole in the road still needed filling in and the top hinge of the screen door was still conspicuously broken. I turned to Mr. Moore and said, "Thanks for driving me home."

The Case of the Irate Witness

by:

ERLE STANLEY GARDNER

selected by:

JERRY GIESLER

My choice is an Erle Stanley Gardner story —for many reasons, the least of which is the fact that I have the pleasure of Mr. Gardner's acquaintance and he has my personal admiration and esteem. I am fond of all of his writings and have been a steady fan of the Perry Mason novels for many years. Thus, there is a special pleasure in being able to select for an anthology of lawyer tales his sole Perry Mason short story, "The Case of the Irate Witness." As in all of his writings, Mr. Gardner tells the story of the kind of lawyer we all admire—the lawyer who champions the cause of the underdog and has no hesitancy in "putting himself out" to serve the best interests of his client.

JERRY GIESLER

S.S.—

The early-morning shadows cast by the mountains still lay heavily on the town's main street as the big siren on the roof of the Jebson Commercial Company began to scream shrilly.

The danger of fire was always present, and at the sound, men at breakfast rose and pushed their chairs back from the table. Men who were shaving barely paused to wipe lather from their faces; men who had been sleeping grabbed the first available garments. All of them ran to places where they could look for the first telltale wisps of smoke.

There was no smoke.

The big siren was still screaming urgently as the men formed into streaming lines, like ants whose hill has been attacked. The lines all moved toward the Jebson Commercial Company.

There the men were told that the doors of the big vault had been found wide open. A jagged hole had been cut into one with an acetylene torch.

The men looked at one another silently. This was the fifteenth of the month. The big, twice-a-month payroll, which had been brought up from the Ivanhoe National Bank the day before, had been the prize.

Frank Bernal, manager of the company's mine, the man who ruled Jebson City with an iron hand, arrived and took charge. The responsibility was his, and what he found was alarming.

Tom Munson, the night watchman, was lying on the floor in a back room, snoring in drunken slumber. The burglar alarm, which had been installed within the last six months, had been by-passed by means of an electrical device. This device was so ingenious that it was apparent that, if the work were that of a gang, at least one of the burglars was an expert electrician.

Ralph Nesbitt, the company accountant, was significantly silent. When Frank Bernal had been appointed manager a year earlier, Nesbitt had pointed out that the big vault was obsolete.

Bernal, determined to prove himself in his new job, had avoided the expense of tearing out the old vault and installing a new one by investing in an up-to-date burglar alarm and putting a special night watchman on duty.

Now the safe had been looted of a hundred thousand dollars, and Frank Bernal had to make a report to the main office in Chicago, with the disquieting knowledge that Ralph Nesbitt's memo stating that the antiquated vault was a pushover was at this moment reposing in the company files. . . .

Some distance out of Jebson City, Perry Mason, the famous trial lawyer, was driving fast along a mountain road. He had planned a week-end fishing trip for a long time, but a jury which had waited until midnight before reaching its verdict had delayed Mason's departure and it was now eight-thirty in the morning.

His fishing clothes, rod, wading boots, and creel were all in the trunk. He was wearing the suit in which he had stepped from the courtroom, and having driven all night he was eager for the cool, piny mountains.

A blazing red light, shining directly at him as he rounded a turn in the canyon road, dazzled his road-weary eyes. A sign, STOP—POLICE, had been placed in the middle of the road. Two men, a grim-faced man with a .30-.30 rifle in his hands and a silver badge on his shirt and a uniformed motorcycle officer, stood beside the sign.

Mason stopped his car.

The man with the badge, a deputy sheriff, said, "We'd better take a look at your driving license. There's been a big robbery at Jebson City."

"That so?" Mason said. "I went through Jebson City an hour ago and everything seemed quiet."

"Where you been since then?"

"I stopped at a little service station and restaurant for breakfast."

"Let's take a look at your driving license."

Mason handed it to him.

The man started to return it, then looked at it again. "Say," he said, "you're Perry Mason, the big criminal lawyer!"

"Not a criminal lawyer," Mason said patiently," a trial lawyer. I sometimes defend men who are accused of crime."

"What are you doing up in this country?"

"Going fishing."

The deputy looked at him suspiciously. "Why aren't you wearing your fishing clothes?"

"Because," Mason said, and smiled, "I'm not fishing."

"You said you were going fishing."

"I also intend," Mason said, "to go to bed tonight. According to you, I should be wearing my pajamas."

The deputy frowned. The traffic officer laughed and waved Mason on.

The deputy nodded at the departing car. "Looks like a live clue to me," he said, "but I can't find it in that conversation."

"There isn't any," the traffic officer said.

The deputy remained dubious, and later on, when a news-hungry reporter from the local paper asked the deputy if he knew of anything that would make a good story, the deputy said that he did.

And that was why Della Street, Perry Mason's confidential secretary, was surprised to read stories in the metropolitan papers stating that Perry Mason, the noted trial lawyer, was rumored to have been retained to represent the person or persons who had looted the vault of the Jebson Commercial Company. All this had been arranged, it would seem, before Mason's "client" had even been apprehended.

When Perry Mason called his office by long distance the next afternoon, Della said, "I thought you were going to the mountains for a vacation."

"That's right. Why?"

"The papers claim you're representing whoever robbed the Jebson Commercial Company."

"First I've heard of it," Mason said. "I went through Jebson City before they discovered the robbery, stopped for breakfast a little farther on, and then got caught in a roadblock. In the eyes of some officious deputy, that seems to have made me an accessory after the fact."

"Well," Della Street said, "they've caught a man by the name of Harvey L. Corbin and apparently have quite a case against him. They're hinting at mysterious evidence which won't be disclosed until the time of trial."

"Was he the one who committed the crime?" Mason asked.

"The police think so. He had a criminal record. When his employers at Jebson City found out about it, they told him to leave town. That was the evening before the robbery."

"Just like that, eh?" Mason asked.

"Well, you see, Jebson City is a one-industry town, and the company owns all the houses. They're leased to the employees. I understand Corbin's wife and daughter were told they could stay on until Corbin got located in a new place, but Corbin was told to leave town at once. You aren't interested, are you?"

"Not in the least," Mason said, "except that when I drive back I'll be going through Jebson City, and I'll probably stop to pick up the local gossip."

"Don't do it," she warned. "This man Corbin has all the earmarks of being an underdog, and you know how you feel about underdogs."

A quality in her voice made Perry suspicious. "You haven't been approached, have you, Della?"

"Well," she said, "in a way. Mrs. Corbin read in the papers that you were going to represent her husband, and she was overjoyed. It seems that she thinks her husband's implication in this is a raw deal. She hadn't known anything about his criminal record, but she loves him and is going to stand by him."

"You've talked with her?" Mason asked.

"Several times. I tried to break it to her gently. I told her it was probably nothing but a newspaper story. You see, Chief, they have Corbin dead to rights. They took some money from his wife as evidence. It was part of the loot."

"And she has nothing?"

"Nothing. Corbin left her forty dollars, and they took it all as evidence."

"I'll drive all night," he said. "Tell her I'll be back tomorrow."

"I was afraid of that," Della Street said. "Why did you have to call up? Why couldn't you have stayed up there fishing? Why did you have to stop and get your name in the papers?"

Mason laughed and hung up.

Paul Drake, of the Drake Detective Agency, came in and sat in the big chair in Mason's office and said, "You have a bear by the tail, Perry."

"What's the matter, Paul? Didn't your detective work in Jebson City pan out?"

"It panned out all right, but the stuff in the pan isn't what you want, Perry," Drake explained.

"How come?"

"Your client's guilty."

"Go on," Mason said.

"The money he gave his wife was some of what was stolen from the vault."

"How do they know it was the stolen money?" Mason asked.

Drake pulled a notebook from his pocket. "Here's the whole picture. The plant manager runs Jebson City. There isn't any private property. The Jebson company controls everything."

"Not a single small business?"

Drake shook his head. "Not unless you want to consider garbage collecting a small business. An old coot by the name of George Addey lives five miles down the canyon; he has a hog ranch and collects the garbage. He's supposed to have the first nickel he ever earned. Buries his money in cans. There's no bank nearer than Ivanhoe City."

"What about the burglary? The men who did it must have moved in acetylene tanks and——"

"They took them right out of the company store," Drake said. And then he went on: "Munson, the watchman, likes to take a pull out of a flask of whisky along about midnight. He says it keeps him awake. Of course, he's not supposed to do it, and no one was supposed to know about the whisky, but someone did know about it. They doped the whisky with a barbiturate. The watchman took his usual swig, went to sleep, and stayed asleep."

"What's the evidence against Corbin?" Mason asked.

"Corbin has a previous burglary record. It's a policy of the company not to hire anyone with a criminal record. Corbin lied about his past and got a job. Frank Bernal, the manager, found out about it, sent for Corbin about eight o'clock the night the burglary took place, and ordered him out of town. Bernal agreed to let Corbin's wife and child stay on in the house until Corbin could get located in another city.

"Corbin pulled out in the morning and gave his wife this money. It was part of the money from the burglary."

"How do they know?" Mason asked.

"Now there's something I don't know." Drake said. "This fellow Bernal is pretty smart, and the story is that he can prove Corbin's money was from the vault.

"The nearest bank is at Ivanhoe City, and the mine pays off in cash twice a month. Ralph Nesbitt, the cashier, wanted to install a new vault. Bernal refused to okay the expense. So the company has ordered both Bernal and Nesbitt back to its main office at Chicago to report. The rumor is that they may fire Bernal as manager and give Nesbitt the job. A couple of directors don't like Bernal, and this thing has given them their chance. They dug out a report Nesbitt had made showing the vault was a pushover. Bernal didn't act on that report." He sighed and then asked, "When's the trial, Perry?"

"The preliminary hearing is set for Friday morning. I'll see then what they've got against Corbin."

"They're laying for you up there," Paul Drake warned. "Better watch out, Perry. That district attorney has something up his sleeve, some sort of surprise that's going to knock you for a loop."

In spite of his long experience as a prosecutor, Vernon

Flasher, the district attorney of Ivanhoe County, showed a certain nervousness at being called upon to oppose Perry Mason. There was, however, a secretive assurance underneath that nervousness.

Judge Haswell, realizing that the eyes of the community were upon him, adhered to legal technicalities to the point of being pompous both in rulings and mannerisms.

But what irritated Perry Mason was in the attitude of the spectators. He sensed that they did not regard him as an attorney trying to safeguard the interests of a client, but as a legal magician with a cloven hoof. The looting of the vault had shocked the community, and there was a tight-lipped determination that no legal tricks were going to do Mason any good this time.

Vernon Flasher didn't try to save his surprise evidence for a whirlwind finish. He used it right at the start of the case.

Frank Bernal, called as a witness, described the location of the vault, identified photographs, and then leaned back as the district attorney said abruptly, "You had reason to believe this vault was obsolete?"

"Yes, sir."

"It had been pointed out to you by one of your fellow employees, Mr. Ralph Nesbitt?"

"Yes, sir."

"And what did you do about it?"

"Are you," Mason asked in some surprise, "trying to cross-examine your own witness?"

"Just let him answer the question, and you'll see," Flasher replied grimly.

"Go right ahead and answer," Mason said to the witness.

Bernal assumed a more comfortable position. "I did three things," he said, "to safeguard the payrolls and to avoid the expense of tearing out the old vault and installing a new vault in its place."

"What were those three things?"

"I employed a special night watchman; I installed the best burglar alarm money could buy; and I made arrangements with the Ivanhoe National Bank, where we have our payrolls made up, to list the number of each twenty-dollar bill which was a part of each payroll."

Mason suddenly sat up straight.

Flasher gave him a glance of gloating triumph. "Do you wish the court to understand, Mr. Bernal," he said smugly, "that you have the numbers of the bills in the payroll which was made for delivery on the fifteenth?"

"Yes, sir. Not all of the bills, you understand. That would have taken too much time, but I have the numbers of all the twenty-dollar bills."

"And who recorded those numbers?'" the prosecutor asked.

"The bank."

"And do you have that list of numbers with you?"

"I do. Yes, sir." Bernal produced a list. "I felt," he said, glancing coldly at Nesbitt, "that these precautions would be cheaper than a new vault."

"I move the list be introduced in evidence," Flasher said.

"Just a moment," Mason objected. "I have a couple of questions. You say this list is not in your handwriting, Mr. Bernal?"

"Yes, sir."

"Whose handwriting is it, do you know?" Mason asked.

"The assistant cashier of the Ivanhoe National Bank."

"Oh, all right," Flasher said. "We'll do it the hard way, if we have to. Stand down, Mr. Bernal, and I'll call the assistant cashier."

Harry Reedy, assistant cashier of the Ivanhoe Bank, had the mechanical assurance of an adding machine. He identified the list of numbers as being in his handwriting. He stated that he had listed the numbers of the twenty-dollar bills and put that list in an envelope which had been sealed and sent up with the money for the payroll.

"Cross-examine," Flasher said.

Mason studied the list. "These numbers are all in your handwriting?" he asked Reedy.

"Yes, sir."

"Did you yourself compare the numbers you wrote down with the numbers on the twenty-dollar bills?"

"No, sir. I didn't personally do that. Two assistants did that. One checked the numbers as they were read off, one as I wrote them down."

"The payrolls are for approximately a hundred thousand dollars, twice each month?"

"That's right. And ever since Mr. Bernal took charge, we have taken this means to identify payrolls. No attempt is made to list the bills in numerical order. The serial numbers are simply read off and written down. Unless a robbery occurs, there is no need to do anything further. In the event of a robbery, we can reclassify the numbers and list the bills in numerical order."

"These numbers are in your handwriting—every number?"

"Yes, sir. More than that, you will notice that at the bottom of each page I have signed my initials."

"That's all," Mason said.

"I now offer once more to introduce this list in evidence," Flasher said.

"So ordered," Judge Haswell ruled.

"My next witness is Charles J. Oswald, the sheriff," the district attorney announced.

The sheriff, a long, lanky man with a quiet manner, took the stand. "You're acquainted with Harvey L. Corbin, the defendant in this case?" the district attorney asked.

"I am."

"Are you acquainted with his wife?"

"Yes, sir."

"Now, on the morning of the fifteenth of this month, the morning of the robbery at the Jebson Commercial Company, did you you have any conversation with Mrs. Corbin?"

"I did. Yes, sir."

"Did you ask her about her husband's activities the night before?"

"Just a moment," Mason said, "I object to this on the ground that any conversation the sheriff had with Mrs. Corbin is not admissible against the defendant, Corbin; furthermore, that in this state a wife cannot testify against her husband. Therefore, any statement she might make would be an indirect violation of that rule. Furthermore, I object on the ground that the question calls for hearsay."

Judge Haswell looked ponderously thoughtful, then said, "It seems to me Mr. Mason is correct."

"I'll put it this way, Mr. Sheriff," the district attorney said. "Did you, on the morning of the fifteenth, take any money from Mrs. Corbin?"

"Objected to as incompetent, irrelevant and immaterial," Mason said.

"Your Honor," Flasher said irritably, "that's the very gist of our case. We propose to show that two of the stolen twenty-dollar bills were in the possession of Mrs. Corbin."

Mason said, "Unless the prosecution can prove the bills were given Mrs. Corbin by her husband, the evidence is inadmissible."

"That's just the point," Flasher said. "Those bills were given her by the defendant."

"How do you know?" Mason asked.

"She told the sheriff so."

"That's hearsay," Mason snapped.

Judge Haswell fidgeted on the bench. "It seems to me we're getting into a peculiar situation here. You can't call the wife as a witness, and I don't think her statement to the sheriff is admissible."

"Well," Flasher said desperately, "in this state, your Honor, we have a community-property law. Mrs. Corbin had this money. Since she is the wife of the defendant, it was community property. Therefore, it's partially his property."

"Well, now, there," Judge Haswell said, "I think I can agree with you. You introduce the twenty-dollar bills. I'll overrule the objection made by the defense."

"Produce the twenty-dollar bills, Sheriff," Flasher said triumphantly.

The bills were produced and received in evidence.

"Cross-examine," Flasher said curtly.

"No questions of this witness," Mason said, "but I have a few questions to ask Mr. Bernal on cross-examination. You took him off the stand to lay the foundation for introducing the bank list, and I didn't have an opportunity to cross-examine him."

"I beg your pardon," Flasher said. "Resume the stand, Mr. Bernal."

His tone, now that he had the twenty-dollar bills safely introduced in evidence, had a gloating note to it.

Mason said, "This list which has been introduced in evidence is on the stationery of the Ivanhoe National Bank?"

"That's right. Yes, sir."

"It consists of several pages, and at the end there is the signature of the assistant cashier?"

"Yes, sir."

"And each page is initialed by the assistant cashier?"

"Yes, sir."

"This was the scheme which you thought of in order to safeguard the company against a payroll robbery?"

"Not to safeguard the company against a payroll robbery, Mr. Mason, but to assist us in recovering the money in the event there was a holdup."

"This was your plan to answer Mr. Nesbitt's objections that the vault was an outmoded model?"

"A part of my plan, yes. I may say that Mr. Nesbitt's objections had never been voiced until I took office. I felt he was trying to embarrass me by making my administration show less net returns than expected." Bernal tightened his lips and added, "Mr. Nesbitt had, I believe, been expecting to be appointed manager. He was disappointed. I believe he still expects to be manager."

In the spectators' section of the courtroom, Ralph Nesbitt glared at Bernal.

"You had a conversation with the defendant on the night of the fourteenth?" Mason asked Bernal.

"I did. Yes, sir."

"You told him that for reasons which you deemed sufficient you were discharging him immediately and wanted him to leave the premises at once?"

"Yes, sir, I did."

"And you paid him his wages in cash?"

"Mr. Nesbitt paid him in my presence, with money he took from the petty-cash drawer of the vault."

"Now, as part of the wages due him, wasn't Corbin given these two twenty-dollar bills which have been introduced in evidence?"

Bernal shook his head. "I had thought of that," he said, "but it would have been impossible. Those bills weren't available to us at that time. The payroll is received from the bank in a sealed package. Those two twenty-dollar bills were in that package."

"And the list of the numbers of the twenty-dollar bills?"

"That's in a sealed envelope. The money is placed in the vault. I lock the list of numbers in my desk."

"Are you prepared to swear that neither you nor Mr. Nesbitt had access to these two twenty-dollar bills on the night of the fourteenth?"

"That is correct."

"That's all," Mason said. "No further cross-examination."

"I now call Ralph Nesbitt to the stand," District Attorney Flasher said. "I want to fix the time of these events definitely, your Honor."

"Very well," Judge Haswell said. "Mr. Nesbitt, come forward."

Ralph Nesbitt, after answering the usual preliminary questions, sat down in the witness chair.

"Were you present at a conversation which took place between the defendant, Harvey L. Corbin, and Frank Bernal on the fourteenth of this month?" the district attorney asked.

"I was. Yes, sir."

"What time did that conversation take place?"

"About eight o'clock in the evening."

"And, without going into the details of that conversation, I will ask you if the general effect of it was that the defendant was discharged and ordered to leave the company's property?"

"Yes, sir."

"And he was paid the money that was due him?"

"In cash. Yes, sir. I took the cash from the safe myself."

"Where was the payroll then?"

"In the sealed package in a compartment in the safe. As

cashier, I had the only key to that compartment. Earlier in the afternoon I had gone to Ivanhoe City and received the sealed package of money and the envelope containing the list of numbers. I personally locked the package of money in the vault."

"And the list of numbers?"

"Mr. Bernal locked that in his desk."

"Cross-examine," Flasher said.

"No questions," Mason said.

"That's our case, your Honor," Flasher observed.

"May we have a few minutes' indulgence?" Mason asked Judge Haswell.

"Very well. Make it brief," the judge agreed.

Mason turned to Paul Drake and Della Street. "Well, there you are." Drake said. "You're confronted with the proof, Perry."

"Are you going to put the defendant on the stand?" Della Street asked.

Mason shook his head. "It would be suicidal. He has a record of a prior criminal conviction. Also, it's a rule of law that if one asks about any part of a conversation on direct examination, the other side can bring out all the conversation. The conversation, when Corbin was discharged, was to the effect that he had lied about his past record. And I guess there's no question that he did."

"And he's lying now," Drake said. "This is one case where you're licked. I think you'd better cop a plea, and see what kind of a deal you can make with Flasher."

"Probably not any," Mason said. "Flasher wants to have the reputation of having given me a licking—wait a minute, Paul. I have an idea."

Mason turned abruptly, walked away to where he could stand by himself, his back to the crowded courtroom.

"Are you ready?" the judge asked.

Mason turned. "I am quite ready, your Honor. I have one witness whom I wish to put on the stand. I wish a subpoena *duces tecum* issued for that witness. I want him to bring certain documents which are in his possession."

"Who is the witness, and what are the documents?" the judge asked.

Mason walked quickly over to Paul Drake. "What's the

name of that character who has the garbage-collecting business," he said softly, "the one who has the first nickel he'd ever made?"

"George Addey."

The lawyer turned to the judge. "The witness that I want is George Addey, and the documents that I want him to bring to court with him are all of the twenty-dollar bills that he has received during the past sixty days."

"Your Honor," Flasher protested, "this is an outrage. This is making a travesty out of justice. It is exposing the court to ridicule."

Mason said, "I give your Honor my assurance that I think this witness is material, and that the documents are material. I will make an affidavit to that effect if necessary. As attorney for the defendant, may I point out that if the court refuses to grant this subpoena, it will be denying the defendant due process of law."

"I'm going to issue the subpoena," Judge Haswell said, testily, "and for your own good, Mr. Mason, the testimony had better be relevant."

George Addey, unshaven and bristling with indignation, held up his right hand to be sworn. He glared at Perry Mason.

"Mr. Addey," Mason said, "you have the contract to collect garbage from Jebson City?"

"I do."

"How long have you been collecting garbage there?"

"For over five years, and I want to tell you——"

Judge Haswell banged his gavel. "The witness will answer questions and not interpolate any comments."

"I'll interpolate anything I dang please," Addey said.

"That'll do," the judge said. "Do you wish to be jailed for contempt of court, Mr. Addey?"

"I don't want to go to jail, but I——"

"Then you'll remember the respect that is due the court," the judge said. "Now you sit there and answer questions. This is a court of law. You're in this court as a citizen, and I'm here as a judge, and I propose to see that the respect due to the court is enforced." There was a moment's silence while the judge glared angrily at the witness. "All right, go ahead, Mr. Mason," Judge Haswell said.

Mason said, "During the thirty days prior to the fifteenth of this month, did you deposit any money in any banking institution?"

"I did not."

"Do you have with you all the twenty-dollar bills that you received during the last sixty days?"

"I have, and I think making me bring them here is just like inviting some crook to come and rob me and——"

Judge Haswell banged with his gavel. "Any more comments of that sort from the witness and there will be a sentence imposed for contempt of court. Now you get out those twenty-dollar bills, Mr. Addey, and put them right up here on the clerk's desk."

Addey, mumbling under his breath, slammed a roll of twenty-dollar bills down on the desk in front of the clerk.

"Now," Mason said, "I'm going to need a little clerical assistance. I would like to have my secretary, Miss Street, and the clerk help me check through the numbers on these bills. I will select a few at random."

Mason picked up three of the twenty-dollar bills and said, "I am going to ask my assistants to check the list of numbers introduced in evidence. In my hand is a twenty-dollar bill that has the number L 07083274A. Is that bill on the list? The next bill that I pick up is number L 02327010A. Here's another one, number L 07579190A. Are any of those bills on the list?" The courtroom was silent. Suddenly Della Street said, "Yes, here's one that's on the list, bill number L 07579190A. It's on the list, on page eight."

"What?" the prosecutor shouted.

"Exactly," Mason said smiling. "So, if a case is to be made against a person merely because he has possession of the money that was stolen on the fifteenth of this month, then your office should prefer charges against this witness, George Addey, Mr. District Attorney."

Addey jumped from the witness stand and shook his fist in Mason's face. "You're a cock-eyed liar!" he screamed. "There ain't a one of those bills but what I didn't have it before the fifteenth. The company cashier changes my money into twenties, because I like big bills. I bury 'em in cans, and I put the date on the side of the can."

"Here's the list," Mason said. "Check it for yourself."

A tense silence gripped the courtroom as the judge and the spectators waited.

"I'm afraid I don't understand this, Mr. Mason," Judge Haswell said, after a moment.

"I think it's quite simple," Mason said. "And I now suggest the court take a recess for an hour and check these other bills against this list. I think the district attorney may be surprised."

And Mason sat down and proceeded to put papers in his brief case . . .

Della Street, Paul Drake, and Perry Mason were sitting in the lobby of the Ivanhoe Hotel.

"When are you going to tell us?" Della Street asked fiercely. "Or do we tear you limb from limb? How could the garbage man have——?"

"Wait a minute," Mason said. "I think we're about to get results. Here comes the esteemed district attorney, Vernon Flasher, and he's accompanied by Judge Haswell."

The two strode over to Mason's group and bowed with cold formality.

Mason got up.

Judge Haswell began in his best courtroom voice. "A most deplorable situation has occurred. It seems that Mr. Frank Bernal has—well——"

"Been detained somewhere," Vernon Flasher said.

"Disappeared," Judge Haswell said. "He's gone."

"I expected as much," Mason said.

"Now will you kindly tell me just what sort of pressure you brought to bear on Mr. Bernal to——?"

"Just a moment, Judge," Mason said. "The only pressure I brought to bear on him was to cross-examine him."

"Did you know that there had been a mistake in the dates on those lists?"

"There was no mistake. When you find Bernal, I'm sure you will discover there was a deliberate falsification. He was short in his accounts, and he knew he was about to be demoted. He had a desperate need for a hundred thousand dollars in ready cash. He had evidently been planning this burglary, or, rather, this embezzlement, for some time. He learned that Corbin had a criminal record. He arranged to have these lists furnished by the bank. He installed a burglar alarm and, naturally, knew how to circumvent it. He employed a watchman he knew was addicted to drink. He only needed to stage his coup at the right time. He fired Corbin and paid him off with bills that had been recorded by the bank on page eight of the list of bills in the payroll on the first of the month.

"Then he removed page eight from the list of bills contained in the payroll of the fifteenth, before he showed it to the police, and substituted page eight of the list for the first of the month payroll. It was that simple.

"Then he drugged the watchman's whisky, took an acetylene torch, burned through the vault doors, and took all the money."

"May I ask how you knew all this?" Judge Haswell demanded.

"Certainly," Mason said. "My client told me he received those bills from Nesbitt, who took them from the petty-cash drawer in the safe. He also told the sheriff that. I happened to be the only one who believed him. It sometimes pays, your Honor, to have faith in a man, even if he has made a previous mistake. Assuming my client was innocent, I knew either Bernal or Nesbitt must be guilty. I then realized that only Bernal had custody of the previous lists of numbers.

"As an employee, Bernal had been paid on the first of the month. He looked at the numbers on the twenty-dollar bills in his pay envelope and found that they had been listed on page eight of the payroll for the first.

"Bernal only needed to abstract all twenty-dollar bills from the petty-cash drawer, substitute twenty-dollar bills from his own pay envelope, call in Corbin, and fire him. His trap was set.

"I let him know I knew what had been done by bringing Addey into court and proving my point. Then I asked for a recess. That was so Bernal would have a chance to skip out. You see, flight may be received as evidence of guilt. It was a professional courtesy to the district attorney. It will help him when Bernal is arrested."